Sexualit

For Dee with love and in memory of Derick Johnson
missed as always.

Sexuality

A Psychosocial Manifesto

KATHERINE JOHNSON

polity

First published in 2015 by Polity Press

Polity Press
65 Bridge Street
Cambridge CB2 1UR, UK

Polity Press
350 Main Street
Malden, MA 02148, USA

ISBN-13: 978-0-7456-4131-7
ISBN-13: 978-0-7456-4132-4(pb)

A catalogue record for this book is available from the British Library.

Library of Congress Cataloging-in-Publication Data

Johnson, Katherine E.
    Sexuality : a psychosocial manifesto / Katherine Johnson.
      pages cm
    ISBN 978-0-7456-4131-7 (hardback : alk. paper) -- ISBN 978-0-7456-4132-4 (pbk. : alk. paper) 1. Sex. 2. Sex (Psychology) 3. Queer theory. I. Title.
    HQ21.J58 2014
    306.7--dc23
                                    2014019992

Typeset in 11 on 13 pt Monotype Bembo
by Servis Filmsetting Ltd, Stockport, Cheshire
Printed and bound in Great Britain by TJ International, Padstow, Cornwall

For further information on Polity, visit our website: www.politybooks.com

Contents

Acknowledgements

It has taken more years than I initially intended to complete this book and I am grateful for the support and patience of family, friends and colleagues throughout this time. Dee Rudebeck, Jude, Emil, Maia and Silas Marwa and Abi Johnson need particular credit for keeping a sense of humour in the moments it seemed that 'the book' was going to become an additional lifelong companion. I only wish Derick Johnson was also still here to see it finished. Given the delays I am particularly grateful to my editors at Polity, Emma Longstaff for originally commissioning the book and Jonathan Skerrett for seeing it through to publication. I am deeply indebted and thankful for the ongoing influence and support of Lynne Segal, who always impressed that interesting work is to be found on the margins and has provided kindness and encouragement through good times and bad. Co-learning, conversations and critical engagements with Paul Hanna, Ed Moreno, Stella Fremi, Stephanie Davis, Matt Adams, Paul Stenner, Jayne Raisborough, Niki Khan and Hannah Frith have all contributed greatly to ideas developed here. Life at the University of Brighton is enriched by the collegiality in the School of Applied Social Science and collaborations with colleagues from the LGBTQ research hub, particularly Kath Browne, Olu Jenzen, Irmi Karl, Nigel Sheriff and Aidan McGarry, who share commitments to social justice and community-engaged research.

The research on suicide and mental health that features in the book would not have been possible without financial support from CUPP, dialogue with Ben Fincham and collaborations with Paul Faulkner, MindOut and Allsorts – vital and vibrant community mental health projects running in Brighton and Hove. Working with Helen Jones, Jess Wood, Jason Saw, Elliot Klimek and service users from both organizations has been life enhancing and I am sustained and encouraged by their passion, activism, friendship and care. I am particularly thankful to Liz for allowing me to use her image from the Focusing the Mind exhibition (Brighton Pride, 2008) in published work. I am also grateful to Michelle Lollo and Caroline Nin for hosting the Paris experience and providing the image (p. 161) to document it, alongside many years of friendship.

Colleagues and postgraduate students in the Department de Psicologia Social, Universitat Autònoma de Barcelona have hosted a number of visits and provided a rigorous testing ground for reflecting on interventions from critical/community psychology and psychosocial studies. I'm particularly thankful to Joan Pujol, Marisela Montenegro and Antar Martínez Guzmán and look forward to future collaborations. Michael O'Rourke, Noreen Giffney and Anne Mulhull need a special mention for running the *The(e)ories: Advanced Seminars for Queer Research* in Dublin. These intensive workshops draw together scholars and practitioners from queer studies, psychology and psychoanalysis and offer a rare opportunity to read closely and collectively while seeking clarification from the author of the text in hand. The impact of the sessions I have managed to attend over the last eight years is apparent in the pages that follow.

Finally, I am grateful for research leave funded by the University of Brighton, which provided extended periods of time for the basic requirements of research: reading, thinking and writing. In 2007 the Department of Gender and Culture Studies, University of Sydney hosted me for five months providing me with access to their excellent library where I did much of the work for chapters 2 and 5. Chapter 5 is an expanded version of an article previously published as 'How very dare you!': shame, insult and contemporary representations of queer subjectivities, *Subjectivity*, (2012) 5, 416–37. I am grateful to Palgrave for permitting me to reproduce ideas, as well as Catherine Tate, Matt Lucas and David Walliams for allowing me to again use extracts from *The Catherine Tate Show* and *Little Britain*. I am also thankful to Jenz Germon, Gilbert Caluya, Cate Thill, Louisa Smith, Raewyn Connell, Jessica Cadwallader, Sarah Cefai, Julie Mooney-Summers, Naimh Stephenson, Jane Ussher and Janette Perez for welcoming me to Sydney and engaging with my research, and to Sally Munt for providing insightful feedback back in Brighton on an early draft of this chapter. Chapter 2 was written at home in Brighton on a shorter period of research leave in 2010. The rest has been carved out, as my colleague Mark Erickson would say, 'in the cracks' of our daily lives. Any errors, limitations and omissions are thus my responsibility, or perhaps I can attribute them to the distractions of Brighton and Sydney; two wonderful cities that provided the backdrop for the writing of this book and home to many queer lives.

1

Introducing Sexuality: towards the psychosocial

Any polarizing of psychology and history cripples the investigation of the issues that both psychologists and social scientists are trying to understand.

Helen Merrell Lynd, 1958, p. 214

The structure of this kind of conceptual impasse or short circuit is all too familiar: where it is possible to recognize the mechanism of a problem, but trying to remedy it, or even in fact articulate it, simply adds propulsive energy to that very mechanism.

Eve Kosofsky Sedgwick, 2007, p. 635

Sexuality: between psychology and historicism

Despite Helen Merrell Lynd's warning polarization between psychological and socio-historical approaches has been an all too familiar feature of late twentieth-century thought, particularly in the field of sexuality. In reviewing prominent theories and debates it is reasonable to claim that this polarization constitutes a 'kind of conceptual impasse', found in many accounts influenced by either Marx or Freud, or latterly Freud and Foucault, whose vital work sets the scene for contemporary understandings of sexuality within academia and everyday life. This book explores the polarization between psychological and socio-historical accounts that are documented well in sexuality studies and somewhat ambitiously proposes an alternative, a psychosocial manifesto that seeks to stitch and mend the polarization. Yet, as Sedgwick states, trying to remedy, or even articulate the impasse is not without its own problems. Specifically, in trying to articulate accounts of sexuality without recourse to a polarization between psychology and historicism invites us to engage with the 'psychosocial', but inevitably within this articulation it is difficult not to fall back on the mechanisms that constitute the split.

The term sexuality can refer to a set of practices or behaviours, a range of feelings or affects, or as a way of categorizing people on the basis of their sexual orientation, sexual identity or political allegiances. The plural, sexualities, is utilized to acknowledge the multiple meanings of sexuality and to recognize that an understanding of contemporary sexuality needs to engage with a proliferation of identity categories, sexual practices, subjectivities, desires and relationship formations, including for example queer or trans alongside more familiar categories such as heterosexual, lesbian, gay and bisexual. This book explores the way in which the term is conceptualized in an array of psychological and social debate, such as neuroanatomy, adolescent development, sexual health, youth suicide, identity politics or gay marriage, and provides access to a range of theoretical perspectives that seek to explain how sexuality is developed, constructed, queered, embodied and transformed.

Since the late 1800s, sexologists and psychologists have tended to promote the view that sexuality has its origins in biological processes underpinned by hormones, drives, and more recently, genetics. In contrast, historians and sociologists point to the social field as the defining force that shapes the meanings given to sexuality and sexual experience. This observation provides the starting point for investigating how polarization produces different forms of knowledge and the impact these have on how sexuality can be experienced in personal and political contexts. Such distinctions are familiar within social science accounts of sexuality, but they are also apparent within the humanities and queer studies. For example, Michael Warner (1993) expressed a similar warning to Lynd in the seminal text *Fear of a Queer Planet*, critiquing the divergence in theories of sexuality particularly between psychoanalysis and historicism. He suggested psychoanalytic approaches have been used to link the political demands of 'lesbians and gay liberation to fundamental psychic structures' (1993, p. xi) in a framework that lacks the necessary subtlety to recognize historical or cultural differences, while historical perspectives that champion difference through social constructionist analysis pinpoint the importance of cultural specificity in identity construction but have not generated new theories for explaining sexual subjectivities. Nevertheless, in more recent years, queer studies has been reinvigorated by a 'turn to affect' and with it the increased application of psychoanalytic concepts and theories, as well as the influence of neuroscience, to develop new tools for describing processes of normalization and resistance, and for rethinking subjectivity.

Elsewhere, mainstream psychology has largely discarded and discredited psychoanalytic approaches in favour of a scientific research paradigm that seeks to understand questions about the aetiology of sexual orientation. These types of research studies attempt to identify causal origins in the hope of explaining why someone might identify as lesbian, gay or bisexual, and these origins are often assumed to be biological, determined by hormones, genetics or neurological structures. Working within the same paradigm, developmental approaches look to establish whether there are models that can explain the processes by which individuals come to call themselves gay, lesbian or bisexual, and these tend to note the influence of both biological and social factors. However, the cultural turn that precipitated a paradigm shift that began to transform the social sciences and humanities in the 1970s heralded the beginning of a radical separation *within* psychology that has further exacerbated the problem of polarization. In the UK, for example, there has been a growing disciplinary trend where social and critical psychologists informed by poststructuralism, feminism and psychoanalysis have either drifted away or have been exiled from more mainstream psychology departments, with many ending up in sociology, interdisciplinary health studies, or more recently in newly created pockets called psychosocial studies. This redrawing of disciplinary borders has been influenced further by the introduction of the research quality assurance process (Research Assessment Exercise [RAE] now renamed Research Excellence Framework [REF]). Much is at stake with government research funding distributed to universities on the basis of how well the submitted departments rate against others within the category they have been entered into. In recent years psychology has been grouped into a category submission of Psychology, Psychiatry and Neuroscience. Within this the work of social, critical, theoretical and even some applied psychologists is seen as detrimental to a strong submission based around experimental, cognitive and neurological research. As a result many of the leading critical voices within psychology, those most likely to engage with socio-historical approaches and to explore the intersections between psychology and historicism have found themselves included in other submissions – most frequently Sociology, or Social Work and Social Policy. Playing the REF game, as it is sometimes referred to, and getting strategic decisions right, is seen as crucial for university funding. Yet, the danger is that this is at the expense of encouraging the theoretical and methodological richness that is necessary to understand complex issues such as sexuality. As I hope to demonstrate in this book, this can only be achieved by reading widely in order to draw across disciplines and intellectual traditions, a process that can be both liberating and terrifying. Resting on the margins of a discipline loosely claimed as 'home' (in this case psychology), looking out towards sociology, women and queer studies, cultural studies or literary theory generates new ways of seeing, feeling and knowing. But when these connections do not gel or you find yourself falling between the gaps of disciplinary debates without an interlocutor, these endeavours can be isolating and disheartening. These are the pleasures and challenges that studies which claim to be transdisciplinary face, and the 'psychosocial' is one such space welcoming those willing to take such risks.

Transdisciplinarity, subjectivity and psychosocial studies

The term 'psychosocial' is widely used in health studies to indicate an interaction between certain psychological and social factors. In this context, it is primarily used within a scientific research framework that seeks to ascertain the influence of each factor (such as personality or income) or delineate between levels of analysis (e.g. bio-psycho-social) (Hollway, 2006). In contrast, in the UK in particular, psychosocial has been developed as a field of study for rethinking the polarization between psychology and historicism. In defining psychosocial studies as 'transdisciplinary', Paul Stenner (2007) notes that those working in this field tend to be 'academic migrants' or 'cross-country scholars' who are concerned with 'real life issues of power, social exclusion and inequality'. Emotion or affect often operate as key topics for transdisciplinary psychosocial studies because of its readiness as a site for 'revisioning' the space between the psychic and the social (Stenner, 2007; Greco and Stenner, 2008). Thus, within this emerging corpus of work we find accounts of love (Brown, 2006), grief (Stenner and Moreno, 2013) or regeneration (Walkerdine and Jimenez, 2012) but produced through theoretical lenses that seek to go beyond either sociological or psychological explanations. For some this is because of the polarization where 'the sociology of emotion . . . continues to afford the intellect and reason too much control over feeling and the irrational', while its alternative, 'an exclusively defined psychoanalysis of affect in which the structural, historic forces in people's lives might be underrepresented', is inadequate (Brown, 2006, p. 6); for others, this is more emphatically because 'psychology ends up killing – or at the very least simplifying – the phenomena of which it desires to speak' (Brown and Stenner, 2009, p. 4).

In an attempt to address these discipline-based limitations, psychosocial studies has encouraged rich theoretical engagement from a range of perspectives including sociology, social and critical psychology, but also feminism, queer, postcolonial and cultural studies, in order to reconsider the relationship between psychic life and social conditions in the making of subjectivity (e.g. Frosh, 2010b). Subjectivity is a key concept that raises its own questions about how we come to experience ourselves as subjects, and whether this can ever really be known. Henriques et al. (1984/1998, p. 3) use the term,

> to refer to individuality and self-awareness – the condition of being a subject – but understand in this usage that subjects are dynamic and multiple, always positioned in relation to discourses and practices and produced by these – the condition of being subject.

In a move towards theorizing subjectivity, those influenced by phenomenology have pointed to how poststructuralist approaches place too much emphasis on discourse, power and control that constitute particular subject positions or identities, rather than the embodied or intersubjective element of this experience (e.g. Johnson, 2007; Burkitt, 2008). Here, in bridging poststructuralism and phenomenology, poststructuralist approaches are associated with establishing the ways identities, such as gender, sexuality, race or class, are constituted through ideological and normative processes, while phenomenological engagements with subjectivity entail ascertaining how someone comes to occupy a particular identity and experience the world in which they reside. Contrasting investments in concepts such as 'identity' or 'subjectivity' are now familiar within sexuality studies and psychosocial studies. It is taken for granted that the influence of social constructionism and queer theory has dismantled any certainty in the stability of identity categories, but identity remains an important concept particularly when thinking about political allegiance and social transformation for groups that are minoritized and oppressed. In sketching out the distinction between identity and subjectivity the social psychologist Margaret Wetherell suggests:

> 'Identity', thus, allows the researcher to investigate what groups and their relations make possible for subjects. 'Subjectivity' tells the story of how a specific self lives those available cultural slots, actively realizes them, takes responsibility and owns them as an agent, turning social

category memberships and social roles into ethical, emotional and nar-
rated choices. (Wetherell, 2008, p. 75)

Given the investment in this book in the concept of subjectivity,
this definition is taken rather unfairly from Wetherell who is summarizing the work of Couze Venn (2006) in order to argue *against*
subjectivity as a productive concept for rethinking the relationship
between the psychological and the social. Yet, in the context of
exploring sexuality which is so often referred to in categorical identity terms, such as lesbian, gay, bisexual, trans and queer (LGBTQ), I
find the subjectivity/identity distinction helpful to acknowledge that
the purpose of engaging the psychosocial is to say something about
how these identities are lived 'either thoroughly or ambivalently', as
well as about where they are located in power structures (Wetherell,
2008, p. 76). To do justice to Wetherell here, it is worth noting that
her concern is that a focus on subjectivity dulls down engagements
with identity, such that issues of intersectionality are overlooked.

The term intersectionality was first outlined in the context of
feminist and critical race studies as a way of moving beyond single
axis attention to difference and marginalization, analysing the intersection of gender and race and their impact on lived experience
within a specific focus, that of problematizing the US legal system
(Crenshaw, 1989). The early interest in the intersection between
race and gender within feminist theory and politics (Crenshaw,
1991) has been greatly expanded in recent years to include demands
for broader attention to how a range of social categories including
gender, race, class and sexuality interact. Yet, the field of studies
is not without its own theoretical, methodological and practical
contentions (McCall, 2005; Nash, 2008). In particular, McCall
questions whether analyses are able to attend to 'the complexity
that arises when the subject of analysis expands to include multiple
dimensions of social life and categories of analysis' and outlines the
strengths and weaknesses of favouring 'anti-categorical complexity', 'intracategorical complexity' or 'intercategorical complexity'
(2005, p. 1772). To explain, anti-category approaches are frequently aligned with scholars who are sceptical about the ability
of analyses of identity categories to say anything meaningful about

the complexity of lived experience. Intra-category approaches are associated with those who seek to demonstrate how categorization results in exclusion and how understanding the complexity of subjectivity can illustrate the limitation of categorization approaches. Inter-category approaches are seen to be useful for demonstrating the links between the category itself and inequality, particularly focusing on analyses of social groups.

Debates about intersectionality return us to similar concerns within the field of psychosocial studies: the relationship between identity and subjectivity and how to stitch together understandings of the psychic and social consequences of marginalization and inequality, which operate through different identity categories and social dimensions. It might be argued that in attending to the psychosocial when theorizing sexuality and subjectivity through a transdisciplinary framework other identity categories such as race and social class remain underanalysed – a limitation that an intersectional approach would address. But, in a recent interrogation of the proliferation of calls for intersectional analyses, Robyn Wiegman (2012, p. 246) has asked 'what does it mean that intersectionality functions today by tacking back and forth between a demand for the particular and a promise that through it every relation of subordination can be brought into critical view?', while Surya Monro (2010, p. 1007) proposes that 'analysis of the interstices between social characteristics is relatively straightforward at the level of the individual, but once group level conceptualization is undertaken a category-based approach is required to a degree'. Thus, this book heeds the warning and seeks where possible to attend to intersectionality, but always within a framework that avoids attaching marginalization and oppression to hierarchical categories of difference.

In conceiving a psychosocial manifesto it is important to resist introducing new polarizations between identity and subjectivity, where one wins out over the other, instead recognizing the analytic purchase of both for specific fields of enquiry and political debate and their interrelatedness. Returning to Wetherell's original point, it can be noted that she too is working within a psychosocial ethos that opposes the polarization of subjectivity and identity because, as she states, 'features conventionally marked out as to do with "subjectivity" . . . are intrinsic to the formation and cultural representation of what gets marked out as "identity" ' (2008, p. 78). Nevertheless, her central concern with theoretical debates in the psychosocial field more generally is whether the movement towards psychoanalytic theory as a way of studying subjectivity 'may end up over-emphasizing interiority and privacy' (p. 78). In this sense, she suggests psychoanalysis might offer a return to psychology and interiority at the expense of the socio-historical, despite recent attempts for psychoanalysis to engage a more social constructionist discourse. This concern that privileging one theory over another results in firstly a split and then the emphasis or polarization between interior and exterior is precisely the outcome that this book attempts to avoid.

Elsewhere, those who utilize psychoanalysis to theorize subjectivity point to the importance that the concept 'unconscious' affords for criss-crossing the interior–exterior divide. Stephen Frosh (2010a, p. 194) states that it can offer this 'in the sense that unconscious ideas are both "in" and "outside of" the subject, neither owned by the "person" nor completely separate'. However, although concepts such as the 'unconscious' are without doubt useful, psychosocial studies is not unified in terms of how the concept is utilized. For example, within psychoanalytically inspired psychosocial approaches there has been considerable debate about the merits of approaches inspired by theorists Melanie Klein or Jacques Lacan (e.g. Frosh and Baraitser, 2008; Hollway, 2008) and whether psychosocial studies should in fact be called *psycho-social* studies. The importance of the hyphen is demanded by some (e.g. Hoggett, 2008) in order to demonstrate that there are *distinctions* between 'inner' and 'outer' which psychoanalysis can purportedly help to both link and disentangle. In contrast, Frosh and Baraitser (2008, p. 354) are critical of Kleinian informed 'psycho-social' accounts where, they argue, 'inner reality' is privileged over 'outer reality', such that 'in Hollway's description of the psychosocial, both elements are theorized as infiltrated by "the" unconscious, which in turn is understood as residing in the "inner world"'. They suggest that the classic psychoanalytic notion of 'psychic reality' might be more psychosocial 'in the sense that it figures something that is never totally "internal". Psychic reality is what the subject *lives in;* this replaces an abstract opposition of the "outer" as against the "inner" with a conceptualization of the "psychic" as that which stands for both.' To emphasize this, the authors draw on the metaphor of the Moebius strip to illustrate psychic reality as 'a folding of space', as a 'hybrid' that is neither in nor out. The concept of 'hybridity' has widespread use in the social sciences and humanities as a means of exploring notions of 'mixedness', with particular purchase in queer studies and critical race studies (see chapter 4), and is of significant value as a mode of thinking psychosocially.

Nevertheless, the purpose of illustrating this small-scale debate about the role of psychoanalysis in British psychosocial studies is to give some insight into the analytic tensions that occur when attempting to think between the poles of psychic and social or, as Sedgwick would have it, attempting to articulate and remedy a conceptual impasse. Unlike these authors my aim is not to demonstrate that psychoanalysis is crucial for this, although it can certainly help, or that a particular school of psychoanalytic thought is better equipped to do so. Rather, I wish to provide the reader with some of the theoretical tools necessary to begin to imagine how concepts such as psychosocial might conjure up alternative ways for understanding sexual subjectivities. Central to this is an engagement with queer theoretical perspectives, which are already hybridized forms that draw across the psychic and social fields. Similarly, I embrace Frosh's (2010a, p. 198) reference to the psychosocial as a 'sutured unit' if 'ill-defined entity' and, despite the risks of reinvigorating the dualism, I propose it as a productive transdisciplinary approach for exploring sexuality and subjectivity.

Towards a psychosocial manifesto for sexuality

The impetus for this book was originally sparked in November 2003 after hearing David Halperin speak at the *Sexuality after*

Foucault conference in Manchester. In a talk that became the basis for his essay *What Do Gay Men Want?* (2007, p. 11), he made the provocative statement that what was needed was a theory of gay male subjectivity 'without necessary or automatic recourse to psychology or psychoanalysis'. At the time I was writing about transgender subjectivity, working in an interdisciplinary sense drawing on insights from feminist and queer perspectives, and critical psychology. As are all critical psychologists, particularly those with an interest in gender and sexuality, I was well schooled in the limitations of psychology and its methods, its normalizing and pathologizing history, its promotion of the rational, free choice making individual over other models of the self, its political conservatism and dispiriting alignment with maintaining the status quo. Yet, this statement troubled me: what would it mean to theorize subjectivity without recourse to psychology? Would it be possible to do away with psychology, to kill it off as Foucault had once suggested?

The second time I heard Halperin give this paper was in Sydney at the *International Conference of Queer Asian Studies* in February 2007, just before his extended essay was published. By then I had secured a contract to write this book, then loosely titled *On Sexualities* that set out a similar structure to the one delivered here. The idea was to provide a comprehensive overview of a range of disciplinary engagements with 'sexualities' as they are developed, constructed, queered, embodied and politicized. The aim was to produce a text that would be relevant to students and academics in psychology and sociology wanting to gain an expanded view of sexualities beyond the one presented in their core discipline. I had just begun researching psychology-based literature for chapters 2 and 3 when I attended the conference, and listening to Halperin on this second occasion irritated me. How, I wondered, could an entire collection of work that had much to say about subjectivity, whether insightfully or not, be dismissed in one phrase: 'without . . . recourse to psychology or psychoanalysis' (2007, p. 11)? Attempting to understand our irritations is always fraught, but this seemed to stem from a perceived unreasonable tendency to collapse psychology and psychoanalysis without proper interrogation

of their similarities and differences, as well as a failure to acknowledge the challenges produced by those doing critical work *within*
psychology and psychoanalysis, which also sought to generate
non-pathologized understandings of queer subjectivities that were
meaningful to the everyday lives of those subjects.

Yet, despite my affective response, Halperin had a point. There
is a problem with the way (for him) gay male subjectivity, but
we might here include all queer subjectivities, are consistently
wrapped up in 'discourses of mental health, the high moral drama
of the individual sexual act, the dichotomous opposition between
rational agency and pathology, and the epidemiology of risk'
(2007, p. 29). In fact, there is much to like about the book that
he published later that year. In it, along similar lines to Lynd and
Warner, he laments that although the impact of Foucault's thesis
removed the 'inner life of male homosexuality' from the realm of
psychology, this was at the expense of exploring queer subjectivities. Thus he argues that in many Foucauldian inspired approaches
sexuality manifests as 'an aesthetics of existence' (p. 8), and lesbian,
gay, bisexual and trans (LGBT) identities have become psychologically empty categories. Nevertheless, his call 'without . . . recourse
to psychology and psychoanalysis' was somewhat undermined by a
belated recognition that not all forms of psychology have partaken
in the pathologizing and individualizing practices that the discipline is renowned for. In fact he states:

> It is not a matter of refuting or rejecting psychoanalysis outright, nor
> of condemning and demonizing the academic field of Psychology as
> a whole – which, after all, includes the radical subfields of social psy-
> chology and critical psychology, so useful for documenting collective
> practices and formations of subjectivity and for locating in subjectivity
> itself a potential site of political resistance. (2007, p. 9)

So the challenge for theorizing subjectivity is less about doing so
without recourse to psychology broadly defined, but more about
the *form* of psychology with which to engage, and the implications of this. This insight injected a second trajectory into the
research for this book. I no longer only read literature from across

disciplinary perspectives for what it told us about sexualities, but also for what it tells us about 'psychology' and the role it plays in producing understandings of sexuality and sexual subjectivities. This introduced a new dynamic into the research process, a new complexity. At times I wondered whether, against my best intentions, I was actually writing a defence of psychology. However, as the research progressed it became clear that 'the psychological is quite literally everywhere' (Brown and Stenner, 2009, p. 4). Not as some monolithic form but as a productive force that is 'being worked out and worked through as a live concern in all aspects of human activity'.

Thus, through the chapters outlined here and expanded in the following pages readers are invited to not only imagine how a 'psychosocial' approach might be shaped for theorizing sexuality and queer subjectivities, but also to rethink definitions of the psychological and its relationship with sexuality and queer studies. We start by considering 'the poles' of the polarization identified here. Chapter 2, 'Developing Sexuality', provides a critical review of core psychological perspectives that have contributed to popular understandings of sexuality as something that is inherent to the individual. The aim of taking 'psychology' as the starting point is to introduce readers who are familiar with general criticisms of psychology, but less so with specific ways these play out in the field of biological and developmental psychology. There are profound conceptual difficulties in attempting to separate sexuality into sexual identities, sexual orientations and sexual behaviours, and empirical evidence that attempts to answer questions about causality is contradictory and contentious. Nevertheless, perspectives such as psychoanalysis, experimental psychology and neuroscience have all played their part in contributing to contemporary debates about sexuality and subjectivity. Understanding how these approaches are problematized *within* psychology is an important tool to help question the way concepts drawn from them reappear later in the book in constructionist, queer and affect theory literature. The final stages of the chapter engage with developmental psychology literature that has discarded questions of causality to focus on the experience of 'growing up gay'. Here, we acknowledge the impact of constructionist perspectives on understandings of identity as a stable category, alongside a expanding concern for the well-being of those who come to call themselves lesbian, gay, bisexual or trans. Chapter 3, 'Constructing Sexuality', considers the second pole of the polarization, historicism, and the way that social constructionist accounts of sexuality have reshaped its conception from condition to role, script, story and discourse. The chapter begins by considering sociological literature and the challenges raised for biological and psychological drive theories, before considering the influence of Foucault and the way that critical and social psychological accounts of sexuality have been informed by these debates. Nevertheless, it is argued that social constructionist critique is insufficient for a psychosocial approach to sexuality and subjectivity, and that there is value in considering the potential of the psychoanalytic and biological concepts it so vehemently rejects if we wish to engage with the rich field of bodies, pleasure and desire. Chapter 4, 'Queering Sexuality', begins this process through an analysis of queer theory as a psychosocial perspective for theorizing sexual subjectivity. The chapter begins by reviewing how queer emerged as a political and theoretical trope for tackling the impasse that had been reached between constructionist and essentialist debates. It revisits the work of queer icons Judith Butler and Eve Kosofsky Sedgwick to consider the relationship between gender, sexuality and identity as analytic categories prior to considering the influence of queer critical race studies for extending the frame of anti-normativity to rethink all forms of categorization and the value of border crossings. In building a psychosocial narrative the chapter interrogates the key principles of anti-identity and anti-normativity to ask whether it is possible to queer psychology, or whether there are limitations with a queer perspective for theorizing subjectivity. If killing off psychology is one particular aim for some queer theorists, others have found sustenance in psychoanalytic quarters, arguing that it is possible to work with psychoanalysis and generate non-normative or non-pathological accounts. In the final section we review the turn to affect as emerging out of the influence of queer theory and ask whether this is actually a return to the psychology of emotions, and what problems this raises if we prioritize feelings over knowledge. Chapters 5 and 6 take a slightly different tack by offering examples of a psychosocial reading of queer subjectivity and politics, drawing on the theoretical and methodological tools built up through the previous chapters. Chapter 5, 'Affecting Sexuality', considers the shift from gay pride to gay shame and the relationship between affect, politics and subjectivity. By engaging with theoretical perspectives introduced earlier in the book, this chapter attempts to link insights from visual and textual observations inspired by cultural studies with a psychosocial concern for the implications of triggering the 'shame scripts' of those who come to call themselves gay. This is developed via a critical reading of two recent British comedy sketches that feature white, gay, male characters to demonstrate the ongoing relevance of shame in the constitution of particular versions of gay male subjectivity against a backdrop of shifting cultural anxieties about contemporary sexuality: in particular, how to talk about homosexuality in a more 'open' and forgiving climate. Secondly, it is argued that if shame and insult mark out certain groups for comic value it is worth considering the possible consequences of this for individual lived subjectivities via the link between affective experiences of shame, discourses of mental health and epidemiological accounts of LGBT 'suicidal risk'. Chapter 6, 'Transforming Sexuality', reconsiders debates from poststructuralism and the paradox of identity for political transformation. The tension between identity-based politics and the importance of recognizing intersectionality for understanding marginalized subjectivities is revisited, before asking whether the 'affective turn' that is associated with queer theorists such as Sedgwick allows us a route out of this impasse via a shift from language, culture and knowing to experience, community and feeling. Drawing on the same examples of gay marriage and mental health and providing readings of political activism and community visual arts projects it considers affective activism as a strategy for transforming queer subjectivities. It is argued that affective activism invites new forms of relating across identity difference producing a vitalist politics that sustains people through their everyday lives (Allison, 2009). The final chapter draws together the strands of each chapter to summarize the vision presented in the book for a psychosocial manifesto and its application to the field of sexuality, subjectivity and the politics of marginalization, reimagining academic endeavours, transdisciplinarity and, ultimately, queer futures.

2

Developing Sexuality

> we are probably better off at this stage of history without yet another
> tentative, ill-supported, potentially false report about the determinants
> of sexual orientation.
>
> Timothy Murphy, 1997, pp. 228–9

Seeking the 'determinants of sexual orientation' is deeply contentious, as well as a methodologically and ethically fraught field of
study, which often results in 'ill-supported' and 'potentially false
reports' (Murphy, 1997). Nevertheless, psychology broadly defined
as a scientific discipline has been at the fore of research initiatives that
aim to establish universal laws that both explain and predict human
sexual behaviour. This goal is underpinned by the Enlightenment
assumption that the psychological subject is a bounded individual,
rational and unified, as opposed to the psychoanalytic model of the
subject as fragmented and repressed, or the postmodern conception
of the subject as multiple, distributed and relational. Furthermore,
scientific psychology frames its understanding of complex phenomena within the epistemological and methodological principles
of positivism that seek to establish cause and effect relationships
between objectively measured and controlled variables. It is from

this basis that the large majority of empirical studies on sexuality are established and evaluated within psychology, particularly in North America, often with a focus on explaining how sexual orientation develops. In an overview of psychological literature from the last 100 years explanations for sexual orientation can be grouped into three broad themes: psychoanalytic models of sexuality, biological accounts of sexual orientation and developmental models of sexual identity formation. However, the scientific study of sexuality and sexual behaviour has almost wholeheartedly been focused on what is seen to be 'abnormal' sexual behaviour. Thus, heterosexuality as a sexual orientation or sexual identity has received far less attention within the scientific and psychological literature, particularly in post-Freudian conceptions, and the term 'sexuality' has become almost synonymous with lesbian or gay lives. As Eliason (1995, p. 821) states, 'rarely has research addressed the question of how heterosexuals achieve a sexual identity, or questioned the stability or homogeneity of this identity, or indeed, asked whether most heterosexuals experience themselves as even having a sexual identity'. It is with this in mind that the following chapter critically evaluates core psychological perspectives for understanding sexuality within a developmental framework in terms of methodological, conceptual and ontological claims, noting where possible, empirical examples of how heterosexual, lesbian, gay and bisexual identities are perceived to develop. The chapter begins by considering the early influence of Freud and his theory of psychosexual development that introduced the notion of biological drives, including the pleasure principle and the death drive, and a model of identity development based around psychosexual developmental stages. In the second section, evidence is evaluated to illustrate the limited support for biological models to explain sexual orientation, considering firstly the role of *hormones, foetal development and gay babies* as well as *neuroscience, gay brains and genetics*. The third section examines more complex models of sexual identity formation that seek to link influences of biological, psychological and social origin to formulate stage or process-related accounts of how one comes to identify as gay, bisexual or heterosexual. Finally the chapter reflects on the limitations of developmental psychological approaches for a psychosocial manifesto.

Freud and psychosexual development

In *Three Essays on the Theory of Sexuality*, Sigmund Freud (1905/1991) established one of the earliest although frequently disputed explanations for the development of sexuality. Freud suggested that infants are born with biologically embedded sexual drives that seek gratification, and that the objects that become sources of gratification lead, over time, to union between impulse and object. Development is theorized as progressing through a set of developmental 'stages', including the oral, anal and phallic stages, followed by a period of latency during late childhood and early adolescence before sexuality emerges again at the 'genital' stage. The movement through these stages is proposed by Freud to be driven by the 'pleasure principle' such that the child seeks delight in an array of erotogenic areas of the body. Yet, as Harding (2001, p. 2) points out, the outcome of arriving at the genital stage is not certain. This is 'firstly because the sexual drive is extraordinarily versatile in its chosen aims and targets, and secondly because the sexual drive conflicts with other psychic demands'. Thus, 'genital sexuality is only one possible outcome of libidinal development'.

There are several crucial elements to Freud's theory of psychosexual development that set it apart from other developmental models. Firstly, rather than seeing sexuality as one facet of identity, Freud positions sexuality, particularly what he refers to as 'libido', as central to the development of the self. It is for this reason that certain forms of personality associated with certain development stages, for example 'anal', have become popularized as a personality characteristic, or even type. Secondly, his theory ties together sexual development with the formation of a gendered self through an emphasis on resolving conflict during the phallic stage of development, between ages three to six. This stage is proposed as pivotal for learning culturally sanctioned sex-roles and sexual preferences, and is illustrated through analogies with Greek mythology stories of Oedipus and Electra. Freud suggests that the Oedipus complex, as indicated through a boy's unconscious desire to become the focus of his mother's attention, is only resolved through identification with the father and the formation of heterosexual preferences. For girls, Freud suggests the Electra complex is resolved by giving up her fantasy of possessing what she lacks (penis) and replacing it with the unconscious desire to have her father's child. It should be noted that these are not literal, conscious desires, but rather for Freud these identifications take place in early unconscious psychic development and go on to govern the types of desires and identifications that emerge in adolescent and adult sexuality. Thirdly, his account of infant sexual development as 'amorphously sensual' opens the possibility for interpretations of sexual identity formation that do not necessarily correlate with a heterosexual orientation. Contra to many critiques, Drescher (1996) argues that Freud did not see homosexuality as a distinctive problem, citing Freud's (1905/1991, p. 56) statement that:

> Psychoanalytic research is most decidedly opposed to any attempt at separating off homosexuals from the rest of mankind as a group of special character . . . it has found that all human beings are capable of making a homosexual object-choice and have in fact made one in their unconscious.

This idea can be traced to Freud's (1925/1991, p. 333) assertion of a 'bisexual constitution' for all human beings. Nonetheless, through what he describes as 'normal development', at the phallic stage the infant disavows their homoerotic desire for the parent of the same-sex and later, at the genital stage, makes a heterosexual object choice determined by their early childhood interaction with parents and caregivers. As Freud (1905/1991, p. 158) summarizes,

> early efflorescence of infantile sexual life (between the ages of two and five) already gives rise to the choice of an object, with all the wealth of mental activities which such a process involves . . . the phase of development corresponding to that period must be regarded as an important precursor of the subsequent final sexual organization.

Thus, for Freud, the object of sexual desire while adaptable during infancy becomes fixed through early interaction. His approach differs from biological models that promote the idea that sexual orientation is determined by biological factors such as hormones and genetics. Yet, this model is also deterministic, grounded in the biology of sexual drives, and allows for little flexibility in the shaping of sexual orientation beyond early childhood. It does, however, permit a more complex account of the relationship between affect and sexuality, for example in his acknowledgement of the relationship between 'anxiety and loss of a person that is loved' (1905/1991, p. 147), the impact of 'shame, disgust and pity' on sexual desire, and the important role 'moral structures' of society play in shaping the direction of sexual instinct in childhood (p. 155).

The problem with Freud?

Freud's theory of psychosexual development has received much criticism from a range of quarters within psychology including empirical psychologists, feminists and those working in gay and lesbian affirmative perspectives. One of the most vocal critiques of Freud's work emanates from the positivistic tradition of psychology. It is not an understatement to suggest that many undergraduate students when arriving to undertake a degree programme in psychology are surprised by how little the work of Freud figures in the curriculum. As Stenner (2007) has noted, if Freud's work is covered this is often through addressing essay questions such as 'Freud or Fraud?' that set out to teach students that his work should be rejected. Much of the criticism of Freud's work stems from its perceived reliance on the methodological insights of introspection. This process confounds the expectation of scientific rigour that has been in place in psychology since the move towards behaviourism, cognition and more recently neuroscience. A second concern that led to the revision of Freud's insights emanated from the value Freud placed on sexuality in the developmental processes. For example, Erikson (1959) modified and extended Freud's theory from a psychosexual model that ended in early adulthood to an eight-stage model of psycho*social* development that required resolving a series of identity crises that supposedly occurred at various points throughout the lifespan.

Critiques of Freud's work can also be found within recent gay and lesbian scholarship in psychology, however accusations that Freud's work was simply pathologizing are less apparent within these accounts. Instead they often emphasize that 'Freud did not regard homosexuals as inherently sick; indeed he believed that they could be content and well adjusted' (Taylor, 2002, p. 159). Yet, Freud's work is chastised for the normalizing and derogatory effects of positioning homosexuality as *developmentally* inferior to heterosexual development. Of particular alarm was the way Freud's theory was been 'embellished' by followers who did seek to pathologize lesbians and gay men by suggesting their sexual orientation was a failure in normal development (Brown, 1995; Taylor, 2002), perspectives that underpinned the inclusion of homosexuality in the first edition of the *Diagnostic and Statistical Manual for Mental Disorders* (DSM) (APA, 1952). The work of US psychiatrist and psychoanalyst Charles Socarides stands as an emblematic example of this type of practice. Socarides (1968) reworked Freud to argue that homosexuality was a form of 'arrested development', suggesting it was the result of intrapsychic conflict such that the homosexual was 'filled with aggression, destruction and self deceit' (1968, p. 67). He was a lifelong proponent of the view that homosexuality was suitable for therapeutic intervention and defended his actions in providing evidence against the American Psychiatric Association's (APA) decision to remove homosexuality from the third edition of the DSM in 1973 (Socarides, 1995). In an overview of psychoanalytic conceptualizations of homosexuality, Drescher (1996) documents how followers of Freud have produced accounts of homosexuality as pathology *and* as normal sexual variation. He argues that no psychoanalytic account is credible in terms of 'scientific facts', rather 'the manner in which psychoanalysts choose to speak, act, and write about these issues is based on their moral and ethical beliefs' (1996, p. 187). Thus, psychoanalytic theories cannot be separated from the cultural and political times in which they are generated. However, in exploring a psychosocial or transdisciplinary understanding of sexuality psychoanalysis can provide ways of thinking about sexual development via a non-rationalist model. It can also help think about the way desire for particular 'objects' is not determined by biology alone, but mediated by interpersonal interactions and the social order. Furthermore, despite Freud's normalizing language it also raises questions about the naturalness of any sexual orientation other than what we have come to call 'bisexuality'. It is perhaps for this reason that Freud's work has had much more influence within queer theoretical perspectives than it ever could given the scientific imperative of psychological studies. While it is rare to find a reference beyond *Three Essays on Sexuality* within psychological textbooks, scholars in queer studies have developed Freud's later ideas, as well as those of Klein and Lacan to offer rich readings and perspectives on pleasure, perversion, shame, disgust, AIDS, homophobia and love. The concept of melancholia has received much attention for theorizing the formation of sexual subjectivities and identities where sexuality as resolution to loss is seen as central. Equally, the 'death drive', a second drive theory that Freud introduced in *Beyond the Pleasure Principle*, has been crucial in defining debates in contemporary queer theory. Here Freud proposed that behind our drive to seek pleasure, to live and to reproduce, is a first instinct 'to return to the inanimate state' that predates life, such that 'the aim of all life is death' (Freud, 1920/2001, p. 39). As Josh Cohen (2005, p. 103) summarizes:

> The thesis of the *death-drive* remains the most controversial and contested of his concepts, reshaping our sense of Freud's own enterprise and opening up new and unexpected roads into the psychoanalytic future. For many in the mainstream of the analytic movement, the death-drive would remain outside the canon of Freud's key terms, an aberrant speculative digression, lacking the necessary grounding in empirical observation and research. For his bolder and more controversial successors, however . . . , it was the very excess, the conceptual 'madness' of the death-drive that made it such an inexhaustible resource for psychoanalytic thinking.

However, the ways in which psychoanalysis has been used and reformulated means within the disciplines of psychology and psychiatry, it has become positioned as a risky perspective for theorizing sexual subjectivity, especially for those who take up non-normative sexual identities.

Biological models and sexual orientation

For those who favour biological explanations 'biology' is seen to determine sexual orientation; it is *the* foundational category with which social and psychological factors interact. As fleshy and bodily beings it is difficult to deny that physiological processes are not involved in all aspects of human behaviour and interaction. Yet, for others, attempts to ground sexual orientation in biology are fraught with methodological and conceptual difficulties, as they frequently fail to acknowledge the role social processes play in shaping biology, as well as being underpinned with moral and ethical dilemmas (Hubbard and Wald, 1993; Brown, 1995; Fausto-Sterling, 2000). Despite these necessary criticisms a series of approaches have been proposed to both explain sexual development and illustrate the vital function of biology in this (Rosario, 1997). In the work of early sexologists we find examples of numerous diagnostic terms to refer to homosexuality, including 'contrary sexual feeling' (von Krafft-Ebing, 1886) and 'sexual inversion' (Ellis and Symonds, 1897/1936). These define and shape an unbroken line of research that has stretched since the mid-nineteenth century to today, consistently conceiving of homosexuality as a biological phenomenon (Rosario, 1997). There are, of course, competing histories about the role of early sexologists in the construction of homosexuality and attempts have been made to rebuff their work as 'psychologizing' and 'pathologizing'. But, as Vernon Rosario (1997) skilfully notes, even contemporary biologists (e.g. Hamer and Copeland, 1994) have joined this dismissal while staking their own claims to biological explanations for homosexuality that ground same-sex behaviour as a variation of nature. These competing histories will be elaborated further in chapter 3, but for now it is useful to attend to the evidence that suggests early sexologists such as Richard von Krafft-Ebing were not simply enemies of homosexuals (Terry, 1999). Rather, they were sympathetic supporters of what might retrospectively be seen as 'sexual minority rights' and used biological explanations to elucidate the many case studies submitted to them by self-identified 'inverts'. As Rosario (2002, p. 81) expands, 'many historians have pointed out that biological models have been popular with inverts and homosexuals (especially men) since the beginning of biomedical attempts to explain same-sex attraction'. Thus, it can be argued that biological studies of sexual orientation can be used for opposing political aims: for normalizing and defending homosexuality, as well as pathologizing and condemning it (Rosario, 1997, p. 3).

However, the focus on biology has always presupposed a particular question, 'what causes the development of a homosexual orientation?' From the mid-1950s, in order to pinpoint the genesis of sexual orientation, the biological tradition increased its focus on the role of hormones in pre- and postnatal development. Key influences within this trend are the work of well-known sexologists Anke Erhardt and John Money (1967; Money and Erhardt, 1972). Money (1988, pp. 11–12) was a lifelong proponent of the impact of prenatal hormones on brain dimorphism and sexual orientation development. He opposed the use of phrases such as 'sexual preference' arguing that: 'There is no option, no plan. . . . One either is or is not bisexual, homosexual, or heterosexual.' Thus, he saw no potential for fluidity in sexual desire despite acknowledging that heterosexual people might engage in same-sex acts and homosexuals might have heterosexual partners, if particular conditions required it. For Money, separating out 'sex acts' from 'sexual orientation' was quite straightforward: the definitive criterion required for a homosexual, heterosexual or bisexual orientation was 'falling in love', and this status is 'locked' into the brain 'prenatally by a process of genetic determinism, or by the determinism of fetal hormonal or other brain chemistries'.

Hormones, foetal development and gay babies

Maternal stress was one of the first areas to be investigated as a potential influence on hormone levels that might effect prenatal development. In 1983 Dörner et al. conducted a study involving 100 men identified as bisexual or homosexual, and 100 men identified as heterosexual. The men were asked to consult with their parents in order to report on any events that had been experienced by their mother as stressful during their prenatal lives. The researchers concluded that mothers of bisexual or gay men were more likely to report instances of 'moderate' or 'severe' stress during pregnancy than the mothers of heterosexual men, and that the types of events that constituted 'maternal stress' included 'war' and 'unwanted pregnancies'. In a conclusion that has been described as 'bold' (Zucker and Bradley, 1995, p. 158) the researchers suggested that the 'prevention of war and undesired pregnancies may render possible a partial prevention of the development of sexual deviations' (Dörner et al., 1983, p. 87). Shameless might be a more appropriate summation of this conclusion given the multiple war zones that exist across the globe and the impact this has on issues far more profound than levels of homosexuality, including the number of undesired pregnancies that result from brutal crimes against women during war. But, in evaluating the findings, rather than address the sentiments underlying a moral agenda, Kenneth Zucker and Susan Bradley critique the study for the absence of a reliability check for the variables 'maternal stress' or 'sexual orientation', before offering the higher rate of absent fathers during war as an alternative explanation for the homosexuality/bisexuality of these men.

In a second widely reported example, Ellis et al. (1988), influenced by Money's (1988) proposition that sexual differentiation of the brain is more sensitive during the second trimester, also found that mothers of gay men recalled experiencing more stress than mothers of heterosexual men or bisexual men. Stress was reported to be more severe during the nine to twelve months prior to their pregnancy as well as during the expected second trimester of their pregnancy, but no difference was found in recollection of stress between mothers of lesbian or heterosexual women. Despite its findings being criticized for statistical flaws (Zucker and Bradley, 1995) and no relationship between maternal stress and lesbianism supported, this study has been drawn on in popular psychology books as a reason to reduce stress during pregnancy, in order to avoid having a 'gay baby' (Pease and Pease, 1998). This is the type of research that critics of psychology have grounds to dismiss out of hand. Yet the slippage from empirically flawed research to popular generalizations has long-term implications for public attitudes towards homosexuality, particularly when the research is held up as a 'scientific truth' that most lay people would have little reason to doubt.

Problematically, the contentious and flawed nature of research findings about the origins of sexual orientation is far less likely to be widely reported. In a mid-century overview of research findings, Richard Green (1979, pp. 120, 130) argued there was 'no definitive conclusion as to the effect of prenatal exposure to sex-typed hormones on postnatal behaviours'. As a result he argued that researchers needed to move forward by 'incorporating all components of the multi-determined nature of human sexuality in the dynamic interface between biological and social systems'. This status has remained the same today despite research into the biological origins of sexual orientation continuing apace over the last thirty years. Since then, maternal stress has been implicated alongside genetics and the consumption of alcohol in dermatoglyphic studies that seek to map out differences in finger ridge patterns in relation to sexual orientation (e.g. Hall and Kimura, 1994). Some have moved away from maternal stress to develop the 'maternal immune hypothesis' that focuses on changes in the uterine environment as a result of successive male births to explain correlations between fraternal birth order and homosexuality in males (e.g. Blanchard and Bogaert, 1996). Others have analysed prenatal exposure to elevated rates of hormones in hormone treated pregnancies as one area of development for understanding sexual orientation (Meyer-Bahlburg, 1995). All of these studies are problematic. Most provide no more than correlations between disparate variables such as 'birth order' and 'sexual orientation' wrapped in the proposition that further study of these 'biological processes' will reveal the determinants of this relationship. Moreover, while none of these researchers claims to have found a causal model for sexual orientation the failure to do so is primarily attributed to methodological limitations, rather than their own epistemological and conceptual starting points.

Neuroscience, gay brains and genetics

In recent years attention has turned to the possibility of mapping difference in sexual orientation within the brain. Neuroanatomist Simon Le Vay (1991) famously published an article in the internationally acclaimed journal *Science* suggesting that one of the nuclei (INAH3) of the anterior hypothalamus was three times smaller in gay men than straight men, and similar in size to heterosexual women. Le Vay's work is remarkably similar in format to that of Dick Swaab and colleagues who have argued that gender identity can also be traced to particular nuclei in the hypothalamus (Zhou et al., 1995; Swaab, 2005). Le Vay's study (1991, 1993) was greeted with much fanfare and widely misreported in the media as the discovery of a 'gay gene'. Murphy (1997, p. 27) points out that 'Le Vay himself protests that he did not prove that "homosexuality is genetic" or some such thing' but suggests the extrapolation of his findings to such conclusions were not helped by his statements such as 'to put an absurdly facile spin on it, gay men simply don't have the brain cells to be attracted to women'. These recent neuroanatomy studies have, however, been used to support the argument that both gender identity and sexual orientation are determined in the brain during prenatal development (Swaab, 2005).

A number of salient limitations and critiques that rebuke the implications of Le Vay's findings are skilfully summarized by Murphy (1997). Firstly, given that there are exceptions to the correlation between INAH3 size and sexual orientation within Le Vay's research sample, Murphy suggests he may have misinterpreted this relationship and it is possible that other factors might predict the size of INAH3. In responding to this Le Vay relies on a familiar defensive block, attributing the exception cases to a flaw in the methodology: 'It is also possible, however, that these exceptions are due to technical shortcomings or to misassignment of subjects to their subject groups' (Le Vay, 1991, p. 1036). But, as Murphy (1997, p. 28) replies, it is unlikely that this error would only take place in the assignment of gay men, 'taking straight for gay, gay for straight – would likely have occurred as well'. Secondly, feminist biologist Anne Fausto-Sterling (2000) also dismisses the simplicity of a model that proposes a rigid binary between categories gay and straight that can be mapped onto a single area of the hypothalamus. Thirdly, it is important to note that these studies are based on brain autopsies. In Le Vay's study the gay male subjects had died from AIDS and it was not possible to control for the effect of drug treatment or disease on the brain structure of these men. And finally, some biologists dispute the very staining techniques that are used to identify clusters of cells suggesting they can create biological artefacts, thus INAH3 may have been manufactured in the research process. Consequently, this study does not afford much in the way of establishing the determinants of sexual orientation. At best, as Murphy argues, it suggests there might be a correlation between INAH3 and sexual orientation. Nevertheless, neuroscience developments have continued apace since the 1990s such that we now find studies increasingly focused on illustrating brain differences via functional magnetic resonance imaging (fMRI) and positron emission tomography (PET). Recently, it has been suggested that these differences occur in the amygdala where again it is claimed that lesbians have the same brain structure as heterosexual men, and gay men as women (Savic and Lindström, 2008). Yet, these findings lead us no closer to an explanation for sexual dimorphism, or even for why when under stressful conditions the volume in blood flow in the amygdala suggests cross-gender connection. Instead, we are left with an empty suggestion that explanations for this difference are probably the result of sex hormones in the womb, or genetics. Much more worrying than whether there are inherited differences is the broader question of what researchers hope this type of research will do. An article published in *Medical News Today* (2011) gives insight into this, couched in its own interpretation of the important intervention the research might have. Citing Dr Jerome Goldstein (director of San Francisco Clinical Research Center, USA) speaking about Savic and Lindström's study at the twenty-first meeting of the European Neurological Society (ENS), the article reports:

> 'We must continue to bring forward data that show the differences or similarities between the brains of homosexuals, heterosexuals, bisexuals, and trans gender persons. Clearly the basis of sexual orientation is in the brain and differences in brain structure and function and the province of neurology', Dr. Goldstein added. 'Neuroscience has much to offer in the area of understanding the origins of all variations of sexual orientation. The neurobiology of sexual orientation and the gay brain, matched with other hormonal, genetic, and structural studies, has far-reaching consequences beyond sexual orientation.' Treatment variations are already emerging as a result of recognition of sexual orientation differences and the advent of gender specific medicine.

This final reference to 'treatment' returns us to the most problematic element of psychological research that seeks a causal explanation for sexual variation. This does not imply the desire to find a biologically determining factor that can naturalize sexual orientation beyond the norm. Instead it carries moral assumptions about the value of sexual and gender variation and raises questions about the ethics of doing research in the field of sexual orientation.

Elsewhere, psychologists have relied on twin studies in order to investigate the possibility of a genetic explanation for sexual orientation. A series of studies by the controversial psychologist Michael Bailey and his colleagues (Bailey and Pillard, 1991; Bailey et al., 1993, 2000) has argued that there is some evidence for a genetic explanation for sexual orientation. For example, Bailey and Pillard (1991) assessed the likelihood of homosexuality in a group of monozygotic twins, dizygotic twins and non-genetically related adopted siblings. In the male sample they found the likelihood of identical twins having a gay or bisexual brother to be 52 per cent, non-identical twins 22 per cent and for genetically unrelated brothers the likelihood was 11 per cent. In the female sample they found a 48 per cent likelihood that identical twins would have a lesbian twin, a 16 per cent likelihood for non-identical twins and a 6 per cent likelihood for adopted sisters. While comparing individuals of varying genetic closeness allows the researchers to acknowledge that social and environmental factors play a role in the development of sexual orientation they do not sufficiently engage with these. Almost half the likelihood for developing a gay identification is determined by something other than genetics in the male sample and this increases to over 75 per cent in the female sample. Thus, while genetics might play a part in development the social environment is as important. Moreover, this study permits little insight into the *ways* in which genetics or the environment might influence sexual development, or the way they interact with each other.

The genetic basis for homosexuality garnered further support from another study involving gay and lesbian siblings reported in *Science* that also received much media attention. Hamer et al. (1993) suggest that male homosexuality is associated with a particular gene on the X chromosome, Xq 28. The implication of this finding is that homosexuality in men is inherited via a genetic link to an uncle on the mother's side of the family (Hyde, 2005). This claim was further supported by a follow-up study (Hu et al., 1995) but a second attempt to replicate the finding failed to do so (Rice et al., 1999). Findings from the data on lesbian siblings found no such link and led the researchers to conclude that pathways of development for sexual orientation are different for males and females (Hu et al., 1995). Again, the evidence for a genetic link is tentative, leading Evan Balaban to the emphatic conclusion that 'they've shown little more than that a group of highly selected men who happen to be homosexual share among them a certain region of the X chromosome at a higher rate than would be expected due to chance' (cited in Murphy, 1997, p. 35). Janet Hyde remains more optimistic that genetics will reveal intriguing insights into the origins of homosexuality. She describes the first full genome scan for sexual orientation in men (Mustanski et al., 2005) as a major breakthrough, as it found evidence for genetic transmission on chromosomes 7, 8 and 10. Despite this, she recognizes sexuality as highly complex and multifaceted and argues that while biological substrates are developmental, they are not necessarily fixed from birth as 'biological phenomena emerge or disappear at various times across the life span' (Hyde, 2005, p. 172). However Hyde looks to modern neuroscience to explain sexual development through an understanding of the interactive processes between genes, the brain and the endocrine system and believes this will materialize through new and improved advances in research techniques and technologies. The truth is out there, still waiting to be discovered – if only we had the right methods. What is more likely is that as neuroscience research techniques become more nuanced and sensitive they will create exponentially more complicated pictures of the sometimes stable, often fleeting relationships between biological substrates. This is because biological phenomena will always be shaped and remodelled by social factors, illustrated by research that shows changes in behaviour and the environment can lead to changes in brain structure (Draganski et al., 2006).

One way for proponents of biological models to acknowledge the complexity of sexuality has been to note that there can be variation and discordance between the categories sexual orientation, sexual identity and sexual behaviour (Bailey, 1995). Thus, some have turned to a 'psychological' definition of sexual orientation that focuses on 'sexual attraction' while acknowledging that sexual identity or sexual behaviour are more readily shaped by social processes (Money, 1988; Le Vay, 1993; Bailey, 1995). This point is interesting because it suggests that biological models of sexual development are not completely blind to the importance of social context in the formation of sexual identity, behaviour and practices. Rather, they are focused on the affective state of sexual desire or attraction as core to sexual orientation, leaving the seemingly less stable relationship between sexual identity and sexual behaviour to more socially informed fields of study. The problem with this approach, however, is that scientific evidence has yet to conclusively support the proposition that sexual orientation is determined by prenatal biological factors and that desire and attraction are not entwined with identity and behaviour. Indicating this, in a recent summation of biological understanding of sexual orientation, is that:

a number of factors seem to influence sexual differentiation of the brain and thus sexual orientation and gender identity. Chromosomal disorders, genetic factors, stress during pregnancy, and medicines taken by the pregnant mother may play a role. Postnatal social factors do not seem to be of primary importance for the development of sexual orientation or gender identity. (Swaab, 2005, p. 656)

What is crucial here though is just how tentative most of the biological findings are. As Blanchard et al. (2006, p. 412) conclude in their publicly funded study of the interaction of fraternal birth order and handedness in the development of male homosexuality: 'Of course, both explanations of the present data, like any other hypotheses that might be advanced right now, are purely conjectural. They are offered largely as a stimulus to further study.' Positivistic psychology regularly rallies attacks on qualitative approaches accusing them of being unable to distinguish between conclusions and conjecture. Yet, speculative explanations abound in biological accounts while continuing to attract large-scale funding because of their claims to a scientific status that will eventually reveal the truth of sexual orientation development. Even more concerning is that when the findings are largely disputed or rejected as both methodologically and interpretatively flawed, the popularity of these explanations and the truths about sexuality they erroneously presuppose continue to circulate in wider domains (Nelkin and Lindee, 1995). Few seem to note the paradox that in the search for biological markers of sexual orientation some of these studies through a focus on social factors such as 'maternal stress' or 'alcohol consumption during pregnancy' already highlight the crucial role that the social environment may play in shaping biology, while implicitly implying a moral agenda that locates responsibility for homosexuality in the behaviour and practices of women during pregnancy. Thus, with a lack of any conclusive evidence for causal models of sexual orientation and the dangers inherent in explicit and implicit moral agendas that underpin this type of research, many critics ask what is the point in pursuing this type of research agenda at all. As Murphy (1997, p. 73) eloquently states in his analysis of the ethics of sexual orientation research:

The origins of erotic desire are not necessarily the most interesting
questions to be asked in regard to homoeroticism. . . . A richer and
deeper understanding is to be found in asking what society has made
of homoeroticism and why. And these questions have little to do with
the size of brain structures, antenatal fetal hormone balances, the X
chromosome, or the density and distribution of finger skin ridges.
These questions are, by contrast, questions about the origin of public
morality and social conscience.

Developmental models of sexual identity formation

Rather than focusing on the unavailing origins of sexual orientation, some lesbian and gay affirmative psychologists turned their
attention to conceptualizing the processes by which lesbians, gay
men and bisexual men and women develop their identity in a
hostile environment (Gonsiorek and Rudolph, 1991). Within this
tradition researchers attempted to account for the psychological
difficulties some lesbian and gay men experienced by suggesting
that the stresses encountered by LGB people can result in elevated
levels of psychological distress (Gonsiorek, 1995; D'Augelli and
Grossman, 2001; King et al., 2003). This approach grew in popularity in the 1970s as clinicians working with lesbians and gay
men noticed certain patterns within their clients' experiences of
establishing a same-sex identity. The processes involved in identity
development have been widely conceptualized through a variety
of 'coming-out' models (Dank, 1971; Plummer, 1975; Cass, 1979)
where a person is seen to move through a series of stages before
'accepting' or 'coming to terms' with their sexuality (Bohan,
1996). The interface between sociology and psychology should
be noted here as these types of models were formulated in both
disciplines: for example, the sociological work of Ken Plummer
(1975, 1981) and Gagnon and Simon (1968, 1973) is frequently
referenced in psychology-based overviews of the process of sexual
identity development, and latter day critiques of models of sexual
identity have drawn on sociological concepts to evaluate develop-

mental models (Troiden, 1979; Gonsiorek and Rudolph, 1991; Brown, 1995; Fox, 1996; Flowers and Buston, 2001; see chapter 3 for more detailed discussion of sociologically informed understandings of identity formation).

Coming out: developing a homosexual identity

The best-known developmental model within psychology was produced by Vivien Cass (1979, 1984, 1990, 1996) who proposed the Homosexual Identity Formation (HIF) model, which involves six stages: (i) identity confusion, (ii) identity comparison, (iii) identity tolerance, (iv) identity acceptance, (v) identity pride, and finally (vi) identity synthesis. Cass (1996, p. 232) suggests there are several pathways of interaction at each stage and that moving through each stage of development brings about a series of changes for the individual, including (i) increased use of the term lesbian or gay to account for and understand oneself, (ii) use of the terms 'lesbian' or 'gay' as an explanation of self within a larger set of interpersonal exchanges, (iii) development of increasingly positive feelings about being a lesbian or gay man, (iv) increasing belief that one belongs to the lesbian or gay social group and strengthening of social ties with other lesbians or gay men, (v) gradual acceptance of positive values about homosexuals as a social group, (vi) increasing independence from heterosexual values and (vii) a gradual shift in the use of the concept lesbian or gay from a means of labelling self to a description of an inner belief in self. Cass (1990, 1996) acknowledges that identity formation is complex and multifaceted and that some individuals will not 'progress' to the final stage if they encounter environmental conditions that are detrimental to identity development. Thus, for Cass, environmental factors such as societal norms, family beliefs and negative events are seen to interact with individual factors (defined as 'needs, desires and learned behaviour') and biological factors (defined as 'level of sexual desire'). This interaction can 'foreclose' identity development leaving the gay or lesbian individual in a state of cognitive conflict that may stall their development, such that they are unable to incorporate new information that will help shape their emotion, cognition and behaviour and lead them into identity pride and synthesis.

Subsequent studies have set about testing Cass's model and there is significant disagreement about its validity and the number of stages that are involved in the process of sexual identity development. Furthermore, competing explanations are offered that favour a 'phase' or more flexible 'process' model of development, rather than multiple, distinct, linear stages of development that a person must move through in order to develop a secure self-identity as lesbian or gay. For example, support has been found for Cass's HIF model in a sample of lesbians and gay men (Cass, 1984) and lesbian women (Levine, 1997), while others (Levine and Evans, 1991) suggest that the model can be just as well explained by four main developmental levels: awareness, self-labelling, community involvement and disclosure, and identity integration. McCarn and Fassinger (1996, p. 521) have proposed an alternative process-orientated model that links personal sexual identity development with group membership development. In a study with lesbians they argued that sexual identity development involved 'two parallel branches that are reciprocally catalytic but not simultaneous' with each branch consisting of four phases including (i) awareness, (ii) exploration, (iii) deepening/commitment and (iv) internalization/synthesis. In a second study with gay men Fassinger and Miller (1997) found support for the four phases, but no evidence to suggest that there is a separation between individual and group identity development. In an evaluation of her own model, Cass (1984) has also suggested that a four-stage process might account for her proposed six stages, but elsewhere she has continued to support the original model (Cass, 1996). Others (e.g. Johns and Probst, 2004, p. 81) have argued that 'sexual minorities view the identity formation process as occurring in two phases, rather than multiple, discrete linear stages'. These phases are characterized by whether sexual orientation is 'fully integrated' or 'unintegrated' into self-identity. This points to the problematic assumptions of linear stage models of development in that they assume only one outcome (Brown, 1995), they do not adequately account for many individuals' experiences of coming out (Rust, 1993; Fox, 1996), and while 'this linear progression is intuitively appealing, extant research suggests that it is far from universal' (Savin-Williams and Diamond, 2000, p. 608).

Despite these critiques, John Gonsiorek (1995, p. 32) argues that 'coming out models are an important theoretical development', as they describe the developmental process that lesbian and gay youths have to negotiate in *addition* to more generic forms of development. Brown (1995, p. 18) suggests that while coming-out models have limitations their strength can be found in the importance they afford to the relationship between 'internal reality and external cultural context . . . demonstrating how social discourse influences the process of naming oneself lesbian [or gay] as well as the meaning ascribed to that name'. This means that comparative analyses with non-western populations while revealing similarities in psychological processes would not be expected to generate the same findings, as Gonsiorek (1995, p. 35) points out:

> this perspective stresses the relationship between the individual, social forces, and sense of self, these differing cultural perspectives are not variations on a theme epitomized by the white, middle-class, North American, English-speaking world. Rather, the entire developmental process and outcomes in the sense of self can vary greatly as the social forces that shape them vary. In other words, as the experiences of diverse groups are observed and described, the model begins to shift qualitatively, rather than merely quantitatively.

In this sense, there can be no one model that adequately explains homosexual identity formation as development will be shaped by the wider social context. As Sears (1989, p. 447) puts it, 'the development of homosexual identity is shaped by the racial and gendered contexts in which the person is situated'. Drawing on a range of studies with lesbian and gay men from non-white ethnic backgrounds, Gonsiorek (1995) demonstrates how multiple personal identities interact resulting in a variety of cultural stresses. For example, black men have been reported as experiencing triple prejudice, for being black in a white heterosexual majority, for being black in a gay white majority, and for being gay in a black heterosexual majority (Icard, 1986). Elsewhere, studies consistently point to gender differences in the developmental process. For example, some researchers note that lesbians are more likely to experience early same-sex attraction as an affectional rather than sexual phenomenon (Sears, 1989; Brown, 1995; Diamond, 1998). This has been supported further by empirical studies that propose a different developmental pathway through sexual identity milestones such as: first same-sex attraction, self-labelling, same-sex contact and disclosure. Ritch Savin-Williams and Lisa Diamond (2000, p. 607) conducted interviews with 164 sexual-minority young adults and found that while the gap from first same-sex attraction to disclosure averaged ten years for men and women, women were more likely to follow 'label first developmental trajectories' while 'men were more likely to pursue sex before identifying themselves as gay'.

Although these concerns with the developmental process of lesbians and gay men arose from an *affirmative* focus, one of the key limitations of 'coming-out' models or models of homosexual identity formation is that they maintain a focus on same-sex practices shielding any developmental processes associated with heterosexuality behind a blanket of normality. As Worthington et al. (2008, p. 22) suggest, despite the range of models applied to lesbian and gay individuals 'there has been only limited progress in the construction of models that apply to bisexual or heterosexual individuals'. In the next section we examine attempts to provide models and theories of sexual development that can incorporate a range of sexual identities, including heterosexuality and bisexuality and consider whether these can be expanded to account for sexuality more generally.

Bisexuality and the disruption of binary sexual identities

Bisexuality has its own established history since being introduced by Freudian psychoanalysis. This history has seen both alterations in its conceptual origins and various impositions in accounts of psychopathology (Fox, 1996; Angelides, 2001). A variety of researchers (e.g. Klein, 1993; Fox, 1996; Lee and Crawford, 2007) have pointed out how the dominant conceptualization of sexuality within a heterosexual/homosexual binary has left bisexuality both 'uniquely conceivable and uniquely inconceivable in Western culture' (Rust, 2000, p. 205). Furthermore, even in the growing discipline of LGBTQ psychology, bisexuality remains frequently misunderstood and marginalized along with transgenderism (Hegarty, 2004; Clarke and Peel, 2007). Ronald Fox (2004) argues that although still marginal, there have been notable transformations since the 1970s that have led to a better understanding of bisexuality. These shifts include the move towards affirmative theoretical perspectives in research on gay and lesbian identity (as documented above) and a gradual questioning from the 1980s onwards of dichotomous views on sexuality. Fox attributes this latter shift to the impact of the work of Alfred Kinsey and colleagues (1948, 1953) on contemporary approaches. Kinsey proposed a model of sexual orientation that drew a continuum from heterosexual, through bisexuality to homosexuality. Others have expanded this to construct more complex models such as the Klein Sexual Orientation Grid (Klein et al., 1985). Klein's approach as outlined in the book *The Bisexual Option* (1993) offers a multidimensional understanding of sexuality as more than 'sexual identity'. For example, the grid consists of variables that are used to measure aspects of sexuality through self-referential time dimensions including past, present and ideal status. The variables provide respondents with the opportunity to represent variation in their sexuality by measuring factors such as: sexual attraction, sexual behaviour, sexual fantasies, emotional preference, social preference, heterosexual/homosexual lifestyle and self-identification. This scale has been used to demonstrate multiple identifications of bisexuality along continuum lines. For example, Weinberg et al. (1994) evidenced different 'types' of bisexuality including what they label as pure, mid, heterosexual leaning, homosexual leaning, and varied types; while Weinrich and Klein (2003) identified what they describe as three bisexual subgroups: bi–gay, bi–straight and bi–bi. Worthington et al. (2008, p. 23) interpret these studies to

claim that they deliver conclusions about bisexuality that counter-
act existent stereotypes. These conclusions are summarized as:

> (a) Bisexuality is a unique and legitimate identity; (b) substantial
> external pressures to conform to the gay–straight binary may result in
> considerable confusion, exploration and uncertainty; and (c) there are
> important within-group differences among bisexual individuals that
> have critical influences on sexual identity development.

These models of bisexual identity should be commended for their
greater attendance to multiplicity in the psychic life of sexuality,
for example by allowing for fluidity in how people might describe
their sexual attractions, sexual fantasies or emotional connections
across a broader spectrum than gay or straight. However, there are
a number of limitations with their foundational categories. Firstly,
while the models discuss different stages or processes in identity
formation, they either assume one of the dichotomous poles as the
starting point for identity construction, such that bisexuality is only
formed once emerging out of either a heterosexual or homosexual
identity, or, in pin-pointing bisexuality on a continuum, they rein-
force the dichotomy by classifying in reference to either the gay or
straight pole (e.g. bi-gay, bi-straight or bi-bi). Secondly, Weinberg
et al. (1994) propose a model of bisexual identity formation that
sees the individual move from a heterosexual identity through four
stages: initial confusion, finding and applying the label, settling
into the identity and continued confusion. This problematically
reinforces the notion that a bisexual identity can never be experienced as stable, presumably because the bisexual person may
always be wondering whether they are really gay or really straight.
Mary Bradford (2004) takes issue with this conclusion on two
grounds. Firstly, she critiques the assumption of the heterosexual-
to-bisexual trajectory in this model suggesting from her own
findings that bisexual people can also move in the direction from
homosexual-to-bisexual. The second critique is embedded within
Weinberg et al.'s (1994) conclusion: the notion that bisexual individuals remain in a state of continued uncertainty that might be
marked with periods of doubts about their own sexual identity.

Bradford (2004) rejects this claim and suggests that with sufficient community affirmation, social action and leadership it is possible to experience certainty in a bisexual identity, despite cultural forces that marginalize it or erase it by labelling it as a transitory 'phase' on the way to the development of a stable heterosexual or homosexual identity. Bradford does this by proposing her own model that sees bisexual individuals move through four stages, including questioning reality, inventing identity, maintaining identity and transforming adversity. This affirmative approach encourages notions of 'self-fulfilment' while reinforcing the importance of validating a bisexual identity – as people who self-identify as bisexual often do experience widespread discrimination or derision in a culture that does little to recognize a lifelong bisexual identification (Barker et al., 2012). Social psychological commentators have labelled this a 'double bind' (Barker, 2004) where bisexuals can experience hostility and marginalization from the lesbian and gay community as well as from wider society.

A third concern that emerges when reflecting on the literature on bisexual identity formation is insufficient attendance to gender difference in men and women's experiences of bisexuality. Bisexuality frequently becomes gender free and few theorists present a sophisticated analysis of how identity formation or commitment might emerge for bisexual men or women. A noted exception to this can be found in the work of Lisa Diamond (2008). Diamond has made a consistent contribution to the developmental psychology literature on same-sex identity, attraction and behaviour in women, whether they identify as lesbian or bisexual (Diamond, 1998, 2003a, 2005, 2008). Diamond (2008, p. 5) outlines the continued debate about whether bisexuality should be conceptualized as '(a) a temporary stage of denial, transition, or experimentation; (b) a "third type" of sexual orientation, characterized by fixed patterns of attraction to both sexes; or (c) a strong form of all individuals' capacity for sexual fluidity'. She points to the importance of longitudinal studies if researchers are to be able to draw conclusions about how sexual attraction might 'change over time', and suggests that there is evidence 'that women's desires are even more situation dependent and less category specific than those of men'

(2008, p. 6). For example, in comparing change over time in a New Zealand cohort study, Dickson et al. (2003) found that over a five-year period 30 per cent of men who reported ever having had a same-sex attraction experienced a shift in their attraction, and two-thirds of these reported the change as attraction towards the same sex. In the same study, the ratios for same-sex attraction and change over time differed for women. They found that of the 45 per cent of women who reported ever having had a same-sex attraction, two-thirds reported a change in their attraction over time and that 80 per cent of these were towards the same sex. Although studies such as these usefully provide further support for the proposal that there may be qualitative differences in bisexual experiences of men and women, Diamond (2008) argues that the study has certain limitations including that follow-up data were measured over a short period and that insufficient comparison was made in the changes experienced by bisexual and lesbian identified women. In an attempt to address these, Diamond (2008) presents an analysis of longitudinal data collected over ten years on female bisexuality from adolescence to adulthood. Her findings indicated that during this time two-thirds of her research population ($n = 79$ lesbian, bisexual and 'unlabelled' women) changed the identity labels they had claimed in the initial wave of data collection, and one-third of the women changed their label more than once. Same-sex attraction, however, remained fairly stable over the ten-year period, but there was a decline in same-sex behaviour. In 1995 most women were engaged in sexual activity with both men and women, but by 2005 most women were pursuing predominantly same-sex or predominately opposite-sex behaviour. The findings led Diamond (2008, p. 13) to argue that,

> there are, in fact, appreciable boundaries between the long-term developmental trajectories of lesbian, bisexual, and unlabeled women, but these boundaries are relatively fluid. Hence the present study supports the notion of bisexuality as a third type of sexual orientation and also supports the notion of bisexuality as a capacity for context-specific flexibility in erotic response. In contrast, the findings are inconsistent

with the long-debated notion of bisexuality as a transitional stage or 'phase'.

In a research climate that pays little attention to the psychology of women's sexuality and even less to that of bisexual women (Lee and Crawford, 2007), Diamond is an important and rare voice. Her analysis of sexual identity, sexual attraction and sexual behaviour enables her to produce a nuanced understanding where sexual attraction to both genders can remain a stable aspect of self-identity even when sexual behaviour with only men or only women might precipitate a change in sexual identity. However, there are also limits to her findings. As with most psychological research Diamond reflects more on the methodological limits of her account, rather than some of the conceptual issues. Diamond points out herself that the study followed a small sample over ten years, and that these women were disproportionately white and middle class. For me, however, there is some conceptual dissatisfaction with a conclusion that insists that bisexuality is a 'third *type* of sexual orientation' (2008, p. 13) yet the 'distinction between lesbianism and bisexuality is a matter of *degree* rather than kind' (p. 5), as well as something inherently contradictory about the notion of 'fluid boundaries'. Furthermore, the study could do more to unpack the shifting personal experiences that might precipitate a switch in sexual identity, particularly given that this underpins her understanding of sexual identity as a fluid naming device that is driven by the motivation of matching sexual practice and identity (we are what we do), rather than sexual identity as some inherent, ontologically stable state that matches a fixed notion of sexual attraction. Finally, her conclusion dismisses the concept of bisexuality as 'a temporary stage of denial, transition, or experimentation' and finds in favour of bisexuality as 'a "third type" of sexual orientation, characterized by fixed patterns of attraction to both sexes'. But, it makes no further reference to the third conception, whether bisexuality is 'a strong form of all individuals' capacity for sexual fluidity'.

Heterosexual identity formation: one model fits all?

If models of sexual identity formation need to attend to the distinction between sexual orientation and sexual identity, how does this division work for the most dominant form of sexuality – heterosexuality? Little research has focused on the ways that heterosexual people achieve their sexual identity, whether this identity is perceived as stable or homogeneous, or even whether heterosexual people experience such a thing as a sexual identity (Eliason, 1995). Some claim that research on heterosexuality as a developmental pathway has lagged behind because as a construct 'heterosexuality qualifies only as a prefabricated way of living that one slips into anonymously. . . . Remove the social institutions which support it, and the whole fragile edifice will collapse.' Furthermore, heterosexuality has its own contested history in the annals of sexology having been coined as a term after that of 'homosexual', and originally to refer to 'an abnormal or perverted sexual appetite toward the opposite sex' (Penelope, 1993, cited in Eliason, 1995, pp. 823–4). In recent years, particularly in the counselling psychology literature, there has been greater attendance to models of identity development and how these might be invoked for majority group identities. Perhaps the most detailed example in the field of heterosexual identity development emanates from the work of Roger Worthington et al. (2002), who promote a model of heterosexual sexual identity development that attempts to reduce the dichotomizing of 'sexual orientation along heterosexual–homosexual lines of distinction and help to eliminate notions of normative-ness regarding heterosexuality' (Worthington et al., 2002, p. 524). Worthington et al.'s conceptual take on the ontological status of heterosexual identity is similar to that proposed by Diamond. Worthington et al. (2002) argue that a distinction should be made between 'constructs of sexual identity', 'sexual orientation' and 'sexual orientation identity' so that sexual orientation can be understood as a stable element within an overall sexual identity that might be more fluid. Thus, they maintain that there is something inherently real and stable about sexual orientation, but that sexual identities can be seen as shaped by social, historical and cultural forces.

They do this by proposing a multifaceted model of heterosexual identity development that includes biopsychosocial influences, individual and social identity processes and developmental stages of development. Biopsychosocial influences include (i) biology; (ii) microsocial context; (iii) gender norms and socialization; (iv) culture; (v) religious orientation; (vi) systemic homonegativity, sexual prejudice and privilege. Parallel dimensions of individual identity development and social identity development also occur within the biopsychosocial context. Individual identity dimensions include: sexual values, sexual orientation identity, preferred modes of sexual expression, preferred characteristics of sexual partners, preferred sexual activities and perceived sexual needs; while social identity processes include group membership identity and attitudes towards sexual minorities. Finally, individual sexual identity and social sexual identity are seen to evolve and interact through various conscious and unconscious *statuses* of development. These include: (i) unexplored commitment; (ii) active exploration; (iii) diffusion; (iv) deepening and commitment to heterosexual identity; (v) synthesis between individual identity, group membership and attitudes to sexual minorities.

It is worth pausing here to reflect on the complexity of this model. In their effort to create a multidimensional model, Worthington et al. (2002) direct much attention to the social domain in both individual and group identity formation drawing our attention to the influence of factors such as the *microsocial context* in which people develop. Although biology is marked out as the first influence on sexual orientation development they resist reifying it as the bedrock for heterosexual identity formation. Instead they argue that biology must also be seen as a 'multistep and multigated process that can lead to substantial variation in anatomy, psychology and behaviour' (p. 503). Furthermore, in contrast to all the models discussed so far, their fluid account of sexual identity is underpinned by a more explicit acknowledgement of how social constructionist approaches have destabilized essentialist understandings of sexual identity (see chapter 3 for full discussion of social constructionism). In addition, Worthington et al. (2002) take care to summarize the limitations of many psychological approaches to understanding heterosexuality. These include: the tendency to perpetuate dichotomous models of sexual identity formation; the limits of 'stage models' for understanding human development compared to more contemporary views of development as a fluid and permeable process; failing to engage sufficiently with dominant societal forces such as 'compulsory heterosexuality' and how they might contribute to heterosexual identity formation; and demonstrating how social identity processes associated with group membership are often overlooked when considering majority group membership identity formation. As such:

> Existing models tend to overemphasize individual identity processes to the exclusion of social identity processes, ultimately failing to consider the impact of group membership affiliations and privilege on the identity statuses of heterosexuals. (Worthington et al., 2002, p. 502)

Perhaps this model is more complex and sophisticated because it emerges out of a counselling psychology perspective. This model is underpinned by a motivation to shine a spotlight on taken-for-granted assumptions about heterosexuality in order to improve psychotherapeutic practice with clients. As such it should be commended for its focus on dimensions such as *gender norms and socialization* that highlight the way competing discourses position men and women in relation to social norms regarding their gendered behaviour and heterosexuality. In contrast to many accounts of homosexual identity development that continue to conflate homosexuality with cross-gender behaviour (Drummond et al., 2008; Reiger et al., 2008; Savic and Lindström, 2008; see Hegarty, 2009 for a critique), they significantly dismantle the confusion between sexuality and gender orientation by transcending dichotomous conceptions of both gender and sexual orientation (Hoffman, 2004). The radical separation of gender identity and homosexuality is supported further by their claim that transgendered individuals can be any sexual orientation. Equally, the model pays due attention to *cultural* and *religious* influences and how they can regulate values and expectations for heterosexual behaviour. A third innovative consideration is the way that *systematic homonegativity, sexual prejudice and privilege* are named as significant components in heterosexual identity formation. This will of course impact on the development of LGB youths as well as those that might be perceived to be L, G or B, but actually identify as heterosexual (Blumenfeld, 1992). However, Worthington et al. (2002, p. 509) go further than this to argue that:

> an equally important aspect of the pervasiveness of homonegativity is that heterosexuality has become defined most critically by what it is not (e.g. lesbian, gay, or bisexual), rather than by what it is, resulting in the relative absence of a true sense of sexual identity for many (if not most) heterosexually identified individuals.

Thus, within this multidimensional model, inevitably influenced by queer critiques (see chapter 4), there is recognition that normative processes shield 'heterosexuality' in a sexual identity spectrum. The authors are keen to make heterosexuality visible as a site of privilege that is maintained through institutional practices and societal norms that allocate resources and opportunities to heterosexual people that are less available to LGB people. Finally, they also suggest that as a heterosexual individual develops a better understanding of their own sexual values, needs and preferences they may become less prejudiced about others as they are likely to develop 'a greater appreciation for and affirmation of sexual diversity' (Worthington et al., 2002, p. 525), a process that sociologists refer to as 'hetero-reflexivity' (Roseneil, 2002).

Despite the many strengths of this model, some elements remain areas of contention or issues for further reflection. Two interrelated concerns stand out in particular: whether the model can or should be expanded beyond heterosexuality to account for all sexual identity formation (Bieschke, 2002), and the problem of accounting for identity intersections in models that attend to majority group identity formation (Hoffman, 2004). In their conclusion, Worthington et al. (2002, p. 525) claim that because they extend sexual identity beyond sexual orientation it is possible to see dimensions that overlap in the development of both heterosexual and LGB identities. From this they make three assertions that raise questions about the notion of separate models for homosexual, bisexual and heterosexual identity formation. These include:

(a) the possible permeability of majority and minority identity modules of sexual identity such that some individuals may traverse more than one developmental pathway during the course of a lifespan, (b) the inclusion of multidimensionality in LGB models of sexual identity such that sexual orientation identity becomes only one of several important facets, thereby increasing overlap in our understanding of sexual identity more broadly, and (c) the possibility of model integration into a more comprehensive understanding of the multiplicity of pathways toward sexual identity available to human beings. (2002, p. 525)

Despite what might be seen as necessary similarities in some aspects of sexual development, Rose Marie Hoffman (2004, p. 379) warns against expanding their model to incorporate all sexual identities. This she suggests 'would obfuscate its standing as a majority identity development model at whose core is the acknowledgement of a privileged status'. This is an important critique as it would be difficult to maintain any critical presence of the power dynamics under which different sexualities are developed within a single model. As it stands, Hoffman (2004, p. 380) also notes the difficulty that arises for majority models of identity development that attend to the specifics of a privileged status such as 'heterosexual' without being able to conceptualize how this identity intersects with other identities such as gender, age, ethnicity, disability and so on. As she surmises,

even though an identity development model may be appropriately limited to one issue and focus on either minority or majority status . . . we must accept the challenge to work to maintain a perspective that recognizes the complexity of the identity intersections within our clients and within ourselves.

These approaches to identity development primarily focus on the processes involved in coming to know and name oneself as lesbian, gay, bisexual or heterosexual through multifaceted notions of developing a specific sexual identity. They also maintain that while this identity might be fluid, the sexual orientation of any individual will be more stable. While all models include the occasional nod to biology in underpinning this stability they do little to explain the internal workings of sexual orientation, as the affective content of desire and attraction and how these become orientated towards particular objects is absent from their analysis. It is this space between the psychic and the social that needs further exploration.

Developing sexuality and the psychosocial subject

As Adrian Coyle (1992, p. 182) has previously noted, the developmental literature is 'rife with overlapping, and opposing conceptualizations, definitions and terminology'. This chapter has illustrated some of these, particularly the conceptual difficulties in separating sexuality into sexual identity, sexual orientation and sexual behaviour. In the early section of the chapter we evaluated theoretical approaches for understanding the development of homosexuality, including psychoanalysis and biological approaches. The approaches have been shown to be lacking in terms of empirical validity as well as for their flawed theoretical basis that consistently conflates same-sex desire and attraction with gender identity transgressions. We then considered 'coming-out' models of identity formation that suffered from a lack of clarity in their own conceptions of development as a stage-like process and dissent over how many stages or phases were necessary. However, there have been notable attempts to move beyond stage-like models for both gay, lesbian, bisexual and heterosexual identity formation and produce a more subtle engagement with aspects of sexuality that may be experienced more fluidly, for example identity and behaviour compared to sexual attraction or orientation. These are welcome additions to the field, but not without their own issues. Perhaps the most pressing concern is whether there is any value in constructing generalized models of sexual identity development at all, whether they be for lesbian, gay, bisexual or heterosexual identity. While essentialist claims for the biological underpinnings of sexual orientation and models of developmental pathways for various sexual identities remain contentious, there is a growing consensus that sexuality is a more pressing issue when considering psychological development across the lifespan (e.g. Badgett, 2003; Garnets and Kimmel, 2003; Patterson, 2008). As such, others have shifted away from research that tries to pinpoint the origins or causes of homosexuality, instead focusing on the implications of 'growing up gay'. Many note the background of discrimination and victimization as a social force that shapes and marginalizes lesbian, gay and bisexual men and women (Harper and Schneider, 2003; Herek, 2003) and a raft of studies have demonstrated the negative impact this can have on physical and mental health, particular for young LGBT people (e.g. D'Augelli and Patterson, 2001; King et al., 2003; Cochran and Mays, 2006; Ussher, 2009). The cultural condition of 'homonegativity' is also seen to have a developmental impact on heterosexual youths. For example, following Blumenfeld (1992), Worthington et al. (2002, p. 508) claim that:

> Homonegative prejudice has a number of influences on development that may not be readily apparent including but not limited to (a) inhibiting one's abilities to form close, intimate relationships with members of one's own gender, (b) adding to the pressure to marry (possibly before one is ready to do so), (c) causing premature sexual involvement to prove to oneself and others that she or he is 'normal': resulting in (d) increasing the chances of teen pregnancy and the spread of sexually transmitted diseases, and (e) reducing the complete transmission of knowledge and information through school-based sex education.

Thus, some have suggested that more effort needs to be made to integrate investigations of sexual-minority issues within mainstream understandings of youth psychology (Diamond, 2003b), while others argue that 'developmental scientists need to seriously reconsider traditional empirical and theoretical paradigms that narrowly define sexual-minority adolescents in terms of those who adopt a culturally defined sexual identity label' (Savin-Williams, 2001, p. 5). In particular, the concern for integration of research on both populations is important as many youths with same-sex attractions identify as heterosexual, rather than gay. Thus any research that is predicated on the basis of self-identification will under-recruit those people who may be engaged in same-sex behaviour but resistant to the identity category lesbian, gay or bisexual (McConaghy, 1999). I will return to focus on some of these propositions in greater detail at various points in the book (particularly chapter 5) when I examine how the burgeoning research on 'risk' which is associated with particular sexual-minority identities are embodied in LGBT experiences of mental health. Before that, I turn in more detail to examine sociological and social psychological critiques of developmental approaches for understanding sexuality. The debate reviewed here demonstrates that social constructionist critiques have begun to filter into more mainstream psychological research and practice. Yet, as the next chapter will illustrate, these critical engagements can be developed much further, to problematize the very concept of 'identity'. It will also acknowledge the crucial contributions that critical psychologists have made in this field to provide further evidence for the necessity of a psychosocial approach to contemporary sexuality.

3

Constructing Sexuality

Once the concept of the homosexual is problematized, what is being studied tends to dissolve, making an isolated history of homosexuality itself problematic (despite foolhardy attempts at writing them).

Jeffrey Weeks, 1998, p. 144

In order to begin to fashion a 'psychosocial' approach to the complex field of sexuality it is important to examine both sides of the polarization, and consider the 'disciplinary wash' that is churned up when departing from either a psychological or sociological base. The previous chapter drove out of psychology towards more sociological perspectives problematizing the concept of a homosexual identity and demonstrating, albeit tentatively, how developmental psychological understandings of sexual identities have become marked and influenced by social constructionist theories. This chapter focuses on the history of sexuality and how it has been constructed, even if this serves, as Jeffery Weeks notes, as a 'foolhardy attempt' to write 'an isolated history', where it is impossible to pin down or separate sexuality from other forms of social categorization. In this chapter social constructionism, and its various manifestations, is considered in greater detail, specifically homing in on its theoretical importance to the field of sexuality studies, bringing us into the terrain of multiple and contested sites of knowledge, discourse, power and subjectivity. Debates over the different forms of social constructionism are complex, covering such perspectives as symbolic interactionism and post-structuralism. They also introduce us to new methodologies for understanding human behaviour: ethnomethodology, a staple of sociological enquiry, and historicism. Both methods require an epistemological shift, away from the positivistic approaches that underpin a science of sexuality towards a greater reflection on social meaning and subjectivity. This does not mean we will find a foundational history of sexuality. Quite the contrary, the history of sexuality is a highly contested area with its own 'historiographical' issues including 'questions of evidence, method, strategy, politics, and identification' (Halperin, 2002, p. 2). For example, the question 'does sexuality have a history?' has been addressed from such contradictory positions as radical lesbian feminism (MacKinnon, 1992) and queer historicism (Halperin, 1993). Both have answered with a resounding yes, even if the histories they present promote competing concern for sexuality's relation to gender oppression or psychopathology. If sexuality were then a consistent, coherent category the proposition that sexuality has a history might draw less attention. Yet, the differences between proposed interpretations of this history take us directly to the guiding principles of social constructionism: the idea that the categories that surround our understanding of sexuality, such as 'homosexual' or 'sexual identity', are socially produced, and their meanings are dependent on the social, cultural and historical resources that are used to describe them.

Socially, historically and culturally informed accounts of contemporary sexuality are rarely considered without reference to the influential work of Michel Foucault, and his now classic series *The History of Sexuality*, fashioned in three volumes (although volume 1 gains most attention in social constructionist accounts). It should be noted that the histories of sexuality considered in this chapter emerge primarily from western writing on sexuality. Foucault himself frequently referred to western civilization in his work, which emerged from a cultural preoccupation with modernist principles of enlightenment, science, truth and technologies of the self. It is in this context that he sought to interrogate the 'interplay of truth and sex' that had been created by the scientific study of sexuality (1979/1990, p. 57). Yet the singular importance of Foucault's genealogical thesis for challenging explanations that root sexuality in essentialist accounts of biological or developmental processes does not go unchallenged. Foucault is frequently credited as a founding figure in poststructuralism and queer theory, particularly in the US. As part of the cultural turn, these approaches have been heralded for dismantling any certainty in identity categories that (as we have already seen) are clung onto in many developmental psychology accounts. Yet, this affirmation is not universal. Some have lamented the tendency to privilege Foucault as the origin of social constructionism (e.g. Rubin and Butler, 1994; Weeks, 1998), while others (e.g. Weeks, 1998; Halperin, 2002) point to the overlooked importance of the sociological work of Mary McIntosh, William Simon and John Gagnon, and Ken Plummer. Jeffrey Weeks' (1977, 1985, 1989, 1995, 2000, 2007) unstinting contribution to the socio-historical field is also frequently minimized in histories that depart from Foucault and traverse towards queer theory, when his work could be seen as 'contemporaneous' or even preceding Foucault (Beasley, 2005, p. 146).

This chapter starts by evaluating the contribution these sociological theorists have made to a social constructionist approach to understanding sexuality, documenting epistemological, ideological and metaphorical shifts through the analysis of sexuality as a role, script and story. It moves on to examine discourses of sexuality, summarizing Foucault's earlier work and its impact on the field of sexuality studies as well as broader debates in social theory across the social sciences, including psychology. Finally, the limitations of social constructionist analyses for understanding sexuality and sexual subjectivities are considered.

First, it is worth pausing to reflect on the structure of this chapter. It is impractical to write these histories *beside* each other, in order to represent them as equal but competing discourses. Therefore, it is inevitable that one will be presented *after* or *around* another. As Weeks points out, attempts at writing a history of (homo)sexuality can prove foolhardy. Even the notion of linking ideas chronologically is not straightforward, when some appear in different continents and languages at different times, and many share core concerns and assumptions. Having learnt my social constructionism during the 1990s from the critiques that promoted a poststructuralist, Foucauldian inspired, discursive approach in critical psychology, I may have a propensity to emphasize these rather than the symbolic interactionist accounts that were produced in sociology during the 1970s (as Jeffrey Weeks does). Nevertheless, in the spirit of transdisciplinarity, I try to avoid prematurely promoting the importance of one contribution over another as each historical narrative has particular implications for generating a psychosocial understanding of sexual subjectivities. Each needs examining in terms of its ability to contribute to an account that incorporates 'the contingency of social categories and identities as well as the material effects of these' (Bicknell, 2006, p. 105). Thus, rather than shape a history that promotes certain key thinkers, the narrative that occurs in the next few pages will be based around the following themes: coming out of oppression; role, scripts and stories; discourses of sexuality; deconstructing sexuality, reconstructing psychology; constructing sexuality and the psychosocial subject.

Coming out of oppression

In the sociological field Mary McIntosh's influential paper 'The homosexual role' is attributed to be a defining moment in social constructionist accounts of sexuality. She first published this essay in the US journal *Social Problems* in 1968, although it has been reprinted since (e.g. Plummer, 1981; Stein, 1990). The precept of the paper was a critique of the embedded notion that homosexuality was a 'condition', with which someone might be afflicted or not. She argued that this assumption had underpinned the scientific search for the aetiology of homosexuality since early sexologists such as Havelock Ellis. In assessing the lack of progress in answering the issue of causality she suggested this was due to it being an ill-conceived question, rather than from a lack of scientific rigour or adequate evidence. Finally, she proposed that the fascination with homosexuality as a 'condition' was driven by social scientists' concern that homosexuality was a social *problem*. She states the argument as such:

> The creation of a specialised, despised and punished role of homosexual keeps the bulk of society pure in rather the same way that the similar treatment of some kinds of criminal keeps the rest of society law-abiding. (1968/1981, p. 23)

These points still carry relevance today, yet McIntosh was writing at a time when the history of homosexuality steeped in criminality and pathology was strikingly close. At this time, homosexuality was still listed by the American Psychiatric Association (APA) as a mental disorder and would remain so until 1973. The Gay Liberation Front was only to form in 1969, in the aftermath of the Stonewall riots, when police raided The Stonewall Inn, a meeting place in New York City for gender and sexuality non-conformists. Two years later Dennis Altman published *Homosexual: Oppression and liberation* that attempted to weave a thesis for social transformation between the two dominant theoretical influences of the day: Freud and Marx, who defined the poles of psychology and historicism. Contra to Freud's assertion that in order to function the social world requires the repression of the messy, chaotic polymorphous biological drives that are innate to all human beings, Altman proposed that sexual liberation would lead to a cultural revolution. Drawing on Herbert Marcuse (1955, 1969), Altman declared that the regulatory structures of capitalist society demanded guilt and renunciation of sexual desires in order to produce the necessarily docile and compliant worker. Altman's psychosocial approach shares a similar revolutionary trajectory to others writing at the time. For instance, Guy Hocquenghem (1978/1993) writing in France in the early 1970s proposed a 'revolution of desire'. Drawing on the anti-psychiatry of Deleuze and Guattari (1972/1983) and Foucault's *Madness and Civilization* (1967) he linked the advancement of western capitalism to the arbitrary division of homosexual desire from heterosexual desire, when desire should be better understood as a fluctuating, 'emergent' state. As Hocquenghem (1978/1993, p. 75) notes:

> In the work of Freud . . . the 'polymorphously perverse' refers to the constitutional bisexuality of men and women – a concept which lies between biology and psychology, for desire ignores scientific divisions. . . . Both heterosexuality and homosexuality are the precarious outcome of a desire that knows no name. If the distinction between biology and psychology thus disappears, it is because desire knows nothing of the separation between body and mind upon which the personality is founded. Nevertheless, this kind of separation is the very life blood of psychiatry and psychoanalysis as an *institution*.

For Hocquenghem (1978/1993, p. 73) homosexuality was manufactured as a psychologically repressive category through penal and psychiatric processes so that 'modern repression demands justifications, an interplay between legal guilt and the psychology of guilt'. Thus, 'what homosexuality expresses – indirectly and in popular form – is desire's disquieting disregard for gender and for persons' (Dean, 2000, p. 239). So the association of a homosexual identity category with desire challenges a foundational assumption of psychoanalysis: '*desire's objects remain essentially contingent*' (Dean, 2000, p. 239, emphasis in original). While this conception of desire has been taken up again in recent queer writing (see chapter 4 for further discussion of the relationship between psychoanalysis and queer theory), for now I focus on the criticisms laid at Altman and Hocquenghem from an emerging social constructionist perspective. Both theorists point to how the 'establishment of homosexuality as a separate category goes hand in hand with its repression' (Hocquenghem, 1978/1993, p. 55), and both saw the liberation of this inherent universal desire as key to radical transformation. These theoretical moves were in light of various 'returns to Freud' (via Marcuse for Altman and Lacan for Hocquenghem) and located in relation to left-wing, anti-capitalist politics. Their approach was based on the liberation of biological drives that have been conditioned in terms of shame and guilt in order to maintain the social order. This required, for Altman in particular, claiming a gay identity, as he saw its revolutionary potential for undermining capitalism and challenging the institutions that had served to pathologize sexualities. Hocquenghem made a similar challenge but through the anti-psychiatry emphasis of Deleuze and Guattari by seeking 'to show how the struggles of homosexuals have challenged the accepted relationship between desire and politics' (Weeks, 1978, p. 40).

Despite the clear potential for a psychosocial theorizing of sexuality, weaknesses in the accounts of Altman and Hocquenghem have been posed. For example, Chris Beasley (2005) summarizes a number of limitations with Altman's libertarian stance. Firstly, she observes how libertarian values have been as productive for the political right as for the left, since they promote an individualism that does not sit easily with a collective approach to destabilize capitalism. Altman has acknowledged that his earlier work did overplay the potential for the simultaneous dismantling of sexual repression and capitalism, conceding that they do not equate to the same thing (Altman, 1999), the result of a psychosocial account that perhaps collapses the 'psychic' and the 'social'. Latterly he has shifted his position to suggest that capitalism can support increased sexual freedom (Altman, 2001). Secondly, Beasley notes contradictions in Altman's political voice where he wavers between strongly essentialist identity claims and simultaneously promoting a political agenda based on gay collectivism. As will be shown, the importance and difficulty of maintaining an anti-essentialist notion of identity is a central tenet in social constructionist thinking, and an ongoing challenge. Altman's investment in the stable identity category 'gay' in order to politically represent the gay community can be attributed to a political movement that sought to move lesbian and gay experiences out of oppression. However, this sits uneasily with the social constructionist challenge to identity categories that have emerged in the aftermath of Gay Liberation. Finally, Beasley also notes a lack of acknowledgement about the concerns Gay Liberation raised for lesbians and feminist – as it almost exclusively focused on male experience, or used the terms 'homosexuality' or 'gay' to refer to men and women without attending to the specificity of lesbian lives or other intersectionalities with class or race. This criticism can be laid at much of the work that emerged at this time including McIntosh's 'homosexual role' (McIntosh [postscript], 1968/1981, p. 44) and Hocquenghem (Weeks, 1978, pp. 36–7).

In the preface to Hocquenghem's republished account Weeks lays out a number of limitations based on his own social constructionist invested reading. Firstly, he argues that Hocquenghem's dependence on the repression hypothesis to account for paranoia and repression of homosexuals in society is over-reliant on Freud's hydraulic/drive theory of sexuality, and cannot account for the shifts in social taboos that have been apparent since the 1970s: something that he would inevitably re-emphasize given the rapid social transformations in the UK in the last decade (Weeks, 2007). Secondly, he suggests that although Hocquenghem usefully denotes the artificial separation of homosexual and heterosexual, his account is unable to sufficiently explain why an individual might enter the symbolic order as either 'homosexual' or 'heterosexual'. For Weeks, Hocquenghem's account privileges the psychological, falling back on the Freudian inspired metaphor of the Oedipal process rather than looking to the wider social context and institutional practices that demand a deeper historical and theoretical analysis of their place in shaping sexual subjectivities. Finally, Weeks (1978, p. 37) notes Hocquenghem's lack of engagement with 'different modalities of lesbian' while relying on an explanatory thesis of male homosexuality that fits established Freudian categories.

Despite their indisputable association with radical sexual politics and contribution to the burgeoning literature that sought to challenge the pathologizing impact of psychological discourses, in the light of emerging social constructionism both these theories were considered insufficiently 'social'. Debates in psychosocial studies have moved on from the primary focus of how social repression constrains libidinal desire (Frosh, 2012), yet in generating accounts that sought to attend to the analytic sphere of the psychic *and* the social there is still value to be found in these endeavours. I return to these ideas in chapter 4 when considering the way psychoanalytic concepts have been challenged and defended within queer studies. For now the focus turns to the principles of social constructionism that underpin the critique applied to these theories that emerged out of symbolic interactionism and was premised on a fundamental rejection of biological, psychological and psychoanalytic accounts for their essentialist assumption that sexuality can be reduced to natural biological drive theories.

Social constructionism: roles, scripts and stories

Working out of the field of the sociology of deviance, McIntosh (1968/1981, p. 33) proposed that homosexuality should be seen as a 'social role', rather than an inherent essence. She drew a distinction between psychologists who are seen as 'diagnostic agents in the process of social labelling' and sociologists who should objectively examine the social processes by which 'people become labelled as homosexual', and how these 'processes connect with mechanisms of social control'. Appearing now in the aftermath of the poststructuralist turn that precipitated queer studies and the radical critiques of stable sexual identities that emanated from it, the phrase 'homosexual role' seems rather staid and outdated. Yet, as Weeks (1998) points out, the importance of McIntosh's work was that it asked a *new* question that opened sexuality up to an original sociological research agenda. It is worth reflecting on the ongoing importance of this epistemological shift and its prolonged influence in a field that, as Murphy (1997) notes, often ignores the moral and ethical implications of seeking causal explanations for homosexuality. Furthermore, given that scientists continue to be funded to research what they see as the biological substrates of homosexuality (as discussed in chapter 2) this is not a debate that has been won. Instead, tension remains between the biological, psychological and sociological sciences about what questions should be asked in the field of sexuality. Within this, the sociological approach to understanding sexuality has often been hindered by a 'restricted emphasis on the mechanics of sex and its links to reproduction' (Epstein, 1994/2002, p. 45). However, as any social constructionist would argue (e.g. Burr, 2003; Gergen, 2009), no research agenda is ever free from the ideological values that underpin it. Thus, McIntosh can be attributed with a crucial moment in this history of sexuality research by suggesting that when questions of sexuality are predicated on a distinction between (homo)sexuality as a 'category' or (homo)sexuality as a 'behaviour', they reveal their epistemological investments in their explanations. The distinction between homosexuality as a category (essence) and homosexuality as a behaviour (performance) and the debates that surround this distinction became known in lesbian and gay studies as the 'essentialist/social constructionist' controversy (Weeks, 1998). A generation of scholars (e.g. Plummer, 1975; Richardson, 1996; Seidman, 2003) were inspired to produce their own criticisms of essentialist accounts that located 'sexuality' within a naturalized, inner truth or essence to the self. In contrast, these critiques promoted socially embedded interpretations where sexuality could not be understood outside the social, cultural, interpersonal and linguistic conditions that had fashioned it so. Therefore, the shift to an anti-essentialist conception of homosexuality as a 'social role' demanded a radical epistemological and ontological move precipitated by the nascent field of social constructionism (e.g. Berger and Luckman, 1967/1991).

Within sociology, early social constructionist accounts were primarily informed by the symbolic interactionist work of Plummer and Simon and Gagnon, and these had a major impact within the sociological field during the 1980s and 1990s before their authority waned as a result of competing Foucauldian and queer inspired influences. Social constructionism, in its symbolic interactionist form, is concerned with 'sexual meaning and the way it is socially constructed and socially patterned' (Plummer, 1982, p. 224). Symbolic interactionism developed out of the pragmatic approach of the Chicago School in the 1920s, with the work of social psychologist George Herbert Mead (e.g. 1934/1967) and sociologist Charles Cooley (e.g. 1902/2001) frequently cited as foundational influences. The focus of symbolic interactionism is on the micro-processes of human interaction and how meaning is produced, negotiated and symbolically sustained through everyday experience. It shares some commonalities with other approaches such as phenomenology, existentialism and ethnomethodology, and is also associated with social cognition and social construct perspectives found in psychology (Plummer, 1982). However, as Plummer argues, symbolic interactionism has focused on human sexuality since Kinsey et al.'s (1948, 1953) research triggered interest in the contribution that sociology could make to understanding sexuality as 'sexual conduct' (e.g. Simon and Gagnon, 1967; Gagnon and Simon, 1973; Plummer, 1975). Plummer summarizes how symbolic interactionist approaches coalesce around the critique of essentialist accounts, which he collectively refers to as 'drive theories': those which reduce accounts of sexual identity or sexual orientation to a biological imperative. This would obviously include the biological reductionist accounts of developmental psychology, but also the psychoanalytically informed accounts of Gay Liberation despite their noted mutual critique of the role psychology has played in pathologizing sexuality. As Ken Plummer (1982, p. 226) clarifies, symbolic interactionism

> heralded the view that sexuality should not be seen as a powerful drive but rather as a socially constructed motive; the adoption of the metaphor 'sexual script' as a framework for analysing the social construction of sexual meaning; the directive to study the social sources from which human sexualities were constructed; the need to view sexual development not as something relentlessly unwinding from within but as something constantly shaped through encounters with significant others; the need to see the importance of wider socio-historical formations in generating the meanings which people in society assumed in their identities; and the importance of stigmatic labelling in the creation of separate worlds of sexual deviance.

This extract draws together key influences in social constructionist and symbolic interactionist thinking, but it is worth noting that not all theorists contribute to each approach equally. McIntosh's paper on the homosexual role drew on labelling theory, while Plummer's (1975) thesis *Sexual Stigma* developed this approach by drawing on Gagnon and Simon's (1973) 'script theory' to illustrate the significant impact stigma can have on how lesbian and gay people experience themselves. Socio-historical accounts are more associated with the detailed analyses of Weeks (e.g. 1977, 1985) and Foucault (1979/1990), yet they all share four elements that set them apart from the developmental approaches discussed in chapter 2. Firstly, they see no truth in explanations that ground sexuality in a biological essence. Secondly, as social meaning is seen to shape our sexuality they attend to a much broader definition of sexuality beyond accounts of identity or orientation to include everyday aspects of sexual behaviour and interaction. Thirdly, they resist analyses of sexuality that categorize sexual behaviours into stable types of people, and prefer to understand human sexuality through a model of complex sexual variation rather than sexual perversion. In this sense 'the pervert' is seen as a historical construct and the label is attached to particular lives through the pathologizing diagnostic techniques of scientific psychology. Thus, for social constructionists, 'sexologists, psychologists and the like who defined the homosexual condition as a fixed set of characteristics' (Weeks, 1998, p. 136) are often the target for critique, even from those working within psychology, as well as those outside. Finally, they resist essentialist notions that reduce sexual orientation to a truth of the self or assume that sexuality develops hand in hand with sexual identity. There is no true or real sexual identity, rather they focus on the way 'individuals throughout their life cycle come to be defined by themselves and others as sexual beings, how they come to hook themselves on to the wider cultural meanings, and how these are renegotiated and stabilized' (Plummer, 1982, p. 236).

The metaphor 'script' is one way of accounting for these communicative processes within a sociological framework. The work of Simon and Gagnon (together and separately), fashioned over some forty years, is central to this theoretical approach within sexuality studies. Scripts, for Gagnon and Simon (1973, p. 19), 'are involved in learning the meaning of internal states, organizing the sequences of specifically sexual acts, decoding novel situations, setting the limits on sexual responses, and linking meanings from nonsexual aspects of life to specifically sexual experience'. Theirs is a socialization approach where sexuality is a learnt behaviour, guided by social and cultural norms, rather than an ingrained natural drive. In an often-cited extract (e.g. Plummer, 1982) John Gagnon outlines the scope of human sexuality as follows:

> In any given society, at any given moment in its history, people become sexual in the same way they become everything else. Without much reflection, they pick up directions from their social environment. They acquire and assemble meanings, skills and values from the people around them. Their critical choices are often made by going along and drifting. People learn when they are quite young a few of the things that they are expected to be, and continue to slowly accumulate a belief in who they are and ought to be throughout the rest of childhood, adolescence and adulthood. Sexual conduct is learned in the same way and through the same processes; it is acquired and assembled in human interaction, judged and performed in specific cultural and historical worlds. (1977, p. 2)

For Gagnon and Simon (1973, p. 22) no sexual behaviour would happen without a script that can define the situation, name the actors and plot the behaviour. Despite being defined as thoroughly social, their approach does not completely neglect the physiological aspects of sexuality. Scripts are also seen as 'the mechanism through which biological events can be potentiated', such that orgasm cannot be reduced to a purely biological event, rather it is the manifestation of biological, social and psychological interactions. Accordingly, 'the social-psychological meaning of sexual events must be learned because they supply the channels through which biology is expressed' (p. 22).

In their earlier work, Simon and Gagnon considered similar questions to McIntosh by seeking to establish homosexuality as a role and destabilize the assumption that homosexuality arose from failed socialization. They criticized the overwhelming focus within studies of deviance on 'exotic' behaviour, rather than more pedestrian, everyday interactions, stating that 'a good deal is known about the homosexual bar or tavern, but very little about the ways the homosexual earns a living, finds a place to live, or manages relations with his family' (1967, p. 213). Thus, by overlooking everyday interaction sociologists would inflate differences based on sexual behaviour and generalize these to entire populations. In contrast, in a rare early account of lesbian sexuality Simon and Gagnon (1967) sought to establish that apart from the obvious difference in desired object choice lesbians shared much with what they considered the conventional sexual development of women. This, they argued, is because lesbians are similarly socialized by the prevailing expectations of a female sex-role prior to the emergence of sexuality. Thus, Simon and Gagnon suggested that lesbians share many customs of femininity with heterosexual women, and the performance of masculinity that marks some lesbian identities and spaces can be interpreted for its social meaning rather than as a representation of biologically rooted 'difference'. Instead, they claim that masculine gender performances enable some lesbians to embody a 'butch' identity while others might pass through this in early stages of identifying as lesbian because it also functions as a marker of group identity that distinguishes lesbianism from heterosexuality.

This demonstrates the anti-essentialist assumptions of social constructionism as Simon and Gagnon resist biologically reductive explanations for gender expression. Instead, they highlight the multiple meanings that particular gender performances may have for identity construction and subjectivity, exploring the relevance of two dominant categorization systems – gender and sexuality. What is also interesting about Simon and Gagnon's approach from a psychosocial perspective is the opportunity to understand sexuality in terms of the broader cultural norms that guide interpersonal interaction *and* the internalized specifics of individualized sexual desire. People will not all follow the same scripts, because we have individualized scripts that trigger our sexual arousal, but there are shared, loose scripts that summarize the norms and expectations of particular sexual behaviours in cultural, historical and gender specific ways. For Gagnon and Simon (1984, 1987; Laumann and

Gagnon, 1995; Whittier and Simon, 2001) scripts work via three interrelated dimensions: cultural scenarios that are transmitted through social and institutional sources such as the media, family and education; interpersonal scripts, which include how individuals interpret cultural norms and guide their social interaction with other actors; and intrapsychic scripts, which provoke motivational elements of arousal and produce commitment to particular sequences of events, desires and fantasies, or 'types'. However, as some commentators point out (Dworkin et al., 2007), these dimensions have not been subject to equal scrutiny. For example, the changing social and cultural context that has the potential to liberate normative heterosexual scripts along gender lines has been the focus of much feminist research (e.g. Seal and Ehrhardt, 2003; Dworkin and O'Sullivan, 2005), but at the expense of understanding how these are enmeshed with changing interpersonal scripts and intrapsychic scripts.

It is useful to reflect on the distinctiveness and interrelatedness of these dimensions by considering a recent study that has employed script theory with the specific focus of examining intrapsychic scripts. Dworkin et al. (2007) set out to demonstrate the impact of a sexual health intervention study to decrease heterosexual women's likelihood of contracting HIV or other sexually transmitted diseases (STDs). The aim was to shift the sexual action sequences in their sexual scripts to include earlier discussion of condom use with a partner. The programme introduced women to new sexual scripts through the domains of sexual initiation, pace setting, sexual decision-making, communication about sexual needs and the timing of condom introduction by encouraging the women to move the discussion to during a date, rather than immediately before intercourse. In a one-year follow-up the researchers found that shifts in sexual scripts occurred in both the experimental and control group leading them to conclude that 'a lengthy assessment interview facilitated comfort with discussing and imagining new sexual behaviors, even for the control group participants who did not receive the intervention' (2007, p. 269). Less clear was which domain of sexual script had been transformed by the intervention. For example, Dworkin et al. (2007, p. 277) emphasize that their

questions about sexual scripts were written to focus on the intrapsychic realm (defined as the motivational elements that produce
commitments to particular action sequences, including desires and
fantasies), but conclude that 'it is difficult to predict how women
would have responded to questions about the other two levels of
scripts'. Thus, while their intervention led to a change in sexual
behaviour it is not clear whether this is because of a transformation
in intrapsychic scripts. It is possible that the transformation may
have taken place in terms of accessing alternative cultural scripts
or through the dialogical relationships during subsequent sexual
communications between partners and the impact this may have
had on interpersonal sexual scripts. In line with this, Dworkin et al.
note that a clearer examination of gender relations and the sexual
scripts of both men and women is necessary in heterosexual health
promotion. However, beyond a call for better delineation of the
levels of sexual scripts for analysis (interpersonal, intrapsychic and
cultural) their study provides little conclusive evidence for the way
that sexual scripts might operate through a model that relies on
distinct levels. Following their own admittance that it is difficult
to distinguish how the scripts operate on different levels, it points
to the possible conclusion that the relationship between cultural,
interpersonal and intrapsychic processes is more 'fuzzy' (Whittier
and Simon, 2001) than a clearly delineated model of script theory
permits.

A more damning critique of script theory is developed by the
feminist psychologists Hannah Frith and Celia Kitzinger (2001).
Frith and Kitzinger work within a discursive psychology framework (e.g. Edwards, 1997) to argue that script theory cannot be
constituted as a social constructionist approach at all as it overly
focuses on scripts as cognitive processes. As it has been shown,
sociological approaches in the social construction of sexuality were
informed by ethnomethodology and symbolic interactionism.
Although similarly focused on social interaction, social psychological approaches to the social construction of sexuality were
informed by the discursive turn in the social sciences. The distinction between discourse and cognition became a key strand of
social constructionism that emerged out of critical psychology in

the 1980s and 1990s and offered a radical critique of the growing trend to understand social behaviour via an analysis of cognitive processes (e.g. Potter and Wetherell, 1987). Cognitive psychology proposes that attitudes, beliefs, memories and mental scripts reside within the mind as real entities, or what might be referred to as intrapsychic scripts. In contrast, discursive psychologists argue these constructs should be understood as 'discursive actions' or 'interpretative repertoires', as something people *do* rather than have (Potter and Wetherell, 1987). Central to this is the methodological shift from measuring attitudes to a discursive analysis of how attitudes and beliefs emerge through interpersonal (linguistic) interaction. Reflecting on the application of sexual script theory to the topic of sexual negotiation Frith and Kitzinger (2001) draw attention to how many theorists working in the area of script theory and sexuality have been as influenced by the cognitive psychology approach to scripts (e.g. Schank and Abelson, 1977; Abelson, 1981; Markus and Zajonc, 1985) as by the Gagnon and Simon version (1973) – despite the importance of the distinction for Gagnon (1990). For them, this means that the use of 'sexual script' is often confused with terms such as 'social message', 'cultural belief' and used to imply something that resides within the individual's head. Thus, Frith and Kitzinger (2001, p. 212) argue that:

> despite the fact that script theory is claimed to offer a fundamentally social (indeed, social constructionist) account of sexuality, it is in fact – even in the *most* social version of the theory, as used in sexuality research – fundamentally cognitive.

Rather than seeing sexual scripts as accurate accounts of the sequential events that occur in sexual encounters, Frith and Kitzinger (2001, p. 227) argue that sexual scripts should be seen as 'script formulations' that serve particular social functions such as accountability and impression management. So, rather than accepting women's descriptive accounts which state that sex is negotiated in a specific way, the authors argue that their focus on the social action of talk 'enables us to explore instead the investments such women might have in talking about sexual interaction in the conventionally "scripted" way'. Thus, the types of scripts that women describe may not be internalized, 'personal scripts' which define their sexual behaviour, rather they may be accounts of dominant cultural norms and expectations for their sexual conduct. In this case, interpersonal scripts provide access to both cultural scenarios and intrapsychic scripts.

This criticism is well founded in relation to the use of the 'script' metaphor to ascertain and predict sexual behaviour. However, it has a number of its own limitations. Frith and Kitzinger take greater issue with the use of script theory that emerges out of a cognitive perspective, but it is perhaps of little surprise that theorists influenced by a cognitive school of thought reduce sexual scripts to cognitive processes. More significantly, their account does not fully engage with the sociological literature on script theory that similarly points to the limitations in the way it can be applied. For example, Ken Plummer (1982, p. 228) notes:

> This general imagery of 'script' is a vivid one in highlighting the relativity of sexual meanings, their humanly constructed nature, and in correcting biological and mechanical imagery. . . . But it is only a general imagery, and many problems remain. In the hands of some researchers, it has become a wooden mechanical tool for identifying uniformities in sexual conduct: the script determines activity, rather than emerging through activity. What is actually required is research to show the nature of sexual scripts as they *emerge* in encounters. Such encounters may be seen as stumbling, fragile and ambiguous situations in which participants gropingly attempt (through such processes as role taking, role making, altercasting and self-presentation) to make 'sexual sense' of selves, situations and others.

Frith and Kitzinger can be commended for producing an empirical account of sexual negotiation that *emerges* from interaction, yet their own interpretation could also be construed as reductive – this time to linguistic processes and 'talk'. By promoting the notion that all scripts emerge through linguistic interaction, Frith and Kitzinger's reformulation of sexual script theory does away with the need for analysing 'intrapsychic' processes, and makes no mention of the way social, psychological and biological processes are enmeshed. For them, scripts are only located in the social world (i.e. cultural scenarios and interpersonal processes). This raises questions about theorizing the specificity of sexual desire and for me provides a weaker psychosocial engagement than Gagnon and Simon's approach as for them *all* psychic life is reduced to the cultural realm.

One of the fundamental problems with the metaphor 'script', as I see it, is that it does not conjure up a vivid enough image to depict 'the relativity of sexual meaning' (Plummer, 1982, p. 228). Although its meaning can be traced to the etymological origins of 'scripture', to something that is 'written', scripts are frequently written *for* people to follow, rather than emerging out of their own interactive processes. This reminds us why script theory has been accused of being deterministic and, perhaps, accounts for the gradual replacement of script with the metaphor 'story' within the sociological literature (e.g. Plummer, 1995). Although a story is also something that can be written it promotes the idea of narrative, agency and action in something that is made up or constructed, albeit from pre-existing resources, but with less emphasis upon the predictive imagery that 'scripts' can inspire. It is the metaphor of the 'story' that is apparent in Weeks' (1995, p. 98) discussion of the paradoxes of identity where identities are described as *necessary fictions*: 'historical inventions . . . imagined in contingent circumstances'. In Plummer's (1995) detailed engagement with the process of *Telling Sexual Stories*, he points to the cultural shift towards practices of narrating the self. These stories include lesbian and gay coming-out stories, but also stories of sexual oppression, rape and surviving sexual abuse. Plummer's thesis is not that these stories are fictional accounts (i.e. made up), but they are stories that could only come into being once the social world was ready to hear them. They are therefore historically and culturally specific and contingent. It is here that the parallels between the social constructionist accounts of sexuality that emerged in sociology alongside the philosophical writing of Michel Foucault become more apparent. Foucault's historical tracing of the explosion of discourse about the 'truth of sex' in modern times was underpinned by an analysis of such practices as the 'confession' that can be found in both religious and psychoanalytic discourse. Plummer's development was to analyse how these transformations had rapidly taken hold in the late twentieth century such that sociologists could now speak of 'the sexualisation of modern capitalist societies' (Evans, 1993, p. 65), the 'democratisation of intimacy' (Giddens, 1991) and 'a new form of life politics' Plummer called 'intimate citizenship' (Plummer, 1996/2003, p. 38).

This movement towards framing sociological concerns with contemporary sexuality within poststructuralist concepts such as 'fiction' or 'stories' is seen by both Weeks and Plummer as a profoundly political process. As Plummer (1996/2003, p. 37) states:

> The stories we tell of our lives are deeply implicated in moral and political change and the shifting tales of self and identity carry potential for a radical transformation of the social order. Stories work their way into changing lives, communities and cultures. . . . In short, *a radical, pluralistic, democratic, contingent, participatory politics of human life choices and difference is in the making.* (emphasis in original)

What their latter day accounts acknowledge is that there is no certainty in identity. These identities that we have come to know as lesbian, gay, bisexual are themselves 'historical inventions', and the practices that brought them into being continue to proliferate new modes of sexuality and new identity categories. Plummer (1995), among others, has made a substantial contribution to our understanding of how 'sexuality is produced via new and politically contingent identities in a postmodern, global world' (Schneider, 2008, p. 88). However, it is Foucault who is widely credited with inspiring scholars from across the social sciences and humanities with his analysis of sexuality as a discourse and sexual identities as historical constructs brought into being through institutional practices.

Social constructionism: discourses of sexuality

> but I do worship him. . . . As far as I'm concerned, the guy was a
> fucking saint.
>
> David Halperin, 1995, p. 6

It is difficult to introduce the work of the historian, philosopher
and public intellectual Michel Foucault without either overstat-
ing or downplaying his influence on debates in sexuality studies,
and the field of social and cultural theory more generally. Some
lament the way that Foucault has come to symbolize the origins of
social constructionism, poststructuralism and queer theory when
there is clear evidence that his ideas did not emerge in isolation,
or may even have been precipitated by discussions elsewhere.
Nevertheless, for many contemporary social theorists in the field
of sexuality there is a requirement and frequently an aspiration
to walk in the footsteps of Foucault. The canon of Foucault's
work may seem vast in an era of academic specialism as it makes
interventions into the history of madness, sexuality and the penal
system. The design and thrust of his ideas are, to paraphrase David
Macey (1993), ineffably tied up with his own life experiences,
including his time in a psychiatric institution, suicide attempts, his
homosexuality, his political activism, and his untimely death from
AIDS-related complaints in 1984. Yet, they continue to speak to
wider social questions of 'what we are, what we think, and what
we do today' (Foucault, 1984, p. 32). His status in the transdisciplinary fold can be asserted given the breadth and complexity
of his work, but this is often because he is seen to have failed the
demands of particular disciplinary practices. As Lois McNay (1994,
p. 1) states, 'Historians have rejected Foucault's work for being
too philosophical, philosophers for its lack of formal rigour and
sociologists for its literary or poetic quality.' This refusal to self-
disclosure or to be placed in a definitive disciplinary home can also
be understood as part of his overall project where he claims, 'The
main interest in life is to become someone else that you were not
at the beginning' (Foucault, 1988, p. 11), or 'I am no doubt not the

only one who writes in order to have no face. Do not ask who I am and do not ask me to remain the same' (cited in McNay, 1994, p. 1). The issue of the confessional in both Foucault's personal and academic life is one that has continued to intrigue Foucauldian scholars (or rather scholars of Foucault) (e.g. Huffer, 2010). Nevertheless, it can be argued that Foucault's legacy is ongoing primarily because his work did not focus on providing answers to empirical questions. Instead it asked new questions that required openness to both method and experience (Apperley, 1997). He furnished contemporary theorists with a methodological toolbox for attending to the relationship between power and knowledge, teasing out the interaction of discourse, disciplinarity, subjugation and resistance, as well as providing a litany of theoretical concepts such as biopower, technologies of self and governmentality that continue to demonstrate their relevance to our social, economic and political lives today (Venn and Terranova, 2009).

While Foucault's work has had an immense impact across the humanities and social sciences, in this section the focus is on his account of the history of sexuality and the role this played in the emergence of social constructionist and poststructuralist thought, particularly in the sociological and psychological fields of sexuality studies. His early work (e.g. 1969) had sought to envisage a methodological mode of historical analysis that identified forms of domination that operated through mechanisms of subjectification, objectification and normalization. It is the first volume of the *History of Sexuality* (1979/1991), *La Volonté de savoir* (*The Will to Know*), which is most frequently cited in social constructionist accounts of sexuality. Here Foucault set out his framework as one that rejected the 'repressive hypothesis' that had dominated the work of Freud. Instead of seeing the relationship between society and sexuality as one of censorship and repression, he posited that it was not a 'uniform concern to hide sex' that permeated society, rather 'a regulated and polymorphous incitement to discourse'. As such, 'What is peculiar to modern societies . . . is not that they consigned sex to a shadow existence, but that they dedicated themselves to speaking of it *ad infinitum*, while exploiting it as *the* secret' (1979/1991, pp. 34–5). As Shane Phelan (1990, p. 423) explains, grasping the meaning of concepts such as 'discourse' and *dispositive* or 'apparatus' are necessary to fully understand the implications of Foucault's position. When referring to discourse, Foucault did not simply imply language in its linguistic form, rather discourses incorporate the very many 'practices that systematically form the objects of which we speak' (1969, p. 49). Elsewhere, Foucault refers to these discursive formations as 'episteme', where the episteme is a type of 'apparatus'. As Phelan states, 'the apparatus "is both discursive and non-discursive, its elements being much more heterogeneous" than those of the episteme' and

> includes in this both such linguistic formations as laws and regulations, scientific and philosophical pronouncements, and nondiscursive structures such as architectural designs and economies. These elements are bounded together by their effect, by their role in a larger strategy that coordinates and structures social relations at a given point. (Phelan, 1990, p. 423)

This overview allows us to reflect on Foucault's genealogical method that was crucial to the analysis of sexuality he offered in volume 1. His historical summary of the shifting meanings that underpin our common understanding of sexuality depicted a distinction between pre-modern and modern conceptions of sexuality. Central to this was his concern with a 'new persecution of the peripheral sexualities entailing an *incorporation of perversions* and a new *specification of individuals*' (Foucault, 1979/1991, pp. 42–3, emphasis in original) that had emerged from the development of a 'science of sexuality' that sought 'to tell the truth of sex' (p. 57). Thus, Foucault set out a thesis that demonstrated how subjects become produced through discourses and demarcated the complex relationship that power has to knowledge. As Phelan (1990, p. 424) summarizes: 'Power [then] is not opposed to knowledge or truth, but functions through it and the systems of meaning upon which it rests. Power operates through discourses that define and legitimise its operation.' The shift to a modern conception of the subject as both the subject and object of knowledge is demonstrated through the well-known claim that scientific discourses reconstituted homosexuality from a set of sexual acts to a particular 'type' of being.

> As defined by the ancient civil or canonical codes, sodomy was a cat-
> egory of forbidden acts; their perpetrator was nothing more than the
> juridical subject of them. The nineteenth-century homosexual became
> a personage, a past, a case history and a childhood, in addition to being
> a type of life form, and a morphology with an indiscreet anatomy and
> possibly a mysterious physiology. Nothing that went into his total
> composition was unaffected by his sexuality. It was everywhere present
> in him: at the root of all his actions, because it was their insidious and
> indefinitely active principle; written immodestly on his face and body
> because it was a secret that always gives itself away. It is consubstan-
> tial with him, less as a habitual sin than as a singular nature. We must
> not forget that the psychological, psychiatric, medical category of
> homosexuality was constituted from the moment it was characterized
> – Westphal's famous article of 1870 on 'contrary sexual sensations' can
> stand as its date of birth – less by a type of sexual relations than by a
> certain quality of sexual sensibility, a certain way of inverting mascu-
> line and the feminine in oneself. Homosexuality appeared as one of the
> forms of sexuality when it was transposed from the practice of sodomy
> onto a kind of interior androgyny, a hermaphroditism of the soul. The
> sodomite was a temporary aberration; the homosexual is now a species.
> (Foucault, 1979/1991, p. 43)

Thus, Foucault's legacy was defined by interpretations of this passage that posited the identity category 'homosexual' as a histori-cal invention brought into being by the disciplinary practices that culminated in the scientific study of sexuality: by the will to know the 'truth of sex'. His historical analysis of practices and pleasures revealed that social and cultural meanings surrounding 'sodomy', 'pederasty' or 'gender inversion' slowly gathered into a field of 'perversity' that was increasingly subjected to measures of social control. Crucially, for Foucault, this process also facilitated the creation of a 'reverse' discourse: 'homosexuality began to speak in its own behalf, to demand that its legitimacy or "naturality" be acknowledged, often in the same vocabulary, using the same categories by which it was medically disqualified' (1979/1991, p. 101). Hence, the persuasiveness of Foucault's thesis for sociologists, feminists and critical psychologists was in the way it enabled the transformation of the accepted wisdom on power and oppression. As Elizabeth Grosz (1995, p. 210) describes, Foucault rendered the notion of oppression considerably more sophisticated by alerting us to the idea that the attribution of social value is not simply a matter of being depicted as passive and compliant, stripped of all forms of resistance. Rather, a position of subordination,

> exerts its own kind of forces . . . its own practices, and knowledges, which, depending on their socio-cultural placement and the contingencies of the power game that we have no choice but to continue playing, may be propelled into positions of power and domination.

Accordingly, the work of Foucault has been inspirational for many of those classified as 'oppressed' for there is always the possibility of a certain degree of agency (resistance) that may enable them to both challenge and transform their position. However, the uptake and application of the ideas in volume 1 has not been without controversy. For example, not all feminists have been convinced or enamoured by the Foucauldian inspired social constructionist approach to the field of sexuality. For them, although the focus on issues of power is crucial they find his engagement with the relationship between gender and sexuality insufficient for the political goal of transforming gender oppression. In a recent special edition of *Sociology* focused on intersectionality two notable feminist sociologists, Stevi Jackson and Sue Scott, have called for the rehabilitation of Simon and Gagnon's interactionist approach in order to explore the intersection between gender and sexuality or, as they state, 'the everyday gendered doing of sexuality in interaction' (2010, p. 812). The concept intersectionality has become central to sociologically informed theorizations of sexuality on the premise that single-axis analyses fail to unpick the complexity of multiple forms of marginalization, for instance the intersection of race, gender, sexuality and social class (Taylor et al., 2010). In revisiting script theory, Jackson and Scott (2010, p. 819) argue that presupposing 'a social, reflexive self, [social interactionism] gives scope to human agency but locates that agency in social context' (p. 821), something they claim the Foucauldian inspired social constructionist approach is unable to do. Yet, rather than drawing to the fore the complexity of theorizing intersectionality, they maintain their critique of Foucault by arguing that a lack of sensitivity to issues of agency in Foucauldian inspired approaches to sexuality has enabled a return to *psychoanalysis* (despite his own rejection of the repressive hypothesis). They propose that for those who wish to resist any recourse to psychoanalysis the straightforward application of Foucauldian ideas about discourse to empirical studies of sexuality fails to do 'justice to the complex interrelationships between discourses (or cultural scenarios) and agency/identity (the intrapsychic)' (p. 820). This, they suggest, is because the application is outside the remit of his original thesis and design of his genealogical method, and leaves theorists seeking to explore *why* individuals might identify with certain 'subject positions' turning to psychoanalytic concepts and explanations (e.g. Hollway, 1989; Butler, 1993).

The limitations of discourse analysis and other derivatives of social constructionism as methodological approaches to the study of experiences of subjectivity have been well documented in critical psychology (e.g. Nightingale and Cromby, 1999; Gillies et al., 2005). More recently, others have made use of the Foucault's later work in the *History of Sexuality* series (volume 3, *The Care of the Self*) in both theoretical and empirical studies in order to better address issues of agency, subjectivity and ethics (e.g. Heyes, 2007; Brown and Stenner, 2009; Hanna, 2013). Jackson and Scott's proposal overlooks these developments. Yet, taking Gagnon and Simon's work and repackaging it as a 'feminist sociology of sexuality' (p. 811) by promoting its social credentials is not sufficient for a psychosocial analysis as the problem of the 'intrapsychic' remains. As Gagnon and Simon concur, sexual scripts emerge out of the interaction between biological, psychological and social processes while for Jackson and Scott there is no room for biological or psychological processes. Flagging the reflexive self as a mode of overcoming questions of agency is equally problematic as it presupposes a *knowing* subject. Moreover, as Gagnon (1977, p. 2, my emphasis) argued, 'people become sexual in the same way they become everything else. *Without much reflection*, they pick up directions from their social environment.' In that case, given the social environment is so dominated by directions to heterosexuality, it is surprising anyone would become lesbian, gay, or bisexual at all.

Although the limitations with the recent invocation of script theory remain, what the Jackson and Scott paper does remind us of is a key debate still at stake in the recent history of sexuality: whether social constructionism is sufficient for theorizing sexuality and sexual subjectivities and the importance of intersectionality (even if this is insufficiently sketched out in this paper beyond references to the relationship between gender and sexuality). Foucault may have demonstrated emphatically the way sexuality shifted from an act to a form of being, and discourse analytic accounts point to multiple discursive possibilities in the constitution of subject relations. Yet, socio-historically informed accounts are limited in terms of engaging with how our sexual subjectivities are formed and open to critiques of socio-cultural reductionism, just as they resist any engagement with psychological or biological perspectives for their own reductionist tendencies. Foucault and McIntosh's contribution was to transform questions about sexuality away from why someone might be gay or lesbian, to how that role emerged in a particular social and historical moment, and its social function. Gagnon and Simon's work points to the importance of holding onto a notion of the 'intrapsychic', however poorly defined this is in relation to interpersonal interaction and the cultural sphere. Nevertheless, the desire for more complex sociological understandings of sexual subjectivities remains, along with the need to understand these in relation to other forms of subjugation related to race, class and geopolitical location, and questions about whether these can be produced without recourse to psychoanalysis or psychology (Halperin, 2007; Jackson and Scott, 2010). These arguments will be taken up in more detail in the next chapter when we evaluate the resurgence of psychoanalysis within queer theory and psychosocial debates. For now the focus continues on how social constructionism emerged in psychology and the impact it had on critical strands in the discipline, as theorists have attempted to rethink psychology's own role in the ongoing construction of sexuality.

Constructing sexuality, reconstructing psychology?

Given that psychology is consistently positioned, in a Foucauldian sense, as a core disciplinary apparatus that both invented sexual identities and pathologized particular sexual practices, it is worth considering how scholars in psychology have responded and contributed to the field of social constructionist ideas. The focused criticism on psychology from sociological quarters and some queer perspectives means it is easy to overlook the fact that we can find evidence of the impact of social constructionist thought in psychology from the early 1970s (e.g. Gergen, 1973). Over the last thirty-five years many have questioned the role of psychology, its contribution to forms of social regulation (e.g. Henriques et al., 1984/1998; Parker, 1989; Rose, 1998), gender and sexuality oppression (e.g. Kitzinger, 1987; Ussher, 1989, 2010) and pathologization (e.g. Parker et al., 1995). The uptake of social constructionist ideas in psychology has been inspired by a range of social theorists including Goffman (1961), Berger and Luckman (1967/1991) and Foucault (1979/1991), as well as those involved in the anti-psychiatry movement (e.g. Szasz, 1960; Chesler, 1972). This is not to say that the psychological discipline as a whole has relinquished its quest to be recognized as an experimental science but, in the UK, Europe and Australasia in particular, social constructionist critique and a reflexive engagement with conceptual and historical debates within the discipline are now embedded in the core curriculum. Yet, rather than advocating a radical rejection of psychology like we find in the early work of Foucault and his queer theorist disciples (e.g. Halperin, 1995) these scholars have sought to rethink psychology, its place in contemporary understandings of selfhood (Rose, 1998), and how critical theoretical perspectives might help to revision the discipline (e.g. Fox and

Prillentensky, 1997; Brown and Stenner, 2009). For example, Henriques et al. (1984/1998, p. 1) in their now classic text *Changing the Subject: Psychology, social regulation and subjectivity* state:

> we do not argue that psychology is or has been a monolithic force of oppression and distortion which constrains and enchains individuals. Rather, we contend that psychology, because of its insertion in modern social practices, has helped to constitute the very form of modern individuality. Psychology is productive: it does not simply bias or distort or incarcerate helpless individuals in oppressive institutions. It regulates, classifies and administers. . . . Further, psychology's implication in our modern form of individuality means that it constitutes subjectivities as well as objects.

Thus, in contrast to rejecting the psychological in constructions of sexuality, their position demands a close critical reading *of* the psychological, and the role it plays in contemporary understandings of sexuality and sexual subjectivities. It was the continued role of psychology in depoliticizing same-sex relationships that underpinned Celia Kitzinger's (1987) *The Social Construction of Lesbianism*. This book was the first of twenty-two published in the Sage Series in Social Constructionism (Russell and Gergen, 2004) and took issue with the 'gay affirmative' research trend that replaced the pathologizing accounts that had dominated developmental psychology until the 1970s. As was demonstrated in chapter 2, the gay affirmative approach sought to address issues involved in coming out and the formation of lesbian and gay sexual identities. Inspired by the politics of radical feminism, Kitzinger claimed that this liberal humanist influence shifted lesbian sexuality into the personalized realm of 'alternative lifestyles', 'a way of loving', 'sexual preference', 'personal fulfilment and self actualization', masking its political stance against the 'patriarchal oppression of women' (p. vii). A more recent retrospective (Clarke and Peel, 2004) has evaluated the impact of Kitzinger's thesis, reminding us of both its radical potential and ultimate flaws. For instance, Coyle (2004) talks of the dramatic impact the book had on his own thinking by questioning the unspoken values of a supposedly objective and value-free psychological science. Glenda Russell and Ken Gergen (2004) locate their evaluation of the work in terms of the division between UK and US approaches to lesbian and gay psychology, or what has more recently been conceived as LGBTQ psychologies (Clarke and Peel, 2007). They commend Kitzinger for taking on the empiricist stance of mainstream psychology and proposing an alternative social constructionist perspective that promotes an anti-essentialist ideological critique. Despite winning a raft of prizes, including an APA award, they lament the way 'LGB psychology in the USA . . . has shown little openness to postmodern perspectives – including Kitzinger's constructionist approach' (Russell and Gergen, 2004, p. 512) such that the 'full force of Kitzinger's challenge has yet to be recognised. Only a minority of LGB psychologists in the USA would seriously question that sexual orientation is an actual, extant trait possessed by individuals' (p. 513). This resistance to the deconstruction of ideas about sexuality and the reconstruction of psychological knowledge within mainstream psychology in the USA demonstrates the ongoing need for critical engagements *with* psychology and the disciplinary knowledge it produces, rather than its outright rejection. This type of endeavour can be found in strength among UK and Antipode based LGBTQ psychologies (e.g. Clarke and Peel, 2007; Riggs and Walker, 2004), including critiques of the heteronormative assumptions that often remain unexamined in social construction itself (Hegarty, 2007).

Yet, from a psychosocial perspective, along with other social constructionist approaches Kitzinger's thesis carries its own limitations. Although she shifts the methodological focus from studies of measurable traits to subjective experience, the accounts provided by her participants are interpreted as 'explaining lesbianism in terms borrowed from the dominant' (1987, p. 123). Thus, whether the women draw on notions of a humanistic language such as 'lifestyle choice', a rhetoric of 'romantic love', or gesture to how 'natural' their sexuality feels, the social constructionist interpretation details their positioning in terms of pre-existing cultural resources that depoliticize their identity. So, in line with other social constructionist approaches, there is little space for the exploration of the complexity of sexual desire, particularly when for Kitzinger lesbianism is 'a political statement representing the bonding of women against male supremacy' (1987, p. vii), and all accounts that point to the personal are dismissed as the outcome of normative psychology. I have some sympathy with Kitzinger's critique of the way psychology as a disciplinary technique contributes to new forms of pathologization (for instance the shift from homosexuality as a mental illness to internalized homophobia as a failure to adapt to one's own homosexuality) and the way gay liberation politics subsumed and erased the specificity of lesbian lives. Yet, her critique is predicated on the basis of a particular school of radical feminist politics, which disables any sophisticated engagement with questions of sexual desire, bodies and pleasure (Segal, 1994) and replaces one set of ideological values with another.

What is needed then are alternative ways of rethinking the relationship between the personal and the political. Relying on qualitative methods of enquiry is inherently problematic, particularly for those working in social constructionist perspectives. If we ask people about their sexuality they will inevitably respond in multiple ways that reproduce the variety of biological, psychological, psychoanalytic, humanistic and socio-cultural discourses that permeate our everyday interactions – revealing ourselves as multiple, fragmented and contradictory. This leaves those who want to work against the disciplinary impact of psychological discourse while simultaneously engaging in questions of subjectivity in a conundrum, as the subjectivities we find will inevitably be formed in line with contemporary values of psychology. This is because

> psychology is not, in the majority of cases, imposed coercively upon unwilling subjects, but is actively sought out by people who have come to identify their own distress in psychological terms, believe that psychology can help them, and are grateful for the attention they receive. (Kitzinger, 1987, p. 38)

In an attempt to 'cruise past social constructionism', Peter Hegarty (2007, p. 53) argues that social constructionist research in psychology finds it difficult to step outside its own binaries because of its reliance on the method of discourse analysis and its underlying assumption that 'the social can be understood as the textual'. Social constructionism can reveal how knowledge is constructed but he suggests we should look to 'LGBTQ communities for possibilities of how knowledge and pleasure might go together more easily' (p. 55). Weeks (1998) also recognized that the essentialist versus constructionist binary (which much of his earlier work was based on promoting) was by the mid- to late 1990s becoming a tiresome and tedious debate. Yet, he laments that the debate stayed primarily in the field of sexuality studies despite its wider implications for sociology. If however we look to how social constructionist ideas took off in UK and Antipodean psychology a significant impact on the critical strands within the discipline can be found. Furthermore, if the criticism at the heart of social constructionist accounts of sexuality was targeted towards psychology for its place in constructing homosexuality as a 'condition', there may be some grounds for a 'defence of psychology'. This is because critical psychologists and those working in psychosocial studies have sought to respond to, integrate and devise their own social constructionist informed contributions to the field, but with a continual regard for the complexity of the 'psychological' in understanding sexual identities and subjectivities.

Constructing sexuality, intersectionality and the psychosocial subject

The influence of social constructionist approaches has been profound, transforming the landscape of both sociological and psychological engagements with sexuality, moving our understanding beyond that of behaviour or orientation to engage with sexual meaning, subjectivity and the relationship between homosexuality and heterosexuality. Despite this, the field is left with a number of conundrums that maintain certain tensions between social constructionist theory, identity and politics. For some, social constructionism introduced a radical epistemological shift demonstrating the way social power operates to marginalize and oppress particular groups while promoting and supporting others. There is nothing 'natural' about these divisions whether drawn on the basis of gender, sexuality, race or class, rather they emerge through institutionalized practices and processes that label and position particular 'others'. However, the uncertainty this introduces into everyday categories such as identity can create political tensions. For example, social constructionist ideas can be mobilized by critics to argue that if homosexuality is not a condition and socially, historically and culturally specific, then there is the possibility that individuals might change. Of course this analysis is embedded in a moral discourse that maintains homosexuality as a social problem, a danger to self and society, and an undesirable state of living. Yet, it is difficult for individual people who come to call themselves lesbian or gay to defend against this type of assertion without recourse to the equally morally dubious power of biological explanations. Moreover, many lesbians and gay men do see their sexual desires and identity as a core aspect of self and see social constructionism 'as a fundamental challenge to their hard fought gains' particularly in a social climate where 'the claim of lesbian and gay activism to recognized minority status may be boosted by the latest fashionable theories of the gay gene or the gay brain' (Weeks, 1998, p. 136). Thus, while many of us accept social constructionist explanations for objects such as 'madness' or identity categories such as 'homosexual', their explanatory power for our own sexual identity and subjective experiences of being lesbian, gay, bisexual or straight can be lacking.

So is social constructionism a sufficient explanation for sexuality and sexual subjectivities? If our interest is in the construction of objects or subject positions then the analytic tools of social constructionism may be enough. However, if we wish to engage with the more complex field of lived experience, how we come to embody certain sexual lives, the rich life of bodies, pleasure and desire, then it is crucial to look beyond any reductionist account – whether biological or social – and to the way that sexuality is always wrapped up with other forms and norms related to a broader power nexus that incorporates gender, class, race and geopolitical location. Focusing on sexuality as the single-axis of oppression fails to acknowledge that marginalization is not universal for those that come to call themselves lesbian, gay, bisexual, or even heterosexual. While acknowledging the importance of sociological calls for attention to intersectionality when theorizing sexuality, a focus on the psychosocial subject points to the possibility of incorporating psychological and biological concepts without necessarily reducing subjectivity to either of these imperatives. This means breaking down some of our disciplinary prejudices and promoting reflexive engagement with the impact of all disciplinary thought. Here, there is fault with the longstanding critiques of psychology and psychoanalysis that have emanated from sociological and more recently queer accounts. These have often fixed psychology as a monolith, failing to engage with transformations that have taken place within the subject since the 1970s and its popularity among lay people as a way of meaning making. It is important to recognize, as the previous chapters do, psychology has not been completely immune to the cultural turn in social theory or how this has played out in the field of sexualities across the social sciences and humanities. In continuing this transdisciplinary dialogue and the potential of a psychosocial approach for sexuality, the next chapter focuses on the emergence of queer theory, its ongoing debates with psychology and psychoanalysis, and the way that psychological ideas and concepts have made their own impact as part of the turn to affect.

4

Queering Sexuality

the very phrase 'social constructionism' has come to seem a hopelessly out-of-date formula in queer studies, and the mere invocation of it makes a writer appear backward and unsophisticated.

David Halperin, 2004, p. 11

If social constructionism has had such a profound impact in sociology and social psychology why, in queer studies at least, is it now considered 'hopelessly out-of-date' and 'unsophisticated'? This chapter outlines queer theoretical engagements that sought to shift debates beyond the entrenched constructionist/essentialist binary, and considers the place of psychoanalysis. By the late 1980s, lesbian, gay and feminist studies were dominated by debates about the merits of essentialist versus constructionist accounts of sexuality, with constructionist perspectives usually winning out. The social constructionist position represented an epistemological shift based on the rejection of biological, psychological and psychoanalytic accounts for their essentialist assumptions that sexuality can be explained through innate biological processes or drives. Yet, many scholars had become tired of this epistemological battlefield and its prohibition of broader discussions of how we experience

sexuality and sexual desire. As is often the case in transdisciplinary scholarship, when we become pinned in by the limitations
of our theoretical or methodological tools it is time to look for
new devices to reinvigorate or unlock new debate. Nevertheless,
designing a way out of an impasse is not straightforward as it is
not possible to know in advance what action will lead to this
outcome. With a certain amount of distance it is possible to highlight some of the key triggers that precipitated the emergence of
queer theory, its multiple theoretical influences and its academic
and social impact. 'Queer' had long been used as a term of insult
for lesbians and gay men, but by the late 1980s it was undergoing
a reappropriation within 'queer cultures'. Of central importance
was the socio-political context of the HIV/AIDS crisis that was
sweeping through queer communities against a political landscape
of a growing conservatism. Thus in similar conditions to those that
underpinned the paradigmatic shift within sexuality studies created
by Mary McIntosh's 'Homosexual role', the explosion of queer
studies entailed asking new types of questions, or finding a new
place to begin.

In this chapter we consider the contribution of key thinkers
such as Gloria Anzaldúa, Lauren Berlant, Judith Butler, Tim Dean,
David Halperin, Gayle Ruben, Eve Kosofsky Sedgwick, José
Esteban Muñoz and Michael Warner in shaping the burgeoning
area that more latterly became known as queer studies. Michael
O'Rourke (2011, p. 104) quite rightly warns against reducing
queer perspectives to a few key thinkers and I am aware that the
predominance of white, North American scholars in this list risks
side-lining other important work, especially that emanating from
within postcolonial and transnational contexts, as well as reinsert-
ing an institutionalized concept of Anglo-American centrality
to this particular vision of queer studies. Nevertheless, for those
unfamiliar with debates within queer theory, as readers coming
from a background in psychology often are, it is important to initially explore the 'canon' in order to consider the possibilities that
queer insights have for a psychosocial approach. The first section,
'Finding a new place to begin', considers the emergence of queer
theory and activism as a means of challenging the constructionist/

essentialist impasse that had gripped sexuality studies in the late 1980s. The second section, 'Queer icons', reviews the early contributions of key thinkers Judith Butler and Eve Kosofsky Sedgwick to the emerging field introducing concepts such as 'performativity' and considering the analytic relationship between gender, sexuality and identity. The third part of the chapter, 'Queering race, hybridity and mixedness', outlines criticism that queer theory often presents a 'white-washed' history of sexuality. It introduces the seminal work of Gloria Anzaldúa and José Esteban Muñoz for rethinking the relationship between gender, sexuality and race, and considers how concepts of 'hybridity' and 'mixedness' have value for a psychosocial manifesto by focusing on all forms of border crossings. The fourth section, 'Queering psychology', turns attention to the relationship between queer theory and psychology to consider the challenges that anti-identity and anti-normative tenets raise for psychology, examining the way queer theory has impacted on critical psychological perspectives and imagining the lessons that might be delivered in resisting disciplinary boundaries and queering psychology. Then the fifth section, 'Theorizing queer subjectivity, killing off psychology?', critically examines David Halperin's call to theorize queer subjectivity without recourse to psychology or psychoanalysis. A response to this is organized around the proposition that what is needed is a reimagining of psychology within a psychosocial framework, exploring the way psychoanalytic concepts are already implicated in some queer commentaries, particularly in relation to the figure of the desiring subject. The final section documents the shift from a focus on desire to affect more broadly to highlight the centrality of queer perspectives in the recent theoretical shift from culture to affect that has impacted across the humanities and social sciences. Attention to affect is seen as a central trope for a psychosocial approach, but it is argued that if the affective turn introduces a new binary between thought and feeling, or knowing and being, it will overemphasize questions of ontology and problematically return us to normative engagements with psychology and biology.

Finding a new place to begin:
the emergence of queer theory and activism

The early 1990s saw a rapid growth in attention paid to the newly coined 'queer theory' and its transformative aspirations. The term's origin is often attributed to Teresa de Lauretis, who used it for a conference call in 1990 at the University of California that sought to theorize lesbian and gay sexualities. While de Lauretis quickly disassociated from the term, the use of queer theory as a reference point grew in popularity during the following decade. Nevertheless, Lauren Berlant and Michael Warner (1995) early on questioned whether an entity such as 'Queer Theory' actually existed, especially one that was deemed to be 'worthy of prefacing with capital letters'. Instead, they preferred to talk of 'queer commentary', or 'commentaries', noting that it is not always *theory* that links queer writing. Others speak of 'queer theories' (e.g. Giffney, 2009) indicating the multiple theoretical influences that feature in these commentaries. Rather than mapping a precise theoretical approach then, it is easier to understand the analytical power of 'queer' by reflecting on what it set out to *do* against the backdrop of social constructionism and feminist debates on sexuality and sexual difference of the late 1980s. Within feminist accounts the emergence of queer theory is often traced back further to Gayle Rubin's (1984, p. 304) argument that the category sexuality should be politically and analytically disentangled from gender. Writing against the background of the feminist sex wars that had divided feminists in the late 1970s and early 1980s, Rubin argued that feminism is the theory of gender oppression and should not be privileged in the theory of sexual oppression as this 'fails to distinguish between gender, on the one hand, and erotic desire, on the other'. Nevertheless, within accounts of early star contributors to the field of queer theory the radical analytic separation between gender and sexuality was less distinct. Judith Butler opposed this call (Osborne and Segal, 1993) and in Sedgwick's work, despite arguing for a 'certain irreducibility' of sexuality to gender (1990, p. 30), the notion 'queer' was conceived as having an intrinsic

relationship *to* gender. This is because the visible markers of gender
identity, such as masculinity and femininity, and the way in which
they map onto male and female bodies are often used to 'read' normative and non-normative sexuality – whether or not that reading
relates to an individual's sexual practices. Thus, queer emerged not
as a new identity property of lesbians and gay men, nor to symbolize same-sex desire (although it has been used in these ways), rather
to queer was promoted as a means of disrupting the normative relation between gendered bodies and sexual desires, a practice open
to all.

Embedded within the original call to queer theory was a commitment to poststructuralism and deconstructionism as a means by
which to rethink sexualities outside a comparison to heterosexuality (as the norm), and as a mode for attending to the way that
gender and race also play a role in the way that we experience our
sexuality. The early days of 'queer' saw a particular focus on sup-
posed forms of deviant eroticism and the limits of sexual identity
categories. You did not have to be lesbian or gay to be queer – in
fact many lesbian and gays were construed as 'vanilla', latterly
'heteronormative' or 'assimilationist', and queer alliances were
formed with some in opposite-sex relations if they were perceived
to be subverting (hetero)normative practices. The social and political context of the late 1980s is crucial to understanding the force
with which queer ideas were taken up, not only in response to
widespread homophobia, but also to the premise that equality
for lesbian and gays could only be achieved by assimilating with
heterosexual values. Queer politics emerged as a retort to the sex
panic triggered by the HIV/AIDS epidemic and set out to challenge the well-established conservatism that maintained a wall of
silence on non-normative sexual practices.

Eve Kosofsky Sedgwick (1985, 1990) is attributed with generating one of the most nuanced theories of homophobia, and this,
along with concepts of homosocial desire and homosexual panic,
was key to her early work on the relationships between men. In
the preface to the second edition of the seminal *Epistemology of the
Closet*, Sedgwick revisited the historical moment in which early
queer theory and activism emerged, recounting the time of an

AIDS emergency and excessive homophobic stigma: a time when the word HIV was never spoken by the US president, yet public discourse focused on containing and marking men and women inflicted by the illness with no cure or care. Thus, Sedgwick (2008, p. xv) reminds us how

> the punishing stress of loss, incomplete mourning, chronic dread, and social fracture, and the need for mobilizing powerful resources of resistance in the face of such horror, imprinted a characteristic stamp on much of the theory and activism of the time.

In the UK, the homosexual panic and stigma associated with HIV/ AIDS soon translated into government policy which regulated that local authorities 'shall not intentionally promote *homosexuality* or publish material with the intention of promoting homosexuality' or 'promote the teaching in any *maintained school* of the acceptability of homosexuality as a pretended family relationship', although neither of these should prohibit discussion 'for the purpose of treating or preventing the spread of disease' (Local Government Act, 1988, p. 27). This type of representation exacerbated social stigma and silence about sexuality in schools through a culture of fear, and tied homosexual subjectivity more tightly to discourses of shame, stigma and disease. Against this backdrop, queer theory and its associated political framework developed through the 1990s raising a number of challenges for the rights-based demands of lesbians and gays. Queer activism sought to provide representation to those who felt marginalized by the mainstreaming of lesbian and gay liberation politics. This included those who could not pass as 'straight' and those who wished to actively resist conforming with heteronormative values in order to be accepted. This tension between assimilation and anti-assimilation has intensified in more recent years as the equality agenda has seen numerous successes internationally through increased access to civil rights via marriage, legal recognition of partnerships and increased acceptance of LGBT families through adoption and access to reproductive technologies. These gains are seen by some queer critics as concessions made at the expense of increased control and regulation of sexuality, contra to the drive to liberate desire. In this model, lesbians and gays are accepted by the state *if* they conform to heteronormative notions of monogamy and the family. To contradict this trend, some queer theorists have sought to highlight the messy and disruptive elements of queer lives that have become hidden by a 'sanitized' Gay Pride movement, as well as challenge normalization processes. The 'Gay Shame' counter-movement (see Halperin and Traub, 2009), coupled with the 'turn to affect' more broadly, returns attention to queer erotic and affective practices that do not sit easily with normative expectations of gender and sexuality. Thus, as queer theory and activism has evolved, arguing for the legitimacy of marginalized subjects and practices (e.g. gender variance, sadomasochism, barebacking) while resisting the delineation of its field of application, it has paid increasing attention to the way other categories of difference (e.g. class, race, ethnicity, disability) intersect within an overarching commitment to a non-normative and anti-identity stance (Hall and Jagose, 2013).

Queer icons: the influence of Judith Butler and Eve Kosofsky Sedgwick

Judith Butler's *Gender Trouble* (1990), often cited as a 'foundational' text in the field of queer studies, drew significant attention to the way that gendered bodies lined up with sexuality within the social order. Central to Butler's thesis were the concepts *heterosexual matrix* and *gender performativity*. Butler argued that the appearance of a stable core gender identity was the effect of the repetition of acts, gestures and spoken desires that produced the illusion of an internal essence. The 'heterosexual matrix' demonstrates the way that bodies, genders and sexual desires have been naturalized in order to regulate sexuality within the confines of reproductive heterosexuality. Thus, gender is 'performative' but appears to be an inherent essence because of the repetition of discourses of masculinity and femininity that have the capacity to produce that which they name. Perhaps the biggest contributions of Butler's oeuvre to

the principles of queer theory was the generation of a deep suspicion of all social norms and a drive to radically separate sexuality
from identity. Here, sexual identities, even non-normative ones
such as gay or lesbian, are seen to present their own normalizing
conditions for conduct, subjectivity and desire. Thus, rather than
mobilizing on the basis of identity categories, proponents of queer
theory argue for political activism based on 'resistance to all norms
– a politics that connects gender and sexual oppression to racial
discrimination, class inequalities, ethnic hierarchies, and national
chauvinism' (Dean and Lane, 2001, p. 7).

Eve Sedgwick's work also drew on the concept of 'performativity' to challenge the naturalization of homophobic and heterosexist
assumptions that prevailed in interpretations of queer lives. One of
Sedgwick's (1990) most important contributions was to attempt
to strike out the pervasiveness of the essentialist/constructionist
debate by calling into question the idea that contemporary modes
of homosexuality *had* actually replaced those identified in historical
analyses of the nineteenth century. Although queer commentaries can be associated with poststructuralist analyses, and therefore
social constructionism, Sedgwick objected to the sharpness of the
contrast drawn between different historical modes of homosexuality (such as 'sexual acts' versus 'gay people'), as found in the work
of Foucault (1979/1991, vol. 1) and Halperin (1990), suggesting
this led to the assumption that homosexuality today was a clearly
defined field. Instead, Sedgwick proposed that the modern definition of a homo/heterosexual distinction had become entrenched
as a result of a lack of consistency in whether it should be thought
of as a minority issue, only of interest to lesbians and gays, or as
an issue that was relevant to all cultural understandings of agency
and subjectivity (Sedgwick, 1990). In her subsequent collection, *Tendencies*, Sedgwick suggested that one of the benefits of
'queer' is that it can be used to refer to 'the open mesh of possibilities, gaps, overlaps, dissonances and resonances, lapses and
excesses of meaning when the constituent elements of anyone's
gender, of anyone's sexuality aren't made (or *can't be* made) to
signify monolithically' (1993, p. 8). Thus, in taking to task the
constructionist/essentialist binary in debates about homosexuality

Sedgwick argued that this terminology should be replaced with an attention to the difference between 'minoritizing' and 'universalizing' strategies. Jason Edwards (2008, p. 40) explains that attention to minoritizing/universalizing:

> seems to record and respond to the question, 'In whose lives is homo/heterosexual definition an issue of continuing centrality and difficulty?' rather than either of the questions that seem to have gotten conflated in the constructivist/essentialist debate: on the one hand what one might call the question of phylogeny, 'How fully are the meaning and experience of sexual activity and identity contingent on their mutual structuring with other, historically and culturally variable aspects of a given society?'; and on the other what one might call that of ontogeny, 'What is the cause of homo-[or of hetero] sexuality in the individual?'

Sedgwick drew attention to the impact of minoritizing/universalizing strategies as an alternative to the constructionist/essentialist distinctions for several reasons. These included that it can do the same analytic work while isolating what she saw as the potentially dangerous overlapping of questions of ontogeny and phylogeny: questions of causality that have preoccupied developmental psychologists (see chapter 2) and questions of social form, the foci of social constructionists (see chapter 3) respectively. In this sense, the essentialist/constructionist distinction repeats the polarization between psychology and socio-historicism. Sedgwick sought a more respectful way of holding onto her first axiom that 'people are different from one another', while guarding against questions of ontogeny (causality) that emerge from a history of trying to weed out the abnormal – even if with careful reconstruction we might be able to untie the abnormal from prior histories via the creation of new meanings (constructionism). For this reason she proposed that the gay-affirmative work that had become more popular in psychology would only do well if 'it aims to minimize its reliance on any particular account of the origin of sexual preference and identity in individuals' (p. 41). This is because frameworks for imaging the answer to questions of causality are 'structured by an implicit . . . fantasy of eradicating that identity'. Thus, Sedgwick argued that queer commentaries should interrogate the homophobic and het-erosexist assumptions found in *all* knowledge, in order to challenge 'the universalising, minoritising, pathologising and normalising tendencies of interpretations' (Edwards, 2008, p. 52). This call ushered in an era of queer commentaries that focused on what these interpretations *do*, providing alternative readings that would 'queer' these interpretations, unsettle and offer different, anti-normative possibilities that often excite and seduce the reader.

While the work of Butler and Sedgwick was heavily indebted to poststructuralist theory, there were differences in how their insights contributed to debates in feminism and sexuality studies. Butler's theorization of the heterosexual matrix was widely cited in feminist debates, with much reflection on whether her account of gender performativity could sufficiently theorize embodiment, or whether it was too *culturally* reductionist. Sedgwick's femi-nist credentials were less acknowledged although apparent. This may be because for some Sedgwick's position as a heterosexually married woman, who identified with gay men and was driven by the political injustices of the 1980s and the deaths of many friends and students from AIDs, aligned her more closely with queer poli-tics than gender politics. Some feminists (e.g. Jeffreys, 2003) have been profoundly critical of queer perspectives for being focused on gay men and the celebration of erotic practices involving domina-tion and submission. Thus, Sedgwick's attention to universalizing/minoritizing accounts has become canonical in queer studies, but less so in feminism. In contrast, Butler's concept 'gender per-formativity', demonstrated through the example of drag, had an enormous impact in feminist theory and on the burgeoning field of transgender studies, where transgender became for some the ulti-mate 'queer trope' (Prosser, 1998). Despite queer theory emerging as a theory of sexual oppression, some of its greatest contribu-tions have been to the deconstruction of normative accounts of gender and gender development as well as the production of anti-homophobic interpretations of queer lives. For this reason, queer theory has not resulted in a radical separation of gender and sexu-ality; rather, as both these scholars imply, it indicates the ongoing intricacies of an analytic relationship between the two.

Queering race, hybridity and mixedness

As the concept intersectionality (Crenshaw, 1991) grew in favour within feminist studies in order to draw attention to the omission of race and its intersection with gender, others began to note a similar trend in queer studies where 'much of the scholarship produced in its name elides issues of race and class' (Johnson, 2001/2013, p. 99). For instance, in his seminal essay 'Queer race', Ian Barnard (1999, p. 200) argued that the separation of constructions of sexuality from constructions of race implies that subjective experiences of race and of sexuality develop independently from each other. All too often histories of sexuality (which can include those presented in this book) 'have "white-washed" the figure of the "homosexual"' (Sullivan, 2003, p. 66), not only failing to engage with the complexity of intersections between sexuality and race, but sometimes omitting to include important contributions from scholars who write about race, sexuality and gender. Gloria Anzaldúa is one such theorist who has made a significant impact in critical race studies, but is frequently overlooked in generalist narratives of the queer canon. Her classic text *Borderlands/La Frontera: The new mestiza* was first published in 1987, prior to Judith Butler's *Gender Trouble,* and provided a new queer lexicon introducing concepts of 'hybridity' and 'mixedness' that sought to account for those who lived in the borders or margins as neither 'insiders' nor 'outsiders'. In the introduction to the fourth edition, Norma Elia Cantú and Aída Hurtado (2012, p. 6) outline how Anzaldúa drew on the experiences of Chicanas who grew up in South Texas to 'establish the border between these two countries as a metaphor for all types of crossings – between geopolitical boundaries, sexual transgressions, social dislocations, and the crossings necessary to exist in multiple linguistic and cultural contexts'. Within her theory the notion of living in the border produces a 'mestiza consciousness' that emerges out of subordination but has the 'ability to "see" the arbitrary nature of all social categories but still take a stand . . . to exclude while including, to reject while accepting, and to struggle while negotiating' and acknowledges that 'oppressions are not ranked nor are they conceptualized as static; rather they are recognized as fluid systems that take on different forms and nuances depending on the context' (Cantú and Hurtado, 2012, p. 7).

This theory introduces concepts that align with queer theoretical endeavours that seek to resist categorization and recognize fluidity, but move beyond considering the interrelationship between gender and sexuality to include race, social class and geopolitical context. Similarly, the theory reverberates with the project of this book – to engage a psychosocial manifesto that resists polarized accounts of sexuality. The form of consciousness that Anzaldúa describes as emerging from living on the borders resonates with that of the 'academic migrants' within psychosocial studies who mobilize disciplinary displacements in order to knit between binary oppositions of psychic and social, identity and subjectivity. These entail multiple criss-crossings that also enable us to say something about experiences of oppression that acknowledge difference but do not fix it to particular subjects. Influenced by the work of Crenshaw, Anzaldúa and Sedgwick, José Esteban Muñoz has also made a significant contribution to queer studies that has important insights for psychosocial approaches. Muñoz draws attention to modes of theorizing intersectionality via the concepts 'disidentification' and 'hybridity', arguing that his thesis on disidentification is 'expanding and problematizing identity and identification, not abandoning any socially prescribed identity component' (1999, p. 29). It does so by foregrounding the notion of loss, or the 'lost object' in our understanding of identification processes, and by offering a method of cultural engagement that 'scrambles and reconstructs the encoded message of a cultural text in a fashion that both exposes the encoded message's universalizing and exclusionary machinations and recircuits its workings to account for, include, and empower minority identities and identifications' (1999, p. 31). Here we see the influence of Sedgwick on his aligned project to sidestep the essentialist/constructionist binary and replace it with a more productive strategy for political engagement that focuses on whether messages universalize or minoritize. The second concept, 'hybridity', supports 'disidentification' by drawing together a range of theories of 'fragmentation' that relate to minority identity practices. Thus, as he summarizes:

> Identity markers such as *queer* (from the German *quer* meaning 'transverse') or *mestizo* (Spanish for 'mixed') are terms that defy notions of uniform identity or origins. *Hybrid* catches the fragmentary subject formation of people whose identities traverse different race, sexuality, and gender identifications. Queers of color . . . are not comfortably situated in any one discourse of minority subjectivity. These hybridized identificatory positions are always in transit, shuttling between different identity vectors. . . . A theory of migrancy can potentially help one better understand the negotiation of these fragmentary existences. The negotiations that lead to hybrid identity formation are a travelling back and forth from different identity vectors. (1999, p. 32)

The term 'queers of color' is frequently use in North American accounts that offer a critical engagement with the interstices of race, gender and sexuality to acknowledge a particular postcolonial context that incorporates the distinctive legacies of African American and Latino subjects living in the USA. In the UK, where discourse has been more recently dominated by references to BME (black and minority ethnic), QTPOC (queer trans people of colour) is growing in popularity as a collective term for political affiliation and action, inevitably influenced by the global reach of queer theory and activism. In recent years, the concept 'hybridity' and debates about its value against alternatives such as 'mixedness' have garnered more attention for understanding subjectivity, particularly race and its intersections. Some point to the troubled history that concepts such as 'hybridity' have in relation to eugenics and racist discourse, preferring 'mixedness' or 'mixing' to 'investigate border crossings and alliances' (Gunaratnam, 2014, p. 4). These concepts and their entwinement with broader, queer imperatives to theorize multiplicity and fluidity sit well with a psychosocial ethos as they promote a 'hybridisation of disciplinary approaches to subjectivity' such that 'attention to hybridity and mixing marks an unfolding exploration of the bio-psycho-social that brings with it possibilities for imaginative thinking and empirical investigations of the energetic networks and forces in which the "mechanisms and means" of subjectivity are enmeshed'.

Queering psychology: critical psychology, critically queer

Queer theory is often positioned in opposition to psychology. This section focuses on two key principles of a queer stance, anti-normativity and anti-identity, to explore the challenges they raise for psychology and the potentials and limitations of queer theory for a critically orientated psychology. To examine the anti-normative stance in more detail it is helpful to revisit a seminal essay in Sedgwick's early work that demarks her version of queer theory and illuminates the importance of unpicking normative assumptions about the relationship between gender and sexuality, and psychology's role in maintaining this. In the provocatively titled essay 'How to bring your kids up gay: the war on effeminate boys', Sedgwick (1991) set out a number of concerns with psychological practice (including psychiatry and psychoanalysis) following the removal of homosexuality from the *Diagnostic and Statistical Manual* by the APA in 1973. Here, Sedgwick drew psychology into the queer terrain by arguing that although homosexuality had been depathologized in terms of 'an atypical sexual object-choice' it had now been 'yoked to the *new* pathologization of an atypical gender identification' (p. 158). This move was signalled by the inclusion of a new diagnosis, 'Gender identity disorder of childhood', which for Sedgwick '*re*naturaliz(es) gender' (p. 159), by problematizing and pathologizing gender expressions in childhood that do not follow normative pathways. Sedgwick pointed out that 'revisionists' within psychology were now prepared to construct positive accounts of 'the homosexual' if the gay man is perceived to be '(a) already grown up, and (b) acts masculine' (p. 156). This she argued left the effeminate boy as 'the haunting abject of gay thought' discarding experiences of effeminacy among boys and men, relegating them to the margins. At the heart of this essay is Sedgwick's concern for a space where 'gay development' might be supported when dominant psychological and cultural doctrines fail to affirm 'some people's felt desire or need that there be gay people in the immediate world' (p. 164). Sedgwick suggests that despite the seeming support for adult gay men and accounts of their resilience, there is always the spectre of 'another option' – where things could have turned out differently. Coupled with parental anxiety that gender non-conformity is an early predictor of homosexuality in their child deemed worthy of psychological intervention from the 'helping professions', this contributes to the continuing discourse that 'growing up gay' is an undesirable outcome.

Twenty years later concerns remain about the way that psychological accounts unintentionally contribute to normalizing expectations about the relationship between gender and sexuality development. What has changed is that criticisms are now targeted more directly towards such accounts within mainstream psychological publications. For example, social psychologist Peter Hegarty (2009) raises a number of similar issues with papers included in the journal *Developmental Psychology* as part of a special edition on sexual orientation across the lifespan (Patterson, 2008). Picking up on Sedgwick's 'gender identity in childhood paradigm', Hegarty is critical of recent studies that seek to establish patterns between the breaking of gender norms in childhood and adult sexuality or gender identity. He warns that studying LGBT development against a 'heteronormative' benchmark inevitably stigmatizes LGBT people, and that studies of this kind are often methodologically and theoretically flawed. For example, he states that:

> Drummond et al. [2008] conflate statistically common gender patterns with normativity in their first sentence (p. 34); describe 'girls with potential problems in their sexual identity development' prior to describing those girls' likelihood of growing up lesbian, bisexual, or transgender (p. 42); describe the breaking of gender norms as a *risk factor* for adult transgender status (p. 42); and note that a high 'dosage' of gender transgression is likely to cause bisexual and lesbian identities (p. 43). (Hegarty, 2009, p. 897)

Lisa Downing and Robert Gillett (2011) remind critical psychologists that queer theory is not just resistant to the norm, but resistant to *any* idea of normative behaviour. They suggest this should appeal to critical psychologists, helping them 'interrogate the normative teleology of its mainstream counterpart' (p. 5). While scholars such as Hegarty are here and elsewhere (e.g. 2007, 2011) attempting to do this, getting queer theory into dialogue with mainstream psychological approaches to sexual development is not easy, particularly when many fail to grasp the analysis that is being made. To illustrate, in a response to Hegarty's critique, Zucker et al. (2009, p. 907) completely miss his point, arguing in their defence that it 'has long been recognised that development (normal vs abnormal, typical vs atypical, common vs uncommon) may be best understood as two sides of the same coin', before proceeding to cite Freud's well-known statement that homosexuals should not be conceived of as a different species, but with a glaring omission from Freud's account which states that this is because we have all made a homosexual object choice in our unconscious. Instead, they revert to invoking the binary oppositions that queering seeks to dismantle, and conclude with a heteronormative flourish that erases Freud's concept of perversion in *all* sexuality in favour of suggesting that research on the mechanisms of homosexuality can inform our understanding of 'majority sexual orientation' and vice versa.

Perhaps it is not surprising that queer theoretical ideas and techniques have remained on the margins of psychology. It was not until 1997 that one of the first papers to explicitly evaluate the implications of queer theory for psychology was published in *Theory and Psychology*. Here, Henry Minton offered an interpretation of queer theory that emphasized its potential for scholars working within critical and community psychology perspectives – those driven by interests in social justice, emancipation, critiquing power relations and resisting dominant norms. In defending psychology against some of the charges against it, he argued that within accounts of lesbian and gay identity formation 'there had been a notable conceptual shift that reflects the movement from liberation to queer theory' (p. 346). Perhaps Minton's task was to persuade those within psychology that queer theory was of value, but his account of it did not fully expand on the anti-identitarian stance that underpins it (Downing and Gillett, 2011). Instead, he suggested, 'Queer theory incorporates identity politics as a theoretical and political strategy, making explicit the notion of a queer identity as the primary site of resistance to normativity and objectivity' (p. 348). For many within queer theory this could be interpreted as 'unqueer', writing a stable 'queer identity' into his reading of the way queer commentaries challenge notions of identity. Although these favour disrupting and delegitimizing 'heteronormative knowledges and institutions, and the subjectivities and socialities that are (in)formed by them and that (in)form them' (Sullivan, 2003, p. vi), queer readings also signify that identity is messy, and 'that desire and thus desiring subjects cannot be placed into discrete identity categories, which remain static for the duration of people's lives' (Giffney, 2009, p. 2). Thus, adventures into the territory of 'queer' extend the social constructionist trajectory of instability in truth that critical psychologists are familiar with but shift it into a more emphatic dismantling of identity categories. Queer was not meant to name a new identity category, rather to signify a movement or approach that requires us to take an actively anti-homophobic stance by uncoupling sexuality, desire and sexual practices *from* identity. Nevertheless, this raises challenges for psychologists, even those working within critical or community perspectives, because the object of study for psychology *is* norms of behaviour, and the subject of research is, most often, the individual, conceived as having agency and a sense of self (whether through social interaction or biology). Thus, Downing and Gillett (2011) suggest that a full engagement with queer theory may require the repudiation of psychology itself, and this may be too much of a demand, even for critical psychologists.

Does orientating towards a queer perspective require the rejection of psychology? Certainly Sedgwick's critique of ontogeny is difficult for some psychological approaches, but primarily for those that maintain a vision of psychology as a science based on a rigorous adherence to positivistic methods, which seek to establish causal or predictive relationships and universalizing truths for explaining human behaviour. Yet, an engagement with Sedgwick's oeuvre suggests an outright rejection of psychology and psychoanalysis is too simplistic. Even though she was highly critical of both, throughout her career she made '"extravagant negotiations among the disparate, competing disciplines" called psychology and psychoanalysis, experimental, clinical, and applied alike' (Edwards, 2008, p. 148), and she drew particular insight in her later work from the social psychologist Silvan Tomkins and the psychoanalyst Melanie Klein. As we have seen, Sedgwick was primarily concerned with developing an anti-homophobic stance, which she saw as dependent on six axioms. These can be summarized as: first, people are different from one another; second, even though gender and sexuality are related they are not coexistent and need to be untangled to understand where and how they overlap and where there is no relation; third, we cannot know in advance whether we should theorize lesbians and gay men together or separately; fourth, debates about nature versus nurture take place against an unstable fantasy of what they might explain; fifth, the search for a paradigm shift might mask the present conditions of sexual identity; sixth, the relation between gay studies and the literary canon is, and should be, tortuous.

Taking these axioms as a starting point enables us to see points of connection between Sedgwick's assumptions and that of psychology – not least in the first axiom that notes the importance of individual differences. Equally, within psychology and psychosocial studies, there are theoretical and methodological perspectives for engaging with sexuality beyond a positivist paradigm, as there are across the social sciences, which share a similar concern for how knowledge is produced. Sedgwick's oeuvre, like most queer commentaries, uses skill in close textual analyses to illuminate alternative readings where identifications and desires of literary classics can be seen to cross gender lines. The textual turn within the social sciences, underpinned by poststructuralism also precipitated an increased awareness of the importance of close reading and analysis of discourse sought to demonstrate the relationship between language, power and representation (e.g. Potter and Wetherell, 1987; Fairclough, 1992; Hegarty, 2007). Nevertheless, the final axiom that highlights the relationship between gay studies and the literary canon is where we might see the least potential for overlap between queer theory and critical psychology or psychosocial engagement. For those working in the applied social sciences dense analyses of literature can seem distal from the everyday experiences of those who come to call themselves lesbian, gay, bisexual, transgendered or even queer. However, according to Jason Edwards (2008, p. 11) Sedgwick was also concerned that 'the urgency, reach and power' of her theoretical models might be limited by only utilizing examples from literary texts. To alleviate this, references to the most pressing contemporary social, cultural and political concerns of queer life, including AIDS and youth suicide, can be found throughout Sedgwick's essays, which means that 'any engagement with her work involves making a commitment to weave and interweave oneself among and between and through and beside the theoretical, the political and the personal' (Giffney and O'Rourke, 2007, p. 8).

The feminist scholar Lynne Segal, Anniversary Professor of Psychology and Gender Studies, offers another critical take on both psychology and queer theory. In *Straight Sex: Rethinking the politics of pleasure* Segal (1994) provides a review of early queer perspectives, particularly those inspired by Butler's account of gender performativity. This excellent book, with its original psychosocial approach that gave space to psychological, psychoanalytic and queer perspectives, was for many ahead of its time. It spoke eloquently to those working in gender, sexuality and feminist study but it had less impact in the field of psychology, where even as I write in 2014 the influence of queer theory is still restricted to a few critical voices working primarily on LGBT topics, and even fewer on the intersections of gender, sexuality and race (see Riggs, 2006 for a noted exception). While Segal embraced the playfulness of queer commentaries that sought to unsettle and provoke feelings of pleasure and desire, she has consistently pointed to its limitations in terms of providing an approach to identity that does justice to our attachments, and a politics that is sufficient for challenging the material inequalities that mark out the lives of those who live precariously, whether from violence, oppression or poverty. Segal's

(1994, 1999, 2008) warm and considered analyses of the impact of Butler's work provide a critical engagement with whether gender and sexuality identity concepts could be wholly discarded, even if we do accept that they are fundamentally contingent, that sediment through performative acts, rather than as foundational accounts of our place in the world. For Segal, anti-essentialist notions of identity are crucial for explanations of individuals, yet she resists the anti-identitarian stance of queer theory arguing that identities have ongoing importance for political affiliation. In response to a colloquium titled *Gender, Sex and Subjectivity (After Judith Butler)* Segal (2008, p. 384) argues that there is no single 'Butler' that necessitates an afterword, rather that Butler is a continuing force in feminist and social theory who has produced a variety of distinct positions in her work since the days of *Gender Trouble*. Segal traces five changes that mark a shift from the anti-identity stance that many within queer commentators attribute to her influence:

> She has moved from primarily semiotic analysis to stressing the significance of the socio-cultural moment; from political abstractions to ethical reasoning; from pivotal concern with gender and sexuality to a general interest in alterity and the face/place of the other; from a Foucauldian engagement with exteriority and performativity to a more psychodynamic interest in interiority and stress upon the formative early years of life; from a rejection of identities into the specific embrace of several very distinct ones, articulated – with a suitable plethora of caveats – in the form of an identity politics. (2008, p. 384)

In this article, Segal states that she is aware that she paints a picture of Butler that draws her away from 'that now mythical Butlerian . . . a Queer icon always expected to jiggle and fragment' (p. 386), by reframing her as one who attends to notions of interiority, ethics of care and politics of belongings. Here Butler is less anti-normative and anti-identitarian, and more concerned with the *way* social norms enable some lives to be liveable, some grievable, and how social norms might be reconfigured via questioning the relationship between theory, politics and social transformation

(Butler, 2004). Thus Segal promotes a more optimistic picture for critical psychologists where it is possible to draw on the insight from Butler and other scholars described as queer theorists in order to explore the psychosocial conditions of gender, sexuality, race and minoritized political action, without giving up on identities all together.

Theorizing queer subjectivity, killing off psychology?

Perhaps the most vociferous attempt to reject psychology in recent times comes from queer theorist David Halperin (2007). In the monograph *What Do Gay Men Want?* he sets out an agenda to find new ways of speaking about gay male subjectivity without 'recourse to psychology' (p. 11). Halperin takes inspiration from a 1981 interview with Foucault where he declared 'the entire art of life consists in killing off psychology' (p. 4). Taking on this mantle, Halperin reviews the current state of lesbian, gay and queer studies to conclude it is too bound up with psychological and psychoanalytic concepts and instead seeks alternative ways to think through the conditions of gay male subjectivity. In this way, Halperin is also seeking to move queer debates beyond the impasse of the essentialist/constructionist debate. Following Warner (1993), he sees that the impact of Foucault's thesis on social constructionist accounts of sexuality removed the 'inner life of male homosexuality' from the realm of psychology but at the expense of exploring queer subjectivities. Thus, he champions a Foucauldian inspired approach to sexuality that enables it to manifest as 'an aesthetics of existence' (p. 8), rather than self-analysis, which he argues requires thinking queer subjectivity outside of psychology. This is because:

> When, for example, it comes to capturing the experiences of loss, grief, and mourning – or desire, attachment, and love – the languages of psychology and psychoanalysis are notoriously impoverished, awkward, mechanical, imprecise, inadequate. We need, in addition

to them, other ways of being able to speak about ourselves, about our experiences, about our emotions, and in particular, about the subjective life of sex and sexuality. (Halperin, 2007, p. 10)

Writing with particular concern for the way that gay men's sexual health practices have been conceptualized in relation to 'risk', 'internalized homophobia' or, within the psychoanalytic frame, 'the death drive', Halperin argues that the challenge is to develop an account of gay male subjectivity that is 'neither individualistic nor psychically empty, neither normalising nor politically defensive' (p. 103). While it is clear that Halperin wants a theory of queer subjectivity that does not conceptualize gay male subjectivity and HIV transmission in relation to pathologized notions of low self-esteem, post-traumatic distress, risk taking and so on, it is not always clear what he wants in relation to psychology. He calls for 'a discourse free from psychology itself and from psychology's tainted opposition between the normal and the pathological' (p. 36) so that we address the question of gay male sex and risk 'uncontaminated by normative thinking about gay men's psychology'. This is because contemporary models of gay male subjectivity are encased in 'discourses of mental health, the high moral drama of the individual sexual act, the dichotomous opposition between rational agency and pathology, and the epidemiology of risk' (p. 29). Here, the point that Halperin makes is that much psychological and psychoanalytic conceptualization of gay male sexuality results in the reinforcement of cultural understandings of homosexuality as sickness.

Nevertheless, on numerous occasions he also states that it is *not* a matter of 'refuting', 'rejecting', 'discrediting', 'condemning', 'demonizing' psychology and psychoanalysis, rather it is about challenging its cultural pervasiveness and escaping concepts of the individual, interiority, norms of healthy functioning and pathology. This qualification moves Halperin in line with the ethos of critical psychologists who seek to understand subjectivity yet lament the way that psychology is entwined with forms of pathologization. The solution that Halperin offers is via the concept 'abjection'. Abjection can be defined as 'something of one's own for which one feels horror and revulsion, as if it were unclean, filthy, rotten, disgusting, spoiled, impure – such that any contact with it becomes contaminating, nauseating, defiling' (pp. 66–7). Even though abjection is commonly associated with psychoanalysis (e.g. Kristeva, 1980), Halperin finds value in it as a concept if it is interpreted as originating from negative societal judgement rather than psychic causes. Thus, Halperin uses 'abject' to interpret gay subjectivity as formed through stigma and rejection, and explains risky sexual practices as a collective response to this type of social humiliation. He concludes by stating that his use of abjection is an attempt to

> leave open the possibility for other ways of thinking about and repre-
> senting human affective life. I have wanted to champion, against the
> monoculture of psychology, a plurality of unsystematic approaches,
> largely sociological and aesthetic in inspiration, which are not the
> exclusive property of any particular discipline. (2007, p. 105)

I am sympathetic to Halperin's concern for the way HIV transmission is conceived in public health policy and, if explained in terms of individual failings or desire for the death drive, the impact this may have on gay male subjectivity. Instead, Halperin is attempting to deliver a more optimistic and applied understanding of queer subjectivity that might better inform intervention models. Nevertheless, to do this within the rhetoric of 'killing off psychology' is somewhat misplaced. For instance, Nicole Vitellone (2011, p. 103) criticizes his account as a 'social psychological understanding of *why* and *how* gay men choose to fuck without condoms . . . that does not go quite far enough' because it fails to engage with the 'normalising discourse of protection' that condom use itself represents. Similarly, Lauren Berlant (2009) suggests that in this account Halperin is moving *towards* psychoanalysis, rather than away from it. Instead of being convinced about the need for a rejection of psychology, readers hone in on the importance of the psychological to Halperin's thesis. In fact the ingredients are in place in order to claim Halperin's approach as psychosocial, even if some (e.g. Frosh and Baraitser, 2008) might question his binary interpretation of the psychic as somehow 'inside' and the social as the 'outside' that gets in. But even if this claim were to be resisted, given his own reliance on the work of contemporary social psychologists such as Peter Hegarty, his attempt to kill off psychology is unconvincing. Even if we were to accept the omnipotence he affords to psychology it seems naïve to suggest that it is possible to generate a discourse free from it. Discourses do not operate in isolation, nor do they remain 'pure' as they collide and entwine with the multiple positions and trajectories that mark out a particular social field. Instead, Halperin's account benefits from being read as a transdisciplinary engagement that meets the intellectual vision of others already working within critical psychological or psychosocial modes, attempting to rewrite and redefine psychology, challenging conceptions of normality and producing accounts that speak to social justice concerns and the emotional conditions of lived experience. I would argue that rather than killing off psychology and psychoanalysis, what is needed is a call to *reimagine* psychology.

Desiring subjects, psychoanalysis and its place in queer theory

Not everyone working in lesbian, gay and queer studies has been as keen as David Halperin to call for the rejection of psychoanalysis as a mode for theorizing queer subjectivity. The edited collection *Homosexuality and Psychoanalysis* (Dean and Lane, 2001) attests to this, providing the case for the potential of psychoanalytic ideas to inform queer theory and commentaries on subjects such as pleasure, homophobia, AIDS and love, without recourse to the pathology that Halperin fears. Dean and Lane begin their defence of psychoanalysis with the frequently repeated claim that Freud was not responsible for the pathologization of homosexuality. On the contrary, Freud stated in that crucial footnote, 'all human beings are capable of making a homosexual object-choice and have in fact made one in their unconscious' (cited in Dean and Lane, 2001, p. 4). In line with the call from Sedgwick to interrogate homophobia in all knowledge, Dean and Lane note the important need for psychoanalysts to analyse 'homophobia, rather than perpetuating it

by treating homosexuality as problem' (p. 4). This they suggest is
a limitation within current practice that resists a radical critique of
heterosexism, and relies heavily on normative accounts of gender
and sexuality development. Nevertheless, what sets them apart
from a social constructionist approach is a refusal to locate the
problem in discursive accounts of homosexuality that can be challenged through a programme of social change. Following Freud,
their point is not to seek the normalization of homosexuality, but
to demonstrate that *all* sexuality is perverse. Thus, they set out a
directive for scholars and critics in lesbian, gay and queer studies to
take seriously the conceptual tools that psychoanalytic theory offers
as 'Freud effectively "queers" all sexuality' (p. 5).

In rewriting the potential of psychoanalysis for queer theory,
Dean and Lane are not offering a defence of the psy industries, or
a unified narrative of how psychoanalysis can explain subjectivity
across the spectrum of gender and sexuality identifications. Instead,
they begin with a cautionary account that reinforces criticisms of
psychoanalysts in practice, outlining the way Freud's original ideas
were distorted after his death and how these reconceptualizations
reinforced the type of psychoanalytic practice that lesbians and
gays have come to associate with pathologization and oppression.
They argue that central to this shift was Sandor Rado's rejection of
Freud's foundational concept of a 'constitutional bisexuality' that
underpins all sexuality as conceived as cross-sex desire and identification at the Oedipal stage of development. Rather than observe
the homoerotic potential in Freud's theory, Rado reconfigured
heterosexuality as natural, mature and biologically driven, relegating homosexuality to the outcome of an immature, pathological
fear of the opposite sex; a fear that could be readily treated within
the clinic. Thus by the 1950s Freud's model of sexual development
was reformulated, resulting in the view that emergent same-sex
desire was 'a radical departure from normalcy, a psychical error
producing deviant tendencies' (Dean and Lane, 2001, p. 14): tendencies that could be 'corrected' through psychoanalytic treatment
programmes that restore men and women to the natural status of
heterosexuality. Even though contemporary psychoanalytic practice has on the whole discarded the curative model in favour of an

affirmative stance towards homosexuality, it does so at the expense of the queer flavour of Freud's original thesis. Nevertheless, despite the obvious problems with psychoanalysis in practice, they note, as Foucault did before them, that it is impossible to conceive of contemporary sexuality without now 'thinking in loosely psycho-analytic terms' (p. 8).

Central to Dean and Lane's defence of psychoanalysis is the claim that 'North American queer theorists have found in psychoanalysis an armoury of conceptual tools for describing social processes of normalization and how they may be resisted' (2001, p. 21). They argue that the influence of Lacanian and Laplanchian psychoanaly-sis has been identified by theorists such as de Lauretis, Leo Bersani, John Fletcher and Mandy Merck as important 'for thinking affirm-atively about non-normative sexualities' (p. 23). In contrast to the biological origins of sexuality within Freudian psychoanalysis, the Lacanian focus on sexual desire as an effect of representation has found favour with queer theorists that have also been influenced by Foucault and the cultural turn. As Lacan locates subjectivity and desire in the unconscious there is a certain impossibility to the task of seeking to theorize sexuality, as it operates beyond conscious and rational processes. Hence, for them, the impasse in theorizing sexual subjectivity that emerged from debates between essentialism and constructionism cannot be addressed through new theoretical tools, because sexuality *is* the impasse. Thus,

> cultural constructions of sexuality are simply responses to a fundamen-tal psychic deadlock that can never be fully interpreted or resolved. . . . Sexuality resists social norms, according to Lacan, not so that some pure form of desire can be liberated from cultural constraints, but because unconscious contradictions cannot be eliminated by imagi-nary or symbolic identifications, whether normative or queer. Owing to the unconscious impasse of sex, sexuality will always be subject to sociocultural constructions, and those constructions will inevitably fail. (Dean and Lane, 2001, p. 28)

This refusal to be *known* has its own queer stance, challenging the notion of fixed meanings, identities, and resisting social norms.

Thus for some queer theorists, Lacanian inspired psychoanalysis offers a conceptual engagement with sexuality that is disruptive and anti-normative and has the potential for generating accounts of desire across gender and sexual orientations that are non-normative. Nevertheless, its reliance on the notion of an unconscious returns us to the psychological in a way that is conceived as unacceptable among some sexuality scholars. Here though, this is not in response to disciplinary debates about the value or limits of psychological explanations, but rather to demonstrate the impossibility of theorizing sexual subjectivity.

For instance, the French theorist Hocquenghem has found renewed favour in queer debates because of his radical critique of the nuclear family and the capitalist state. Couched within the potential for queer commentaries, Dean and Lane offer a different interpretation of Hocquenghem's classic *Homosexual Desire* than that of Jeffrey Weeks (discussed on page 50). In chapter 3, we noted two limitations raised by Weeks in the foreword to this book. Firstly, he suggested the account was unable to sufficiently explain why an individual might enter the symbolic order as either 'homosexual' or 'heterosexual'. Secondly, Weeks was critical of the central engagement with the Freudian metaphor of the Oedipal complex, privileged over a historical analysis of institutional practices and the social context that enable the shaping of particular sexual subjectivities. Weeks is, of course, viewing Hocquenghem's account through the lens of social constructionism, but it is precisely because of these failures that Hocquenghem's work has appealed to queer theorists. As Dean and Lane argue, Hocquenghem's protest against the whole of the Oedipal system enables desire to escape from a concept that reinforces and normalizes the nuclear family. Thus, they suggest that by 'resisting imperatives to consolidate the shifting sands of erotic desire into identity categories, Hocquenghem reinterprets and politicizes Freud's theory of polymorphous perversity' (p. 20). Here we can see parallels with the anti-identity and anti-normative stance that binds queer perspectives and the value that can be found in earlier texts when read through new lenses. After Sedgwick's charge at the essentialist/constructionist impasse, the criticisms posed by

Weeks can be interpreted within a framework of ontogeny and phylogeny, raising questions of causality and form that from a queer perspective should be discarded and replaced by an analysis of the minoritizing/universalizing impact of conceiving sexuality in relation to the family structure of the Oedipus myth. According to Hocquenghem, it is the family that creates 'anti-homophobic paranoia', and this criticism has recently re-emerged in a powerful analysis of 'familial homophobia' by the queer writer and activist Sarah Schulman. As Schulman (2009, pp. 41–2) states,

> a standard ethic regarding homophobia in the family has not yet been articulated. Instead of focusing on the homophobia as the subject of inquiry, the great distortion has been to interrogate the origins of homosexuality. . . . In order to develop a vision of how to eradicate homophobia within the family, we must reject completely any framework that maintains homosexuality as a category of deviance that needs to be explained and instead focus entirely on the origins of and solutions to homophobia. This means focusing on the perpetrators, their motives, consciousness, and actions with the purpose of creating deterrents necessary for gay people to have healthier emotional lives.

The sentiments of Schulman echo Sedgwick's call for an anti-homophobic stance but they also give credence to concerns raised by affirmative psychologists who talk about the impact of 'minority stress' (Meyer, 2003). LGBT movements emerge via the gathering together of people who rarely find support for dealing with discrimination and oppression within their family of origin. According to Meyer, in contrast to growing up in a context of racial or ethnic difference the family of the gay adolescent or adult is not perceived as a resource for tackling oppression and discrimination, rather it is often the source of the distress. Although Meyer problematically fails to acknowledge that some people experience multiple forms of oppression (e.g. race and sexuality) and that these are not necessarily hierarchical, Schulman differs from the affirmative psychological perspective and attacks the assumption that this is a problem of the individual, a problem that many of us come to accept as something we have to face alone. She argues that this is due to a lack of third party intervention. Thus, she calls for widespread acknowledgement that familial homophobia is a cultural crisis that can only be addressed by transforming the expectations of how queer people should be treated within their families. In order to do this, we rely on those who have the power to intervene on our behalf, those brave enough to give up their privileged status as heterosexual and speak out against homophobia. This is a call to arms against homophobia and requires the action of friends, siblings, parents, teachers and therapists to challenge the normative situations that enable homophobia to quietly but persistently underpin family relationships.

The turn to affect and the return to psychology

The focus on desire, rather than identity, has been central to queer perspectives over the last twenty years. Lately, along with a more general shift within the humanities and social sciences, there has been increased concern for understanding the power and potential of a wider range of feelings within the field of queer studies. The affective turn, as it has come to be known, is defined by Patricia Clough as 'a transdisciplinary approach to theory and method' which is used to 'grasp the changes that constitute the social and to explore them as changes in ourselves, circulating through our bodies, our subjectivities, yet irreducible to the individual, the personal, or the psychological' (2007, p. 3). Ann Cvetkovich (2012, p. 3) helpfully cites a long list of areas of enquiry that can be collated under the rubric of the 'affective turn'. These include:

> cultural memory and public cultures that emerge in response to histories of trauma; the role of emotions such as fear and sentimentality in American political life and nationalist politics; the production of compassion and sympathy in human rights discourses and other forms of liberal representation of social issues and problems; discussions of the politics of negative affects, such as melancholy and shame, inspired in particular by queer theory's critique of the normal; new forms

of historical inquiry, such as queer temporalities, that emphasize the affective relations between past and present; the turn to memoir and the personal in criticism as a sign of either the exhaustion of theory or its renewed life; the ongoing legacy of identity politics as another inspiration for the turn to the personal; continuing efforts to rethink psychoanalytic paradigms and the relation between with the psychic and the social; the persistent influence of Foucauldian notions of bio-power to explain the politics of subject formation and new forms of governmentality; histories of intimacy, domesticity, and private life; the cultural politics of everyday life; histories and theories of sensation and touch informed by phenomenology and cultural geography.

Thus, the affective turn does not introduce a single, new trajectory within social theory, rather it offers a clustering of interest in rethinking the relationship between thought and feeling, knowing and being, across a range of topics. Within this list we see themes central to those considered in this book, particularly the focus on rethinking the relationship between psychic and social life, the potential of psychoanalytic paradigms and a general desire to move beyond the impasse of constructionist/essentialist or performative/materialist debates that have exhausted scholars with their circularity and tedium. Interest in the cultural politics of emotion (Ahmed, 2004), queer attachments (Munt, 2008), queer phenomenology and orientation towards particular objects (Ahmed, 2006), alongside the desire to explore affects such as shame and melancholy have become the staple of queer enquiry over the last decade. This 'turn to affect' has also emerged alongside new forms of historical enquiry that unpick linear, normative ideas about time and challenge concepts of futurity, introducing new phrases into the queer lexicon such as 'no future' (Edelman, 2004) or 'chrononormativity' (Freeman, 2010), while binding conceptions of historical engagement with emotionality via 'feeling backwards' (Love, 2007) or 'cruel optimism' (Berlant, 2011). These ideas will be explored in more detail in the next two chapters. For now, I want to demonstrate that the explicit turn towards questions about feelings within queer studies has entailed a *return* to psychological and psychoanalytic perspectives, and to argue that the growth in interest in psychosocial approaches is closely aligned with this affective turn in order to better theorize queer subjectivities and politics beyond notions of queer performativity.

Within queer perspectives examples of the affective turn can be traced to two theoretical moves in the work of Eve Sedgwick. First was her engagement with concepts drawn from the work of object-relations psychoanalyst Melanie Klein. Sedgwick argued that much literary criticism, including elements of her own, emerged from a paranoid-schizoid position where anxieties were managed by the practice of splitting, such that texts were perceived as having 'good' or 'bad' characteristics, or in the context of queer readings, could be perceived as 'transgressive' or 'repressive'. Sedgwick was not simply against paranoid readings, there are plenty of examples where perceiving negative intent can be dismissed inappropriately as paranoia. However, she noted limitations in the transformative potential of a reading practice that she perceived as trapped within a cycle of shame dynamics. As Edwards (2008, p. 110) summarizes:

> Sedgwick has pondered whether the ongoing repetition of shame dynamics might not provide a plausible explanation for why genera-tions of scholars shaming, criticising and exposing various repressive ideologies within a wide variety of texts has not necessarily made our world a significantly less oppressive place.

As her oeuvre developed she increasingly argued against binary distinctions, in this case she suggested that embracing Klein's 'depressive position' offered an alternative approach for literary criticism that might generate 'reparative' readings: ones that are profoundly ambivalent, and which can mitigate against anxiety by recognizing and empathizing with both good and bad char-acteristics. This practice, she argued, might be more politically fruitful and transformative for queer interventions than those that rely on an ethics of suspicion, as 'the ambivalent depressive posi-tion is a potential route out of depression and into something more complex, open, unexpected and different' (Edwards, 2008, p. 111). Muñoz (2006, pp. 676–7) picks up this line of thinking within his own later project that seeks to 'engage different psychological and phenomenological discourses in an effort to theorize affective particularity and belonging'. Here, Muñoz directly refers to the benefits of Klein's concept of 'positions', rather than the developmental stage model found in Freudian psychoanalysis as a means for theorizing affects, particularly the relationship between *feeling brown* and *feeling down*. In offering his own reparative readings of 'brownness' and 'whiteness' he attempts to stitch critical race theory, queer critique and Kleinian object-relations in a way that offers 'a certain kind of hope' where 'the loss and guilt that underlies the subject's sense of self' can be tolerated (p. 687).

The second and aligned shift within Sedgwick's writing was a renewed focus on the transformative potential of the negative affect 'shame' for the field of sexuality, triggered by the rediscovery of the work of Silvan Tomkins, a social psychologist interested in systems theory and affect. Sedgwick first introduced his ideas in a paper on shame and the cybernetic fold (Sedgwick and Frank, 1995, p. 7) which prefaced an edited collection of his work *Shame and its Sisters* and reappeared in her own text *Touching Feeling* (2003). What Sedgwick found in the work of Tomkins, that she said was missing from Freud, was an openness to the way that affects such as desire or shame can become attached to objects in indeterminate ways. For her this enabled a psychological engagement with the affective dynamics of sexuality within an anti-homophobic framework, because it found 'a different place to begin'. However, in maintaining her objection to binary contrasts that lead to hierarchical splits between good and bad interpretations, she acknowledged that this required scholars to engage with biology and cognition, and may even result in acknowledging that some responses are innate – the sort of interpretation that constructionists would dismiss as essentialist.

Another trope within the turn to affect in the humanities and social sciences has emerged from the Deleuzian-influenced work of Brian Massumi (2002). Massumi also relies on a return to the psychological, via recent experimental studies from neuropsychology, to claim that affect is distinction from cognition and emotion, such that affects are 'irreducibly bodily and autonomic' (p. 28). Drawing on an experiment about cognition and volition in a paper published in *Behavioral and Brain Sciences* in 1985, Massumi argues that this distinction between affect and cognition is captured by a half-second delay between the occurrence of the affect and the subject's ability to make sense of the situation that triggered the affect. In this model, 'cognition or thinking comes "too late" for reasons, beliefs, intentions, and meanings to play the role in action and behaviour usually accorded to them' (Leys, 2011, p. 443). The uptake of this proposition has not been without suspicion, primarily because of the validity and consequences of the type of psychological knowledge that is reintroduced. For example, critical social psychologist Margaret Wetherell is highly critical of the way that scholars in the humanities have utilized these sorts of psychological studies to support a notion of the autonomy of affect. She suggests that this work is based on an unsubstantiated premise that she refers to as the basic emotion hypothesis that relies on evolutionary biological assumptions. While many have taken the work of psychologists such as Silvan Tomkins, and his more recent followers in neuroscience, such as Paul Ekman or Antonio Damasio, as evidence to support a shift in emphasis from knowing to feeling, Wetherell argues that the science claims on which this is based are controversial and questioned by many who work in affective neurosciences.

The transdisciplinary scholar Ruth Leys notes similar concerns. As a professor of humanities and a historian of life sciences, having trained in psychology before developing a research focus on the history of psychiatry, psychoanalysis and neuroscience, Leys also raises problems with the validity of the studies on which the affective turn is based. In addition to the scientific critique, she asks, '*Why* are so many scholars today in the humanities and social sciences fascinated by the idea of affect?' (2011, p. 435, my emphasis), suggesting that what drives affect theorists

> is the desire to contest a certain account of how, in their view, political argument and rationality have been thought to operate. These theorists are gripped by the notion that most philosophers and critics in the past (Kantians, neo-Kantians, Habermasians) have overvalued the role of reason and rationality in politics, ethics, and aesthetics, with the result

that they have given too flat or 'unlayered' or disembodied an account of the ways in which people actually form their political opinions and judgments. (p. 436)

Leys suggests that the theories of affect offered by both Massumi and Sedgwick are problematic for conceptualizing the role of agency in political action, as they are overly deterministic, reduced to innate and demarcated emotions (fear, shame, disgust, joy, etc.), and they relegate any sense of intentionality. Wetherell concords that the 'vagueness and confusion of Massumi's account of affect . . . , its lack of specificity and psychological naivety, risks, I think, undermining rather than sustaining critical political thought and action' (Wetherell, 2012, p. 126). In the context of queer theory, which is concerned with doing, and unsettling normative assumptions, how affect is conceptualized may not be a problem if it results in transformation. For theorists such as Lauren Berlant (2011) the affective turn can be described as a moment in 'ideological history', and following Sedgwick its impact might be to shake up an entrenched impasse, to increase the possibility of political transformation as a means to challenge oppression. Certainly there is a need to be cautious about any return to psychology that reduces experience to autonomic biological responses. Yet, given Sedgwick's commitment to unsettle binary thinking I see more possibility in her approach to affect in queer theory. Sedgwick argued that there had been an overemphasis on questions of epistemology (knowing) at the expense of ontology (being), but this does not imply that she would encourage an entire shift to the other pole. Her legacy as found in the work of scholars such as Berlant and Muñoz, alongside the championing of a new 'reparative turn' for queer feminism (Wiegman, 2014), is a desire to write between affect and intentionality, feeling and knowing, past and future. Here, concepts such as hybridity and its associated methods can develop a psychosocial flavour:

hybridity forewarns us that we need to think more carefully about the ontology, politics and circumstances of subjectivity, it does so from a semantic field that is itself pluralised and wandering, with a to-ing and fro-ing between material and cultural definitions, and attempts to transport terms from one domain to the other (Yao, 2003). Discussions weave between the empirical, theoretical, technological and experiential and are spoken through the languages of the natural, social and human sciences, autobiography, fiction, literary criticism, art, activism and social policy. (Gunaratnam, 2014, p. 5)

Queering sexuality and the psychosocial subject

What I hope this chapter has demonstrated is that queer theories, or commentaries as Warner and Berlant would state, *are* psychosocial. Engagement with psychoanalysis and affect theories demonstrates the desire to get into the conceptual space that is drawn between the psychic and the social to better understand queer subjectivities, even if the understanding produced is contingent. Like Frosh, I am interested in how psychoanalysis 'can help bridge this particular gap' (2012) but in contrast I am less wedded to demonstrating the way that a particular school of psychoanalysis over other affect theories might aid with this. Perhaps, in line with queer principles of unsettling or undoing normative assumptions, this is underpinned by admiration for Sedgwick's drive to find a different place to begin in order to side-step entrenched impasses which result in binary oppositions and good or bad interpretations, and a concern for more recent engagements with concepts of hybridity and mixedness. At the same time, it must be acknowledged that the return to psychology as a way of reshaping political action has unintended consequences. For some (e.g. Wetherell, 2012) this includes the reintroduction of unfounded evolutionary and biologically reductionist principles and the proposition of political action without subjects or subjectivity. I am also suspicious of cultural approaches that promote notions of affectivity without sufficient engagement with the individual experiences and trajectories of the subjects within that space. In addition, there are other unintended consequences that occur with a return to psychology within an uncritical framework that relate to the role of psychology in the perpetuation of neoliberalism. The psy disciplines with their focus on the individual, social norms and self-management have served neoliberalism well (Rose and Miller, 2008). In *Cruel Optimism* Berlant (2011, p. 53) states that affect theory is 'another phase in the history of ideology' and that if we are to address the neoliberal impasse we must train our affects by writing about them to offer alternatives to normativity. This might take place by intuiting affective eruptions, connections, activisms and momentary escapes from an otherwise stifling existence. But, affectivity and affective management in particular (training our affects) is a crucial tool that oils the cogs of neoliberalism and its proliferation. Thus, in Foucauldian terms, the affective turn offers an alternative to the impasse of regulation versus resistance, but affectivity has the potential to introduce a new mode of governmentality. If the task is to train our affects to allow for the possibility of intent to meet affect, which is always mediated by ideology, can we do this in ways that challenge oppression and social injustice, and can we know that we are not simply re-proliferating the conditions of neoliberalism?

5

Affecting Sexuality

Can there be a homosexual subject who is *not* formed from shame?

Sally Munt, 2008, p. 95

Following the transdisciplinary ethos of this book this chapter examines the way the affective turn that has permeated the humanities and social sciences has shaped the agenda in contemporary concerns about sexuality through two examples. To maintain a focus on psychosocial approaches to help theorize queer subjectivities this chapter considers the shift in emphasis from gay pride to gay shame, and the relationship between affect, politics and subjectivity. Of course the affective life of queer subjectivity is much more than just 'shame' but the purpose of this chapter is to examine the role of shame and insult in the formation of queer subjectivities, particular those of gay men. If affect is conceived as an embodied understanding, or as a sense or feeling that provides an interpretation of the social conditions within which we reside it is little surprise that shame features so heavily in queer accounts. As Munt (2008, p. 95) asks, 'Can there be a homosexual subject who is *not* formed from shame?' Homosexuality has a long history of abjection, religious condemnation and state persecution, and in any form of psychosocial framework we must acknowledge that such a context will shape the psychic reality of those who come to identify with the LGBTQ continuum, even if their own lives are marked more or less by prejudice in distinct ways. Heteronormativity, the cultural bias that favours heterosexuality and normative gender presentations, is the backdrop to all queer lives; government legislation and social and public policy provide another. For instance, contemporary understandings of sexuality are shaped by debates about the legitimacy of 'gay marriage', concerns about homophobic bullying and attacks, and the condition of LGBT people's mental health, each of which can be implicated in individualized experiences of shame. By engaging with theoretical and methodological perspectives introduced in earlier chapters of the book, this chapter attempts to link insights from visual and textual observations inspired by cultural studies with a psychosocial concern for the implications of triggering the 'shame scripts' of those who come to call themselves gay. This is developed via a critical reading of two recent British comedy sketches that feature white, gay male characters. The focus on the intersection of gay male sexuality and 'whiteness' in British comedy is not purposeful, rather it indicates that within the limited number of representations of queer lives on UK television these are most frequently of white, gay men. The analysis put forward demonstrates the ongoing relevance of shame in the constitution of particular versions of queer subjectivities against a backdrop of shifting cultural anxieties about contemporary sexualities: in particularly how to talk about homosexuality in a more 'open' and accepting climate. Secondly, it is argued that if shame and insult mark out certain groups for comic value it is worth considering the possible consequences of this for individual lived experience via the links between shame, discourses of mental health and epidemiological accounts of LGBT 'suicidal risk'.

Shame and sexuality

Shame, disgust and the social order have been consistently posited as crucial elements in sexual development. Freud (1905/1991) suggested that shame, disgust and morality are the mental forces that regulate and repress sexual instinct, linking this to biological drives that become fixed in early development. In contrast, Silvan Tomkins suggests that Freud's theory of biological drives tied to the binary of expression/repression and fixed in relation to particular objects is limited for explaining affective experience. While noting the inherent biological realm of affect, Tomkins and his followers suggest a more flexible biological system with additional possibilities than affects simply being switched on or off by particular objects. For example, Stenner (2004, p. 172) suggests that:

> Even if it is granted that certain innate triggers of affect exist (such as pain and hunger as triggers of distress), affects, due to their biological flexibility, rapidly take on far more complex, learned and meaningful *social* objects which 'trigger' them just as effectively.

Furthermore, in seeing affect as indifferent to particular objects in that 'any affect may have any "object" ', Sedgwick and Frank (1995, p. 7) suggest that unlike most psychological propositions of the twentieth century Tomkins' work is notable for its absence of homophobia and heterosexist teleology. This they concur is not from a 'concerted antihomophobic project or marked gay interest', but rather from 'finding a different place to begin'.

Central to Tomkins' thesis is the notion that shame is amplified by the cultural requirement to hide shame, rather than acknowledge it. For Tomkins, one consequence of the process of learning that shame must remain hidden is a 'rapid luxuriant growth of shame in connection with sexuality' where the child is 'motivated to hide his shame and his sexuality as well as his other sources of shame'. Yet shame is not a standalone affective response to particular events but, according to Tomkins, only works tangentially as an inhibitor to interest and enjoyment such that the 'innate activator of shame is the incomplete reduction of interest or joy' (in Sedgwick and Frank, 1995, p. 134). Thus, unique events or inter-actions will have different 'shaming' affects for different individuals depending on the residue levels of interest or enjoyment for indi-vidual actors involved. While recognizing that shame is connected to sexuality per se, given the socio-historical conditions that have overwhelmingly construed same-sex desire as a forbidden pleasure, Tomkins' approach is useful for thinking about the particular way that shame might be experienced in relation to *queer* sexuality and identity formation as both collective and individual psychic reality.

The theme of shame has returned to the forefront of sexuality studies (e.g. Ahmed, 2004; Moore, 2004; Probyn, 2005; Stein, 2006; Bersani and Phillips, 2008; Munt, 2008; Halperin and Traub, 2009) as part of the wider affective turn in social and cul-tural studies. The psychosocial project has therefore begun in this area of queer studies as theorists draw on a range of concepts in relation to thinking through the psychic life of queer subjectivi-ties. In *Queer Attachments: The cultural politics of shame*, Sally Munt (2008, p. 95) reflects on the psychic and political consequences of shame via a detailed analysis of a range of cultural texts illustrating its role in constructions of sexuality, gender, race and class. In *Insult and the Making of the Gay Self*, Didier Eribon (2004, p. 6) confers with the socio-historical analyses of sexuality that states 'figures of homosexuality are always specific to a given cultural situation', yet he argues that there appears to be something persistently recogniz-able about gay subjectivity across history. Reworking Foucault, and drawing on the sociologist Pierre Bourdieu, Eribon argues that for gay men and lesbians the 'experience of insult is one of the most widely shared elements of their existence' (p. 18). Eribon recognizes that certain challenges to the heteronormative sexual order have been made, but claims that these have done little to transform its continued universal dominance over the course of the last century, such that:

> there is a particular type of symbolic violence that is aimed at those who love members of the same sex and that the schemas of perception, the mental structures, that underlie this violence (doubtless largely

based on an androcentric worldview) are more or less similar everywhere.

This, he continues, 'explains the sense that gay men and lesbians
might have of their relation to gay and lesbian experiences from
another country or another historical moment when they read
works that reconstruct those experiences' (p. 6). In this statement Eribon is proposing that there is something 'universal' about
queer subjectivity through the feelings we experience in relation
to 'dissociated lives', 'dissociated personalities', 'self concealment',
'shame' and 'self hatred' (p. 4) but, importantly, this is not a naturalized way of being, rather one that comes about through practices
of subordination that have changed very little in the last 150 years.
This historical analysis of the affective conditions of queer lives is at
odds with recent UK sociological analyses of sexuality that suggest
a range of practices and technologies have transformed both
homosexual and heterosexual intimacies (e.g. Giddens, 1992), as
well as challenged the 'homo/hetero divide' (e.g. Roseneil, 2002).
Given the very recent social transformations (e.g. civil partnerships, adoption rights) that have taken place in relation to equality
legislation that have arguably transformed the intimate lives of
lesbians and gay men (see Weeks, 2007) and increased the visibility
of non-normative sexual identities and relationships, it might be
helpful to address this changing environment in order to reflect on
why shame has become increasingly embraced as a key trope in
sexuality studies.

Shame and media representations of queer lives

Much of the recent engagement with shame and insult has come
from analyses of literary lives such as Proust and Wilde (Eribon,
2004) or cultural texts such as films, novels or contemporary art
(e.g. Probyn, 2005; Stockton, 2006; Munt, 2008). A continuing
focus on media representations and television cultures (e.g. Munt,
1992) can help ascertain how ideas about the lives of minority

groups are transmitted into the wider social fabric of contemporary Britain. In an empirical study of primetime BBC TV, *Tuned Out*, the lesbian, gay and bisexual advocacy group Stonewall found that gay people were five times more likely to be portrayed in what they describe as 'negative terms' rather than 'positive terms', and that over 70 per cent of representations of gay lives occurred in entertainment shows rather than documentaries or news programmes. They also found that gay sexuality was frequently used for making jokes or as insult and relied heavily on clichéd stereotypes. To highlight some specific findings:

- During 168 hours of programming gay lives were represented positively for six minutes and negatively for thirty-two minutes.
- Lesbians hardly exist on the BBC – 82 per cent of references to gay sexuality were about gay men.
- 51 per cent of gay references were designed for comic effect. (Cowan and Valentine, 2006)

In her own transdisciplinary engagement with 'shame' Elspeth Probyn (2005, p. 86) employs Tomkins and Sedgwick to draw attention to the cultural conditions of shame and its importance for rethinking identity. What is especially useful from this text for my argument is her proposition that 'popular representations of sexuality can provide fertile ground for the airing of shame'. Probyn suggests that:

> As TV increasingly shows a wider range of identities and actively attends to the representations of marginalized or previously excluded groups, it allows for a greater circulation of images of specifically gendered, sexed, and raced shame [which] allows individuals a specific reexperience of the shame of their gender, sex, or race [such that] . . . While a lack of representation may have been painful, it may have been less shaming.

In line with this analysis, then, being represented for comic effect may be perceived as 'negative' by and for lesbians and gay men, among others. However, these representations perform a social function as well as demonstrating the ongoing relevance of shame in the constitution of queer (particularly white, gay, male) subjectivities by mapping onto contemporary insecurities and anxieties about sexuality within a culture that privileges 'whiteness' and 'heteronormativity'.

Comedy queer

The queer character has been a customary feature in comedy sketches, whether as the target of the joke, or more commonly through a performance of rampant innuendo, such that the spectre of queer life can consistently be found in mainstream comedy shows. However, following the content analysis of Cowan and Valentine (2006), the queer character that is frequently represented for comic effect on UK television is the white, camp, gay male. In an attempt to ascertain the social function of comedy, Michael Billig (2005) suggests that mockery and ridicule are powerful forces that regulate and maintain social norms. For Billig (2005, p. 176) there are three paradoxes in humour:

> The first paradox is that humour is both universal and particular. The second paradox is that humour is social and anti-social: it can bring people together in a bond of enjoyment, and, by mockery, it can exclude people. . . . The third paradoxical feature is that humour appears mysterious and resistant to analysis, but it is also understandable and analyzable.

Following this, despite the paradoxical nature of humour, it is proposed that a humour that consistently relies on gay or camp references provides a social function in terms of creating a social bond and maintaining heteronormative values; some people may experience this form of humour as funny, while others will be left unmoved to laughter; we cannot predict exactly what we will find funny or the way in which it will bond or divide us but there is much in humour that is understandable and open to analysis. In one attempt to analyse the role of humour in the construction of English cultural identity, Andy Medhurst (2007) argues that, on the whole, comedy has been overlooked in academic debates that seek to theorize identity. For him, this oversight is unfortunate because comedy tells us something about conflict as well as pleasure and, drawing on James English (1994), 'Comic practice is always on some level or in some measure an assertion of group against group, an effect and an event of struggle, a form of symbolic violence' (cited in Medhurst, 2007, p. 14). Thus, following Billig and Medhurst, an analysis of comedy sketches might tell us something about the conflicts, tensions and taboos that imbue contemporary representations of sexuality, 'since texts and performances are always produced and consumed in specific cultural and historical contexts' (Medhurst, 2007, p. 10). It is with this in mind that this chapter proceeds to address issues of shame and insult by analysing two recent British comedy sketches that feature 'gay characters' or, more accurately, caricatures of 'gays': Derek Faye (*The Catherine Tate Show*) and Daffyd Thomas (*Little Britain*). Both of these comedy shows consist of a series of characters that say something about social relationships and cultural stereotypes of gender, race, class, age and sexuality that circulate in contemporary Britain, although they speak to concerns elsewhere having also had international appeal.

Reading Derek Faye

Derek Faye was a regular character in *The Catherine Tate Show* (2004–8) played by Tate. The central thread of the sketch is that Derek, who is depicted as 'camp', is read in a variety of situations as 'gay', much to his indignation, despite frequent references to his male companion, Leonard Mincer. However, rather than this being a genuine mistake, the sketch ends with a humoristic twist that reassures the viewer that the original reading of Derek as 'gay' is the correct one. The following extract is a transcript of one such sketch:

Derek Faye, *The Catherine Tate Show.*
Reproduced with permission of Catherine Tate.

Derek standing outside toilet in wedding venue. People are dancing in
the main room at the end of the corridor, muffled music can be heard
in the background. Tonia comes down the stairs towards Derek in her
bridesmaid outfit.

Derek: Mother's in there Tonia. Won't be two ticks. Locks are wonky
so I'm keeping dixie.

Tonia: Wasn't it a lovely wedding Uncle Derek.

Derek: And as for Naomi's frock dear, a symphony in cream. I wept
when I saw those page boys. Not everyone can carry off the
munchkin look but they did her proud.

Tonia: I wonder who will be married next in the family?

Derek: Could be you Tonia. You still courting that Darren?

Tonia: It will be two years in June [smiles]. No sign of a ring yet
though [pause]. Hey it might be you and Uncle Leonard?

Derek: [long pause, mouth open] I beg your pardon.

Tonia: You and Uncle Leonard. You know. You can now, one of
those civil partnerships.

Derek: What on earth are you insinuating.

Tonia: I'm just saying you and Uncle Leonard could have a gay wedding.

Derek: Gay wedding? Gay Wedding!

Tonia: Yes, I just thought it might . . .

Derek: How Very Dare You! I've never heard the like.

Tonia: I'm sorry Uncle Derek. Are you not?

Derek: Gay dear, who dear, me dear, no dear. Just because a man mind's his ps and qs and isn't all at sea with a mascara wand you assume he travels up the chocolate escalator.

Tonia: I didn't mean to upset you.

Derek: 25 years mother and I have been putting money in a Christmas card for you and this is the thanks we get. Marry a man. Marry a MAN. How very, very dare you. [Tonia drops her eyes to the floor]. And I'd avoid a calf-length skirt in future if I were you dear. Your ankles are too puffy.

Derek [knocks on toilet door]: Mother. I'll be in the bar.

Opening bars to *YMCA* [by the Village People] strike and Derek struts down the corridor in time with music, pausing briefly to fling his arms into a Y, before striding towards the door to the bar and the dance floor.

Following Tomkins, the visual markers of affects such as shame and disgust can be read through the face. Derek's affective response to being read as gay, 'Marry a man?', is shown not in terms of shame, as that would be denoted through the dropping of the eyes, looking away, rather, the direct eyeballing and flared nostrils indicate contempt and disgust. To me this signals a reversal of the shaming of gay lives, as it is his niece who Derek attempts to shame through his catchphrase 'How very dare you!' In her discussion of the potential for rehabilitating shame Probyn suggests that 'it makes a certain sense that the subordinated may have more nuanced skills at shaming than the privileged' (2005, p. 87) and this is one possible interpretation of the process at play in this sketch. Although Derek claims to be insulted, 'I have never been so insulted', he goes on to insult her in his reference to her puffy ankles. Yet, we are never allowed to be convinced that Derek is not gay, as throughout the clip we are given knowing cues to read him as gay through his camp persona: his reference to her as 'dear'; his appreciation of the 'aesthetics' of the wedding; references to sending money with his mother for twenty-five years. Derek notes, as many theorists have done, how gender performance and sexuality have become incorrectly conflated: 'Just because a man minds his ps and qs and isn't all at sea with a mascara wand you assume he travels up the chocolate escalator.' This reference is offensive to/and about gay men, but Derek's reaction to being called gay can also be read as one of 'shameful denial' as the final clip shows. The niece is correct in her reading, as Derek dances down the hall to *YMCA*. Derek is gay/must be gay, but will not admit it.

Taking this sketch in the context of many episodes a clearer outline of the character is shaped and developed that is revealing about cultural shifts in attitudes towards homosexuality, particularly in the UK. There is a core message in the clips that 'being gay' is not something to be ashamed of. All the sketches follow the same format: woman running newsagent asks Derek for advice as a 'supportive mother': 'we think our son is gay, should we ask him or wait until he tells us?' 'Friendly Spanish taxi driver' offers to take Derek and Leonard to a bar called Homolulu with 'nice pretty boys in shorts'. 'Concerned doctor' asks if Derek would be interested in attending the gay men's health clinic. Man in the music shop offers tickets for sale to Gay Pride: 'It's Gay *Pride*' he stresses in response to Derek's depoliticized dismissal 'gay *party*'. Bonnie Langford replies: 'I've got lots of gay fans' when asked for an autograph dedicated to Derek and Leonard. In this sketch we see Bonnie respond to Derek's usual 'insulted' line with the retort 'there is nothing wrong with being gay you know'. Collectively these reveal stereotypical understandings of gay men's lives: alienated from families because of their sexuality; drinking and dancing; risk of HIV; Pride as political; fans of female artists and musicals. Yet, in telling the audience a positive message about being gay through exemplary straight characters the problem with gayness remains visible but reformulated. 'Disgust/contempt' are still present, but not from some homophobe as gays, lesbians and straight allies might expect, rather they stem from the 'gay' character. 'Shame' is now all of our 'shame' (the gay and straight viewer), shame and withdrawal from Derek because he is unable to be 'out' or 'proud' about being gay. Derek is a closet homosexual in a culture that no longer requires it. Furthermore, when the 'real insult' arrives, it is cast by Derek in his seemingly endless supply of crude references to anal sex as synonymous with a gay male identity: 'backdoor deirdre', 'receiver of swollen goods', 'climbing the chocolate escalator'; or in a derogatory comment to the person who has identified him as gay. This, I argue, makes for both normative and queer readings of a sketch show that illustrates contemporary anxieties among both gay and straight people about how to respond to gay sexuality in a shifting cultural climate of 'equality' and 'openness', but ultimately at the expense of the gay man who is unable to 'come out'.

Similar issues in relation to shame and pride are addressed in the *Little Britain* (2003–6) sketch involving Daffyd Thomas (played by Matt Lucas), famed for his catchphrase 'I am the only gay in the village'. The village is presented as a small, rural community in Wales. In contrast to Derek, Daffyd is an 'out gay man', highly visible in terms of 'gay pride' in his consistent confirmation of his gay identity made particularly visible through a variety of tight-fitting PVC outfits as he engages in local 'action' campaigns on behalf of 'the Llanddewi Brefi Gay and Lesbian Liberation Front. Me!'

Reading Daffyd Thomas

In this clip Daffyd is in the local pub wearing a see-through vest, sitting on a bar stool.

> Daffyd: Another Bacardi and coke please Myfanwy. Oh bloody hell Myfanwy I'm so down.
> Myfanwy: Oh why's that Daffyd?
> Daffyd: It's so hard being the only gay in the village. Oh I just dream of the day I can meet other gays who understand what it's like to be a gay.
> Myfanwy: Oh, I was gonna tell you. I was talking to old Ma Evans and she's got a new lodger from Cardiff. And guess what? He is a gay!

Daffyd Thomas, *Little Britain.*
Reproduced with permission of Matt Lucas and David Walliams.

Daffyd: What, in the village?

Myfanwy: Apparently yes. I told her to send him over here tonight so you could meet him. [In walks David Walliams in tight blue PVC top and black PVC shorts and large spiked dog-collar.] This must be him now.

DW [sits on stool next to Daffyd]: Hello. Can I have a Bacardi and coke please? Ooh, you must be Daffyd.

Myfanwy: There you go? I'll leave you boys to it.

Daffyd: No, don't go . . . [pause] Just passing through are you?

DW: Oh no. I've got a job here at the florist and I'm looking for somewhere to live. I saw a very nice cottage but that's another story hee, hee, hee [titters behind hand]

Daffyd: Is it?

DW: Yes [looks confused]

Daffyd: And you claim to be a gay do you?

DW: Oh yes, I am and Mrs Evans said I should come and talk to you coz you're the only gay in the village. So now you're not. Coz there's two of us [clinks his glass against Daffyd's]

Daffyd: NO. You are not a gay. I am gay.

DW: I AM gay.

Daffyd: All right then. If you're gay who played Dorothy in the film the Wizard of Oz?

DW and Myfanwy: Judy Garland.

Daffyd to Myfanwy: How do you know that?

Myfanwy: It's easy. Everyone knows that.

Daffyd: All right then. This'll get you. Who is the gay character in *Are You Being Served?*

Entire pub responds: Mr Humphries.

Daffyd: Was it?

Entire pub: YES

Daffyd: That's very subtle then. I always thought it was Captain Peacock. He's the one with the moustache.

DW: Well I seem to have passed your gay test so I must be gay.

Daffyd: No. You are not a gay. I am the gay. You are probably just a little bit poofy.

DW: I AM gay. I've had sex with men and everything.

Myfanwy: That's more than you've had Daffyd.

Daffyd: SHUT UP Myfanwy. I AM the only gay in this village and that's that.

DW: Oh. Maybe I should go.

Daffyd: Yes, back to Cardiff. We've already got one gay in Llanddewi Brefi. We don't need another one.

DW: Well goodbye then [gets off bar stool and walks toward the door]. PROVINCIAL QUEENS.

Myfanwy: Daffyd Thomas, you bloody fool. You could have had a bit of cock there. Oh, 'I'm the only gay in the village', you're full of shit you are.

Daffyd: That's exactly the kind of homophobic attitude I've come to expect in this village [slams drink on bar]. Good day [walks out]

Daffyd's narrative is consistently one of frustration at being a 'lonely gay' because of his isolation from other gay people as he is 'the only gay in the village'. The sketch shown here raises issues about what constitutes a 'gay identity', as despite his emphatic claims to 'be a gay' Daffyd does not pass his own 'gay test', does not recognize the reference to 'cottaging', and has never had sex with a man. This is a central theme through many of the sketches with Daffyd patrolling the borders of who can and can't be gay (i.e. no one else passes his test) despite him always being the least experienced in same-sex behaviour, and the least likely to recognize other people as gay or lesbian. Examples of this include asking for an HIV test at the sexual health clinic despite never having had sex with a man and insisting on introducing a 'Lesbian and Gay (including Bisexual)' section in the library when a well-used section already exists that he has not discovered. Similar to the Derek Faye sketch it is the camp character that is most oblivious to the well-known cultural references to queer lives, cues that are familiar to everyone. Furthermore, despite constantly being on the lookout for homophobia, Daffyd is the most homophobic person in the village: he rejects the various attempts made by other villagers to connect him to a gay community; insults other gay men, for instance shouting 'Get back you gay bastards' and blocking their entry to a gay night in the pub he has organized; he resists an invitation to act as a referee for a lesbian couple's application to adopt by responding: 'but you're two great minge-munchers . . . gay marriage, adoption, I don't know, what's wrong with sitting at home watching TV getting moist every time Sandi Toksvig comes on'. In terms of linking this to broader contemporary anxieties this sketch plays with changing cultural norms to suggest that wider acceptance of gay lifestyles means gay people may no longer feel 'special' in their gayness, nor should expect to be rejected on the basis of their sexual orientation. Here, Daffyd is often the conservative character while other villagers, who Daffyd presumes to be straight, are confident in mentioning sexual practices such as 'rimming', 'fisting' and 'minge eating' in their everyday speech illustrating their knowledge and openness around same-sex sexual practices. At other times, the 'straight' villagers discuss their own ambiguities or sexual fluidity, using phrases such as 'bi-curious', much to Daffyd's discomfort. As in the sketch with Derek, it is the gay character who is the most insulting and who we are left laughing at for his failure to move on and embrace how times have changed. However, in this case, Daffyd points to issues of queer assimilation and the blurring of the homo/hetero divide (Roseneil, 2002), and he can be read as either 'the miserable gay who refuses to be happy in a more accepting social environment', or as representing a certain resistance to this invitation to assimilation by maintaining a queer sensibility that is justifiably predicated on a historical expectation of insult, rejection and the shame/pride binary.

Nevertheless, while the gay characters presented here are mocked or the target of the joke, they cannot *simply* be read as functioning to maintain social bonds around the dominance of heteronormative values across a homo/hetero divide through an act of joining together to laugh at gay people. Instead, these sketches are part of a process of both maintaining and transforming social values and bonds in a culture that is challenged by the equality agenda, albeit at the continued expense of the flamboyant, out gay man (Daffyd) and the closet homosexual (Derek). The overwhelming message in both shows is times have moved on, it is OK to be gay, WE are over homophobia and relaxed about same-sex relations, YOU need to get over it too (either by coming out or toning down). This enables the formation of new social bonds and a confidence in being open about non-normative sexuality among white men for the straight viewing audience (particularly in *The Catherine Tate Show*). However, these sketches also contain messages for lesbians and gay men about assimilation, and who gets to assimilate, as well as allowing for alternative readings of resistance and ongoing re-experiences of shame through the inevitable conclusion that gay people who are either not out or too out are a source of humour and shame. However, from a psychosocial perspective, 150 years of oppression cannot be overturned rapidly and the shame and insult that underpins our subjectivities is key to our psychic reality, while the material conditions that constitute it are still readily experienced by many people who come to call themselves lesbian or gay.

'Coming out' of shame: queer politics and suicidal distress

The sociologist Janice Irving (2009, p. 70) proclaims that 'shame has come out of the closet' and that this has had myriad impacts on sexual politics. In fact, the trend to air and make shame visible within queer studies can be traced back to the halcyon days of 'queer' in the early 1990s. As noted in the recent collection *Gay Shame* (Halperin and Traub, 2009, p. 6), 'In 1993, in the first article in the first edition of *GLQ: A Journal of Lesbian and Gay Studies*, Eve Kosofsky Sedgwick argued that queer identity and queer resistance are both routed in originary experiences of shame.' As Sedgwick (2003) notes: 'shame-humiliation throughout life can be thought of as an inability to effectively arouse the other person's positive reactions to one's communication' (p. 37) and that 'for certain ("queer") people, shame is the first, and remains a permanent, structuring fact of identity' albeit 'one that has its own, powerfully productive and powerfully metamorphic possibilities' (pp. 64–5). As such Sedgwick argues that:

> asking good questions about shame and shame/performativity could get us somewhere with a lot of recalcitrant knots that tie themselves into the guts of identity politics – yet without delimitating the felt urgency and power of the notion 'identity' itself. (p. 64)

Thus, after two decades of a Gay Pride movement that sought to celebrate gay lives, the ensuing discontents that have permeated queer writing and politics demonstrate that despite its triumphs (Weeks, 2007) gay pride, as both personal and political motif, has not been completely successful in shaking off or transcending its relationship with gay shame. These discontents have often been expressed in relation to the way the Gay Pride movement has seemingly required coalescence with or assimilation into heteronormative culture and that it has been deemed a necessary price to pay for social acceptance and equality. But, as Heather Love (2007, pp. 10, 30) argues:

'Advances' such as gay marriage and the increasing media visibility of well-heeled gays and lesbians threaten to obscure the continuing denigration and dismissal of queer existence. One may enter the mainstream on the condition that one breaks ties with all those who cannot make it – the nonwhite and the nonmonogamous, the poor and the genderdeviant, the fat, the disabled, the unemployed, the infected. . . . The invitation to join the mainstream is an invitation to jettison gay identity and its accredited historical meanings. Insofar that identity is produced out of shame and stigma, it might seem like a good idea to leave it behind. It may in fact seem shaming to hold onto an identity that cannot be uncoupled from violence, suffering and loss. I insist on the importance of clinging to ruined identities and to histories of injury. Resisting the call of gay normalization means refusing to write off the most vulnerable, the least presentable, and all of the dead.

The blossoming of a 'gay shame' movement has done much to queer the neoliberal tendencies associated with 'gay pride' that have contributed to wider social acceptance of (primarily) gay men through marketing practices and their financial ability to consume. However, within efforts to re-examine areas that may have been marked off limits by a sanitized pride movement there is a conspicuous absence of the consideration of mental (ill) health as one of the tropes of gay shame. Within the pride movement we might see this as a reluctance to engage with the psychological discourses that pathologized same-sex love and desire as a form of mental illness (e.g. APA, 1952) that lives on in calls to theorize queer subjectivities 'without necessary or automatic recourse to psychology and psychoanalysis' (Halperin, 2007, p. 11). Yet this may well have its own silencing impact for a wider understanding of the personal costs of coming out of shame. For instance, while it might be politically transformative to note how shame and insult are parodied and performed in relation to gay male subjectivities in popular culture skits in order to explore cultural anxieties over contemporary sexuality, elsewhere research has shown how 'shame' and 'humiliation' can powerfully impact on young people's processes of sexual identity formation (Hillier and Harrison, 2004) and may well be implicated in the elevated rates of suicide and suicide attempts reported among LGBT people (Johnson et al., 2007; King et al., 2008; McDermott et al., 2008).

Over the last decade a concerted amount of research has argued that LGBT people carry an increased 'risk' for mental health problems, including suicide attempts. In 2003 the first UK based large-scale study compared the mental health of lesbians, gay men and bisexual men and women with heterosexual men and women and found that LGB people under forty were three times more likely to have considered taking their life (King et al., 2003). Elsewhere in the literature, of particular concern is the issue of suicide attempts among LGBT youths, which are within the psychology literature frequently attributed to 'situational' factors such as homelessness, family rejection and bullying at school (Rivers, 1998). Taken together these factors have been explained as 'minority stress', which Meyer (2003, p. 674) defines in terms of an individual psychology resulting from 'experiences of prejudice events, hiding and concealing, internalized homophobia, and ameliorative coping processes'. There is less research on the suicidal behaviour of LGBT adults, with most of the studies available only focusing on LGB people, but these suggest that if victimization continues into adult life so too do elevated rates of contemplated suicide and self-harm (Warner et al., 2004). The few studies that have focused specifically on transgendered people find elevated rates of suicide and suicide-related behaviours among both adults and adolescents (e.g. Israel and Tarver, 1997).

The most recent report to be published in the UK presented a systematic review of 'mental disorder, suicide, and deliberate self harm in lesbian, gay and bisexual people' (King et al., 2008, p. 70) and concluded from a meta-analysis of twenty-five studies that 'LGB people are at higher risk of suicidal behaviour, mental disorder, and substance misuse and dependency than heterosexual people'. The risk described is equated to a two-fold excess for suicide attempts in the previous year for both men and women, and a four-fold excess in risk for gay and bisexual men over their lifetime. It is important to note here that the majority of studies are talking about suicidal thoughts and behaviours, not actual suicides. Following Halperin, it is also important to caution against a wholesale acceptance of the 'at risk' narrative and find alternative ways of talking about this psychological distress that resists coupling it with certain identity categories via discourses of mental illness. If we look to wider socio-cultural understandings of suicide and suicidal distress we find explanations that fall outside individualized mental health problems. For example, research has shown that to mitigate against suicidal feelings it is important to be able to locate a 'future self' in a cultural narrative (Chandler et al., 2003), and the elevated rates of suicide found in some indigenous populations may be explained in relation to cultural erasure. Similarly, Katrina Roen et al. (2008, p. 2096) note that suicide is not primarily about a psychological state (such as mental illness), but is 'a response to a psycho-social dilemma concerning the desperate need for connection with others in tension with the inevitable difficulties inherent in that connection'. This definition sounds remarkably like Sedgwick's account of shame-humiliation in the context of queer identity and queer resistance (described on p. 138). Thus, as Sedgwick notes in her reading of Tomkins, shame may be open to 'reframing, refiguration, transfiguration and deformation' (pp. 62–3) but surviving individualized experiences of shame in relation to sexuality is highly dependent on accessing cultural resources that enable the reconfiguration of the affective state. This process is made harder by the isolating impact that shame has and its potential to direct itself inwards by attacking the self (Lester, 1997) if the intense affective state cannot be released via connection and communication with an/other.

In order to give some insight into the way that shame can operate to obfuscate and isolate I turn to an example taken from a qualitative study with LGBT people who had attempted suicide (Johnson et al., 2007). Developed within a policy context that was promoting a discourse of LGBT suicide risk based on findings from large-scale quantitative studies, the aim of the project was to explore *why* some LGBT people felt suicidal. Informed by the work of Knizek and Hjelmeland (2007) the research made the assumption that suicide is not an unintentional act rather a way of communicating in an extreme situation. Intentionality is difficult to ascertain, particularly in the context of a suicide attempt.

Yet, Knizek and Hjelmeland's approach to better understand the psychosocial context of suicide attempts is helpful in drawing attention to its relational nature that involves both intentional and unintentional forms of communication. In order to address this empirically, Knizek and Hjelmeland follow three analytic steps: firstly, analysing the emotional status of the suicidal person, secondly, analysing the content of the suicide account to define the action radius, and finally, analysing the process that led towards suicide. It is with these principles in mind that their interviews were analysed.

Here, in order to track the affective dynamics of shame an example is presented from one participant. In a lengthy section of interview a young, white, gay male participant described a suicide attempt made when he was fifteen after being bullied and 'humiliated' at school. The incidents involved people calling him 'gay' and 'queer boy', leaving him feeling 'ashamed' as he was unable to respond to the laughter and jeers. What is apparent is the way that shame continues to operate throughout the account he provided three years later as he circles around the key issue that precipitated his suicide attempt. Using Tomkins' affect theory as a way of framing the process at play gives us some insight into the psychic power of shame theories and the potential communicative power of the act. The extract begins shortly after the participant tells the interviewer he took an overdose on returning home from a bullying incident at school, but was found by his mother and taken to the hospital where he survived the suicide attempt:

I: What helped you at that time?
R: At that time the counselling sessions were quite supportive. I found sort of talking to someone that I've never met before, never seen in my entire life, and it just, I knew he knew nothing about me, he knew nothing about what had happened – so it was easiest to tell him what went on and how I was feeling because I knew that he wasn't connected to the school, he didn't know any of my friends, he didn't know my family and he, basically I knew **he wasn't going to say anything to anyone**. I found that a lot easier to get my feelings out in the open.

Here, we see in detail the way that the participant attempts to keep the 'shame' hidden. The importance of talking to a counsellor is explained in terms of his isolation from other key contacts in the participant's life, school, friends, family, summarized in the statement 'I knew he wasn't going to say anything to anyone'. And yet, at this point it is not apparent what the 'anything', the embodied kernel of his 'shame-humiliation' is.

> I: Why was that then? Why were you able to talk to him as a stranger?
> R: it enables basically yell it all out and get everything out of your system that you have wanted to for ages but you haven't had a chance to and personally I felt that was a positive thing for me – just getting it out. Because I'd been keeping it bottled up – I hadn't bothered telling anyone and by not telling anyone, which is one of the main reasons I probably took the overdose because if I'd told someone before then it might have helped me and **if I had told basically someone before about how I was feeling, I might not have felt basically suicidal at that point.** I wouldn't have had it all bottled up inside me.

Here, the participant acknowledges that being able to speak about the source of his 'shame' (i.e. the thing he wants to keep hidden) might have had an impact on translating the affective state into a more positive outcome – 'I might have not felt suicidal'. The participant points to the importance of communication in the dispersion of suicidal feelings, yet, he has still not spoken in this interview about what it is that is 'bottled up inside'. What is it that needs telling? Why is he so reluctant to tell people he is being bullied and called 'gay'?

> I: So you said it was easier to talk to strangers. When you were bottling it up were you looking for people to tell or . . .
> R: At the time I sort of, I think I was and I wasn't. I didn't (pause) know of anyone I could tell at the time and I didn't want to tell anyone that I knew personally at the time basically I just (pause) was, **I was sort of worried that they, if they thought I was being bullied because I was gay, they might think I was gay too.** And, . . . I just sort of was trying to deal with it in my own way as well, I was

trying to deal with it without dragging other people in. Because, **at the time I think I saw it as a positive thing, whereas now I sort of realise that was a negative thing to do** – to try and deal with it myself where really deep down I knew I couldn't. . . . And, when I look back at it now, I was like, it was a kind of stupid thing to do because by doing that, it just brought more weight on me and basically more pressure on myself. **And, I think now, if I hadn't done that and kept it to myself then I might not have took an overdose – I might not have felt suicidal. The way I perceive it now anyway.**

In this final section the participant moves into a position of identifying as gay. He states his concern as 'if they thought I was being bullied because I was gay', rather than 'if they thought I was being bullied because *they thought* I was gay'. This distinction gives support to Tomkins' notion that shame is activated when there is an incomplete reduction in interest and excitement. Tomkins suggests that once shame has been activated it can be reduced by a reactivation of interest or excitement, however the likelihood of this depends on our own individualized shame theories. For Tomkins an affect theory 'is a simplified and powerful summary of a larger set of affect experiences' (in Sedgwick and Frank, 1995, p. 165). Thus, shame theories alert us to the possibility or imminence of shame and enable us to collate strategies for minimizing shame. They are conditioned through past experience, but are open to adjustment through new experiences. However, because of the socio-historical conditions that continue to construe same-sex desire as forbidden, and in quite vicious ways in the school playground, shame appears particularly risky for those who are experiencing emerging sexual interest that violates cultural norms. Crucially, what we might be seeing communicated in elevated accounts of suicide ideation and attempts among some LGBT people is not a desire to die, but a desire to connect, to come out of shame.

This account fits the well-known cultural narrative about queer youth suicide. In Rob Cover's (2012) transdisciplinary account of vulnerability and queer youth suicide he seeks to bridge psychological and sociological understandings of suicide via cultural theory in order to configure

> suicide not as either the outcome of depression and other mental health issues, nor as the product purely of socio-environmental factors, such as homophobia and discrimination, but as the flight from unbearable pain for which some young queer persons are vulnerable in terms of a vulnerability produced socially but which can produce mental health concerns that sit alongside suicidality – mutual symptoms, not necessarily in a chain of causality. (2012, p. 14)

In understanding suicide as the relationship between affect and action this analysis construes the suicidal act as a flight from pain. The question, nevertheless, is why is this felt so acutely by some adolescents? One possible answer is that as adult sexuality begins to emerge the youth enters into a 'liminal space' (Stenner and Moreno, 2013) where affect (desire) and cognition (understanding of what it means to be gay) dramatically collide creating an intense dissonance. In our extract we see the participant express that he did not want people to think he was gay, while others spoke about the sheer sense of fear of being that 'thing' that was spoken of in such detrimental terms. At this stage, the queer youth has few cultural resources to help mediate against the negative knowledge he holds, while feeling desire and attraction that implies he might be gay. Sensing there is no way out can also underpin feelings of 'hopelessness' or, as Schneidman (1993) describes, an intense 'psychache' that is socially debilitating and acutely isolating. This state is common to the affective dynamics of suicidal distress, and has been central to the framing of interventions for queer youth suicide. For example, Cover (2012) analyses the *It Gets Better* online campaign that provides short videos from LGBT people narrating their own accounts of how they managed to make it through difficult times, promising that 'in the future' they will find a better place to live. Attempting to foster 'future thinking' is a possible suicide intervention strategy as a way of mitigating feelings of hopelessness. Nevertheless, whether a suicide attempt ends up being interpreted as a 'suicide' or as a 'cry for help' is highly contingent and our participant was incredibly fortunate to live, found in time by his mother. Sara Ahmed (2006, p. 103) tells us that 'It is useful to recall that the word "contingent" has the same root in Latin as the word "contact". . . . Contingency is linked in this way to the sociality of being "with" others, to getting close enough to touch.' It is therefore necessary to consider the role of contingency in understanding youth suicide and the importance of interpersonal 'contact' in suicide intervention and prevention. Contingency draws our attention back to the individual experiences that more readily trigger desire or shame, to the sociality of being able to 'touch', or be 'touched', to the ability to access resources that might scaffold affective experiences in new and more productive ways.

Shame, sexuality and the psychosocial subject

This chapter has illustrated how comedy and humour play a significant cultural role in both creating and deflecting shame and insult. It also tells us something about the conflicts, tensions and taboos that underpin contemporary cultural concerns about the changing conditions of queer lives in the UK. Comedy sketches such as Derek from *The Catherine Tate Show* and Daffyd from *Little Britain* are part of the process of refiguring and transforming shame: they are complex in their engagement with queer subjectivities and they demand a variety of readings around processes of 'rehabilitating' or 'reappropriating' shame in relation to new forms of openness about non-normative sexualities. At the same time, the Stonewall report on representations of gay people on TV usefully shows how gay people, lesbians in particular, are still seriously underrepresented in most genres, overly represented in 'entertainment' and particularly comedy, and that the BBC should address these critiques. This concern also applies to other minorities who are also made absent by a preponderance of middle-class whiteness, or only represented in particular contexts that perpetuate stereotypes about race and class, as well as their intersections with gender and sexuality. Yet, the request for greater circulation of more or better representations of the diversity of queer lives does not provide an end point for 150 years of insult and oppression. Instead it brings with it possibilities for both (hetero)normalization and further re-experiences of (gay) shame. Without setting up some simplistic urban/rural divide, it should be noted, as some of the participants in the Stonewall focus group discussion of *Little Britain* did (see Cowan and Valentine, 2006), that Daffyd was perceived to be popular among urban-living gay men and lesbians because of his ironic take on a gay male identity. But, for those people who *are* the 'only gay in the village' it can be a painful and embarrassing reminder of their difference and isolation within communities that reject what might be referred to as 'cosmopolitan' values. Similarly, characters presented in comedy cannot simply be seen as either positive or negative representations of LGBT lives as these cultural resources become integrated into the very fabric of contemporary queer subjectivity: for example, Derek's catchphrase 'how very dare you!' was rapidly taken up by gay men, lesbians and heterosexuals across the world (facilitated by social networking sites such as YouTube). As such, the transformative possibilities of shame point to a possible exit from histories of oppression. Yet, those who work in the field of youth suicide caution that young people need to learn about the messy emotions entailed in becoming a sexual subject and that interventions are required to become resilient to the impact of shame (e.g. Cover, 2012). Gay men, lesbians and queer subjects more generally may only be able to partake in the transformative elements of shame if they have already developed a certain psychosocial security in their emerging identities and desires that enables them to survive individual experiences of shame. This is inevitably shaped by their own trajectories and sensitivity to shame theories, and bolstered by access to social/community support, queer or otherwise, that provide resources for mediating and reappropriating experiences of shame through affective reconnection. For others, shame can remain an isolating, risky and ultimately deadly affective state.

6

Transforming Sexuality

all kinds of politics are hybrid forms.

Lisa Duggan, 2003, p. 83

This penultimate chapter continues to build a psychosocial manifesto for the field of sexuality as it is developed, constructed,
queered, affected and ultimately transformed. Central to a psychosocial engagement that offers the possibility to transform sexuality
is the acknowledgement that identities are important for political
engagement, if inherently instable. In order to explore this further
this chapter picks up themes introduced in the last chapter to consider the role of identity, subjectivity and affect in political action
via a discussion of the contemporary tropes 'gay marriage' and
'mental health'. In attempting to work between polarized accounts
of 'identity and subjectivity', 'affect and knowledge' or 'culture and
economy', the presented analysis also considers politics as 'hybrid
forms' (Duggan, 2003, p. 83), and attempts to avoid denigrating
'identity politics', while engaging with some of their limitations.
In recent years, as neoliberalism has expanded and left politics have
been squeezed, some have attacked 'identity politics' that focus on
issues of representation of gender, sexuality and race for failing to

sufficiently engage with class-based analysis of capital and production. This line of argument unhelpfully introduces a polarization, one that Lisa Duggan (2003) defines as between love and money. She argues this leads to a reduction in the potential of political alliances between those who are concerned with social inequality and social justice; another impasse that limits the possibility for transformative action. A central issue for contemporary debates about sexuality is how to create transformation that also offers a critique of neoliberalism and the lives it permits to be lived well, without practices for transformation becoming part of the apparatus of facilitating its proliferation. The socio-economic context in which the desire for political transformation is located has shifted dramatically over the last thirty years. The identity politics of Lesbian and Gay Liberation emerged during the 1960s and 1970s alongside a range of social movements associated with left-wing politics that sought liberal reforms for minority groups via a broad based critique of social, cultural and economic policies. The practices for transformation associated with these movements frequently included public dissent, political rallies and mobilization. Lisa Duggan (2003, p. 67) notes that in the US (and echoed in other western economies) the slow shift right in politics that has occurred since the 1980s has meant that these forms of activism for equality have been replaced by 'lobbying, litigation and fundraising . . . even as the operative definition of "equality" narrowed dramatically enough, in some liberal reformist circles, to make peace with neoliberalism'. For her, the crisis around AIDS against the background of Reagan and Thatcher's policies was a key turning point where transformation was achieved by dual strategies, those informed by liberal reform and radical activism. This is of crucial importance for hybrid forms of politics as debates about sex and sexuality now take place within a global context, enabling the possibility of international alliance under the banner of a human rights discourse, cultural homogenization via a neoliberal economic agenda, and resistance through local alliances and radical cultural projects.

This chapter begins by reconsidering 'Poststructuralism and the paradox of identity' for theorizing political transformation and considers whether the 'affective turn' that is associated with queer theorists such as Sedgwick allows us a route out of this impasse via a shift from language, culture and knowing to experience, community and feeling. Clare Hemmings (2005) sums this up as a debate between epistemology and ontology, and about poststructuralism's seeming failure to engage with a distinction between the two. So, in her reading of Sedgwick she states:

> Part of what makes critical theory so uninventive for Sedgwick is its privileging of the epistemological, since a relentless attention to the structures of truth and knowledge obscures our experience of those structures. She advocates instead a reparative return to the ontological and intersubjective, to the surprising and enlivening texture of individuality and community (2003, p.17). (Hemmings, 2005, p. 553)

Thus, Sedgwick's book *Touching Feeling* is now associated with a critique of the 'cultural turn' that has gripped the humanities and social sciences since the 1970s, offering a potential way out of an epistemology that has supposedly ignored embodiment, investment and emotion. However, as Hemmings points out, the vision of poststructuralism painted by Sedgwick (and Massumi) in order to support the drive towards ontology and feeling is contested. For instance, Hemmings claims that much existing feminist theory has always endeavoured to engage with a 'vast range of epistemological work that attends to emotional investments, political connectivity and the possibility of change' (2005, p. 557). We also readily find these endeavours in critical psychology, critical race, psychosocial and queer studies, particularly through examples of poststructuralist infused phenomenology (Gillies et al., 2004; Ahmed, 2006), process-orientated psychology (e.g. Brown and Stenner, 2009) or psychoanalytically informed psychosocial approaches (Frosh and Baraitser, 2008). Following in this tradition, in this chapter I focus on the affective dynamics involved in contemporary activism around 'gay marriage' and 'mental health' and the potential for transformation. In doing so consideration is given to the politics of ambivalence and concepts of affective activism, affective dissonance and affective solidarity as they interact with identity, subjectivity and experience.

Poststructuralism and the paradox of identity

As the affective turn has gathered pace influencing scholars across the humanities and social science, engagements with affect theory have been proposed as a way out of a particular 'impasse' resulting from the cultural turn that preceded it, namely the limitations of binary, either/or categorizations within the field of sexuality as epitomized by the constructionist/essentialist debates of the 1980s and 1990s. Of course it was Sedgwick (1990) who took an early strike at the pervasiveness of the essentialist/constructionist debate by calling into question the idea that contemporary modes of homosexuality *had* actually replaced those identified in historical analyses of the nineteenth century. To recall, Sedgwick objected to the sharpness of the contrast drawn between different historical modes of homosexuality such as 'sexual acts' versus 'gay people', suggesting this led to the assumption that homosexuality today was a clearly defined field. Subsequently, Sedgwick suggested that one of the benefits of 'queer' is that it can be used to refer to 'the open mesh of possibilities, gaps, overlaps, dissonances and resonances, lapses and excesses of meaning when the constituent elements of anyone's gender, of anyone's sexuality aren't made (or *can't be* made) to signify monolithically' (1993, p. 8).

This move provided the threads of the anti-identity stance of queer theory; nevertheless poststructuralist engagements with sexuality continued apace as the field of application has sought to include a wide variety of people, practices and experiences over the last twenty years. A longstanding tension within poststructuralist informed accounts has been between questions over the stability of identity categories while they have necessarily become caught up in an expanding labelling approach in order to be 'inclusive' of a range of differences. We now have LGBTQ perspectives (e.g. Clarke and Peel, 2007) and sometimes LGBTQIU (including intersex and unsure) as abbreviations to identify those who may engage in non-normative sexual or gendered theorizing and practices. This is not completely naïve, as increasingly attention is paid to the notion of 'intersectionality' in order to better understand the way sexuality is mediated and constrained by other identities such as race, gender and social class. But debate circulates about how we might theorize this. Following Foucault, Wendy Brown (2005, p. 124) argues that the power systems involved in constructing us as gendered, raced or sexual subjects are different in their formation, yet inseparable from the subject. Thus, for her we cannot conceive of these situated categories as interlinked or intersectional as they are the result of 'largely noncomparable forms and styles of power'. In contrast, Surya Monro (2010, p. 1007) suggests, 'Analysis of the interstices between social characteristics is relatively straightforward at the level of the individual, but once group level conceptualization is undertaken a category-based approach is required to a degree.' Furthermore, in attending the multiple forms of difference, the proliferation of what are in effect identity categories is inescapably bound to the paradoxical practices that the history of sexuality has taught us. As Ken Plummer (1981, p. 29) argued thirty years ago:

> with all these categorizations comes the paradox: they control, restrict and inhibit whilst simultaneously providing comfort, security and assuredness. On an even wider scale, categorizations are attempts to order and structure the chaotic, complex and undifferentiated. To search for complexity is to undo categorization; to search for order is to categorize. Both seem necessary and thereby hangs the twist.

For Plummer, the twist is an enduring feature: all our poststructuralist lessons show us the problems of labelling for limiting experience, but without the label he doubts whether the sexual freedoms that were attained by Lesbian and Gay Liberation would have materialized. A decade later, in the emerging light of queer theory, Epstein (1994/2002, p. 51) urged sociologists to remember:

> The point is not to stop studying identity formation, or even to abandon all forms of identity politics, but rather to maintain identity and difference in productive tension, and to rely on notions of identity and identity politics for their strategic utility while remaining vigilant against reification.

In this context identity politics remain important, as they are a means to a form of recognition, even if the form of recognition can never do justice to the complexity of subjectivity. Recently, in the UK, we have seen this in campaigns to improve bi-visibility within LGBT collectives and to challenge bi-erasure within the wider public domain through calls for equality in policy and practice (e.g. Barker et al., 2012). The limitations of this mode of activism is that it is difficult not to end up with reified notions of sexual identities, because in making claims for rights, justice and equality there are tensions in presenting the complexity of experience that others might want to see. Nevertheless, if we accept that the lives of lesbians and gay men have improved on the basis of identity politics it would be churlish to suggest that other minorities give up on identity as a strategy for transformation because our poststructuralist and queer lessons suggest we should be beyond notions of identity stability. Others, however, question whether we need new political strategies given that identity politics failed to deliver the new modes of being that radical social movements sought to produce.

Worlds won and lost

Contemporary sociological understandings of how we live now offer a number of possibilities for lamenting the fluidity and instability in 'liquid lives' (e.g. Bauman, 2003) or maintaining hope that the transformations in erotic and intimate lives that have taken place over the last fifty years enable new modes of relating and reflecting (Giddens, 1992). Jeffrey Weeks (2007) offers a particularly optimistic account of the achievements of the latter, stating 'the world we have won has made possible ways of life that represent an advance not a decline in human relationships, and that have broken through the coils of power to enhance individual autonomy, freedom of choice and more egalitarian patterns of relationships' (Weeks, 2007, p. 7). Weeks' argument is that in each time period over the last five decades there are identifiable gains and losses. Thus he attempts to create a sense of the present that avoids pointing to a decline in stability and values of morality that might be aligned with the liberal right, as well as resist radical queer arguments that argue the gains that have been achieved for LGBT people have only occurred because of the strategic needs of neoliberalism.

Nevertheless, since the 1990s critics suggest that the 'gay pride movement' has become co-opted by neoliberalism, such that freedoms and protection are only afforded to a particular type of lesbian or gay man who has achieved 'equality' as a result of new business opportunities to profit from consumerism and the 'pink pound'. In my own engagement with queer life I remember a particular instance of this in the late 1990s. Living in London at the time, I attended the first Summer Rites party in Kennington in 1996. This was an attempt to offer something more local, less commercial, a more intimate gathering than the annual London Pride parade that had turned into a large-scale, corporate, party in the park. The following summer, Summer Rites had also grown in size and was held in Brockwell Park, Brixton – a previous venue of Pride. It was a cool, grey and rainy affair with many people huddled under trees and in the dance tents. Visible signs of commercialism had expanded with one particularly memorable marketing technique delivered by the cigarette manufacturer Benson & Hedges. With many revellers soaked from the downpour the free t-shirts on offer, along with other merchandise, were already appealing. The t-shirts distributed were not the usual ill-fitting, over-sized freebies that would normally stay hidden in a bed-wear draw before being discarded: these were styled, cut to fit a toned, male body, with a V-neck and capped sleeves. They were produced in black with the all-important branding delivered in small gold detailing on the breast pocket: *B&H*, along with the slogan, '*Fancy a fag?*' Clearly marketed at a particular gay male audience these illustrated the growing awareness of a new market opportunity to exploit, along with the multinational's increased knowledge of the trends that appealed – fashion, but also the queer strategy of redeploying terms of insult as a form of playfulness and humour. And, they did make people smile, and offer inclusion and recognition of their desires and identity. Yet, it is difficult to overlook the more pernicious technique of neoliberalism at work; co-opting radical political strategies to sell products to a long-time marginalized, hedonistic and pleasure-seeking crowd.

What can be made of this situation? Some responded with an acerbic 'Anti-Gay' cultural critique (e.g. Simpson, 1996) that mocked the 'gay is good' mind set as unthinking in its unrelenting purchase of anything that was packaged and sold as 'gay' while failing to notice that increased recognition and 'acceptance' was achieved on the basis of maintaining cultural stereotypes and vapid consumption of trivial and facile cultural objects. While there are legitimate concerns about the co-opting of non-normative cultures by neoliberalism, others have noted the inherent limitations of an increasing trend to blame 'identity politics' for collectively drifting to the right, pinning hope on liberal political reforms while falling for neoliberal charms. For instance, Lisa Duggan (2003, pp. 70–1) argues passionately that:

> To seize the opportunities of the twenty-first century, progressive social movements need deeper and broader analyses of the workings of neoliberalism. . . . One of the primary blocks to this kind of analysis, and to the growth of social movements to redistribute resources downward . . . is the split within the progressive-left. . . . Within the U.S., the specific dynamic of identity-based political formations drifting rightward into neoliberalism's embrace, while being denigrated and dismissed on the progressive-left with increasing ferocity, is a self-propelling, self-defeating, utterly antiproductive spiral of political schism. The more that identity and cultural politics are represented as the irresponsible, trivial, divisive 'other' of serious left analysis and organization, the more constituencies seeking equality may be alienated from the left and abandoned to claim redress through liberal reform alone. This alienation of potential constituencies drains the left of creativity and vitality as well as reducing its body counts. And, without the analytic and organizing energy found within the identity-based political formations, the progressive left has no hope of effectively grasping the forces it seeks to arrest and reverse – those promoting antidemocratic inequality on multiple fronts.

A particularly bleak example of the anguish felt by some on the left at the failure of radical politics to deliver the new world that social movements from the 1960s and 1970s sought can be found in Jonathan Rutherford's (2007) *After Identity*. He argues that identity politics set out to promote collectivity, the social value of equality and empowerment through challenging political power structures. Yet, rather than achieve equality by elevating personal and moral consciousness through modes of collectivism and transformation of institutional practices, he suggests the dramatic changes that have ensued are not a result of left politics. Instead, capitalism and consumerism are credited for legislative victories that have accrued equal rights and opportunities for minorities such as lesbians and gays, at the same time that neoliberalism has accelerated the historical transformation of the category 'the individual'. This, he suggests, has led to a more atomized existence, greater financial disparity between rich and poor, and elevated rates of mental illness from a loss of belonging, hope and political purpose. Drawing links with the cultural turn that demonstrated non-essentialist notions of self and identity and the importance of relationality and contingency, Rutherford argues that identity as something that is performed or done has been co-opted by the commercial market to be played out in relation to consumption, work and social status. For Rutherford, being 'after identity' entails finding new ethical modes of being to promote more egalitarian social relationships. In order to achieve this, following Ricoeur, he suggests that left politics have been too focused on notions of freedom and equality, at the expense of the third concept, fraternity. Thus he argues for a reinterpretation of 'the ideal of fraternity as the ethical framing of political and economic relations and principles. From its old incarnation as a limited and gender biased expression of solidarity, it becomes a reparative ethic of common life' (2007, p. 35).

Reparative readings, hybridity, community

A reparative ethic is also central to Sedgwick's turn to feelings as a new mode for political transformation. Her call to foster reparative readings is predicated on a critique of a long historical privileging of epistemology over ontology. For Sedgwick the turn to affect returns us to the ontological and the intersubjective, in ways that vibrate with a desire for feelings, community and experience rather than language, culture and knowing, which have become associated with epistemological and paranoid critiques. This might also resonate to some degree with Rutherford's call to reimagine fraternity as a mode to develop connections and a sense of belonging. It also recalls how concepts of hybridity and community have always been crucial for those writing with attention to how oppression is experienced. Hybridity because, following Anzaldúa (1987), rather than replace one mode of activity with another we need to be able to 'hold multiple social perspectives while simultaneously maintaining a centre that revolves around fighting against concrete material forms of oppression' (Cantú and Hurtado, 2012, p. 7). Community because, as Audre Lorde (1984, p. 111) proffered, 'Without community there is no liberation, only the most vulnerable and temporary armistice between an individual and her oppression. But community must not mean a shedding of our differences, not the pathetic pretense that these differences do not exist.' Thus, we must continue to negotiate the tension between dissolving communal identity categories which progressive politics require to organize, and proposing such categories on the basis of sexuality while attending to differences of gender, race and social class. By offering an analysis of the aspirations, tensions and compromises entailed in what is known as the 'gay marriage' debate, in the next section I examine the potential of this approach for developing affective connections across identity differences in a way that does not seek to draw divisions between cultural and economic politics, or denigrate the achievements and role of identity in fostering political allegiances. In order to offer a cultural context that is different to the dominance of US-based analyses so often found in queer studies, I draw on subjective experiences taken from Europe, specifically the UK and France, with some reference to Australia.

For and against gay marriage

Civil partnerships were introduced into the UK in December 2005. Since then, the Office of National Statistics' (ONS) provisional figures for 2012 suggest that 7,037 civil partnerships have taken place, with the average age of men 40.0 years and women 37.6 years. Since the law change I have been to a number of ceremonies, including latterly my own in December 2011, and have struggled personally with mixed feelings about the concept as well as the contradictory arguments that have ensued. Debates about 'gay marriage' can be deeply polarized, with some within queer perspectives (e.g. Brandzel, 2005) despairing of the inherent 'homonormativity' in such a desire, arguing that this is another example of assimilation with heteronormative values. Others more optimistically see it as a furthering of the transformation of erotic life, suggesting that if we follow the conservative line of why they reject calls for equality in marriage it points to a different and more significant victory that redefines all forms of relationships and erotic intimacies. As Weeks (2007, p. 184) states:

> Logic would usually suggest that de-heterosexualizing marriage by promoting same-sex unions/marriages is a potentially transgressive and subversive assault on its heteronormativity, an undermining of its corner-stone role, and a destabilizing of the hetero–homo binary that constitutes the gendered and sexual order. That is clearly what the conservative movements assume, and why they are so violently hostile to same-sex marriage.

What is clear from talking to friends and colleagues is that motivation for entering into a civil partnership or same-sex union is highly dependent on the individual lives of those involved. The act opens up a range of emotional encounters and affective experiences including love, fear, shame, joy and ambivalence, which are inevitably shaped by our familial, class, race and ethnic heritage. For some, as is often the case with same-sex relationships, the couples do not originate from the same country and the act allows them to live together when other legal structures would see them deported or unable to work. For others, the act allows them to celebrate their love and life together in a way that is experienced as politically important to recognize the impact of liberal equality reforms and protection from discrimination within the law. Some, often those from white, middle-class, conservative backgrounds, find their lover given greater recognition within their family, easing relationships now that the state has given 'permission' to the family to appoint value to the relationship. While this can be disappointing if parents had not been brave enough to speak out against homophobia before, the new comfort that the family takes from state-legislated respectability can make day-to-day relations easier. For others, the spectre of a day of recognition and celebration is a painful reminder of a lack of acceptance and shame within the wider family as crucial members such as parents or grandparents refuse to attend, re-enacting the homophobia that may have marked earlier experiences of discussing their sexuality in unsupportive environments. Finally, as in my own experience and in others', is a form of dissonance that locates subjects within an impasse between heteronormative critique, the desire for celebration and acceptance, and the potential to 'queer' weddings, that can end with an ambivalent positioning. Given rhetoric in the debates *for* gay marriage is dominated by notions of love and equality (see for example Amnesty International's campaign, *Love is a Human Right*) how is it possible to stand *against* gay marriage, and therefore against equality? Particularly when those who do take this stand are often doing so within a vicious language of hate speech, fire, wrath and religious condemnation. For this reason, a recent experience of attending a pro-gay marriage march in Paris during December 2012 offered an opportunity to reflect more on mixed emotions and ambivalence, and their place in accounts of affect, identity and queer politics.

Emotions in politics have always mattered, even if Jeff Goodwin et al. (2001) suggest that the dominance of models of the human as 'rational and instrumental' within the social sciences has precluded the role of emotions from political analyses for over thirty years. In demonstrating *why* emotions matter for understanding politics and social movements they point to the importance of 'affective bonds' for connecting people and maintaining our investments in social networks, and the central role of emotions such as anger, pride and shame for motivating action. This is certainly true when I reflect on how I found myself on a large political demonstration marching for gay marriage in Paris, December 2012. I had not travelled to Paris for this demonstration. My motives for being there were personal although related, tied up with meandering friendship networks and a surprise first civil partnership anniversary weekend break for my partner. The timing was a coincidence, but like many incidences of queer activism it was a chance to meet up with old friends and new, walk through city streets, and party in the evening. Pictured in the centre of the image below is Caroline, who originates from Paris, who I have known since the mid-1990s when we both lived in London. Unbeknownst to me, my (now) partner, Dee, also lived in a north London warehouse with Caroline shortly after she arrived in the UK from Australia in 1996. Alongside Caroline is Michelle, an old friend of Dee's from Australia, where they first met in Melbourne in the early 1990s, but developed their friendship in London during the same mid- to late 1990s period. Michelle returned to Sydney after a couple of years in London and is someone who Dee and I have spent time with on various visits to Sydney over the last decade. Next along is Dee, another Australian national, who has lived in the UK for sixteen years, and we together for twelve years. Finally, I am on the end, looking up to those who are watching the march out of their Parisian windows. Caroline and Michelle started their relationship six years ago when Caroline was visiting Australia for work and have since been struggling to find a way to live and work in the same country, until France finally voted yes to same-sex unions in the summer of 2013.

So here we are during a four-hour long procession through the streets of Paris that was estimated to include between 60,000 and

Taken during pro-gay marriage protest in Paris, 16 December 2012.
© Michelle Lollo, reproduced with permission.

150,000 people demonstrating for equality for same-sex relationships and parenting in law. An early thought that occurred to me
as I looked around at those partaking and those watching from
the pavements and windows above was, 'I wonder what Foucault
would have made of this?' Of course feelings of pride, shame,
fear as well as the comfort of being together were readily available and interspersed through moments in the day, as was a sense
of ambivalence about what we were marching for. Similarly, the
situation was ripe for paranoid readings of these affective responses,
particularly when you have a limited grasp of the French language,
so no immediate access to the meanings of chants or slogans that
were being displayed on placards, leaflets and badges. In this situation, reading affectively is crucial if others are to be interpreted
as for or against gay marriage, as an ally or a threat to safety. To
produce a paranoid reading is not entirely misguided: the following week another rally took place, this time attended by similar
numbers campaigning against gay marriage and for the sanctity of
the family and accounts of homophobic attacks regularly occurred
in the media. Yet, following Sedgwick, paranoid readings entail

the epistemological uncovering of systemic oppression rather than preparing the affective and reparative ground for social change. Thus, analysing the role of ambivalence might offer a more productive and reparative engagement than paranoid interpretations of the pride/shame binary, and of who is for or against gay marriage.

Ambivalence and affective dissonance

In the field of sexuality our politics have most often been conceptualized around the emotional dynamics of a pride/shame binary. The trope of gay pride was central to the identity politics of lesbian and gay liberation from the 1970s onwards as activists sought social change through a rights-based agenda, campaigning for freedom of sexual expression and later equality for same-sex relationships. In many countries significant social changes have taken place that have seen homosexuality shift from pathology and sin, worthy of incarceration, to an established minority identity with legislative protection against discrimination in the workplace, and the legal recognition of same-sex relationships and families (via access to IVF treatment and adoption). Gay pride has been a dominant political strategy in order for lesbians and gays to 'come out of shame', yet, as Deborah Gould states in an analysis of early AIDS activism and the shift from community love and pride to militant social action:

> we cannot adequately understand lesbian and gay politics . . . without paying close attention to the role that ambivalence and attempts to manage it play in shaping lesbians' and gay men's self understandings, feelings about themselves and society, interpretations of their situations, and political subjectivities and actions. (2001, p. 142)

For Gould, ambivalence emerges because lesbians and gay men are caught in a complex web of identifications and desires that link them to shame and guilt as well as pride and celebration, where at times we may feel ambivalent about our own self in a heterosexual society that provides conflicting messages about acceptance and rejection. We recognize this in the political tension that recent debates about gay marriage raise, not only for those on the conservative right, but also within the field of queer politics. It has been interesting that the recent UK press coverage about gay marriage has focused on religion, splits in the Conservative Party and marriage tax breaks. Less attention has been given to the deep ambivalence that many lesbian and gay people feel about the notion of gay marriage: we must of course be *for* gay marriage, because how could we possibly be against equality, standing alongside religious and conservative critics of homosexuality as a sin and against nature? Nevertheless, there is uneasiness about what gay marriage demands in terms of lifestyles to be adhered to, that it is ultimately an act of assimilation, normalization and of gaining a place at the table to sit side by side with heterosexual oppression. Similarly, there is little engagement with how these feelings are amplified or diluted by other forms of difference within an LGBT collective. Jeffrey Weeks takes a more sympathetic view, suggesting that marriage between same-sex couples has the potential to transform both normative meanings and everyday practices involved in intimate relationship formation. Although he does not specifically discuss the affective dimension Weeks is alluding to the space between the poststructuralist binary of regulation or resistance that underpins that other split category of assimilation/anti-assimilation. In thinking through this space it is helpful to return to Gould's conception of the role of ambivalence in lesbian and gay politics and the necessity of 'assessing the psychological repercussions of growing up and living in a heterosexist society' (2001, p. 139) as one potential explanation for feelings of ambivalence. As she states:

> From early childhood, they are socialized into, and often assumed to be fully part of, that society. Many of their significant relationships are with heterosexuals, and they often share many of the hopes and expectations as straight people. Their social conditioning and consequent ambivalence about their sexuality might bolster their attraction to society and their desire for social acceptance by arousing an anxiety that heterosexuals are in some sense *right* in their condemnation of homosexuality. On the other hand and simultaneously, lesbians

and gay men have historically articulated disillusionment, anger and antipathy toward a state that institutionalizes inequality and a dominant society that sanctions hatred toward 'queers'. Lesbian and gay attraction to society is diminished by what many see as state and societal allowance, even approval, of the deaths of hundreds of thousands of gay men from AIDS and laws that criminalized homosexual sex, prohibited gay marriage, expel homosexuals from the military, and exclude lesbians and gay men from discriminatory protection. Even while fearing that dominant discourses about homosexuality might be right, lesbians and gay men mix ideas of rights and justice [in the US] with their same-sex experiences of sexual pleasure and emotional connection, nourishing a belief that in fact *they* are normal and right and that a homophobic society is the problem. (p. 138)

Putting aside the 'othering' language tone of them and us, Gould points to a legacy of oppression that leaves queer subjects in the conflicted position of both desiring acceptance and belonging, while simultaneously questioning or rejecting the embrace of the bully. Of course we cannot assume that all lesbians or all gay men will feel this in the same way, as their experience of rejection and oppression will depend on how else they are located in systems of gender, race and class. Nevertheless, perhaps there is a fluid system of identification and disidentification that is experienced by many. As early gay liberationist Martha Shelley (cited in Gould, 2001, p. 138) says, 'Sometimes we wish we were like you, sometimes we wonder how you can stand yourselves.' While this offers a psychosocial engagement with unacknowledged affective responses such as ambivalence there is little in Gould's account that questions whether this ambivalence might offer transformative possibilities or the potential to connect in ways that foster new collaborations, new participatory communities or collectives. More recently, Clare Hemmings (2012, p. 148) has suggested that political transformation can begin from individualistic experiences of affective dissonance if we can move to a collective capacity based on affective solidarity. Here, the concept *affective solidarity* 'draws on a broad range of affects – rage, frustration and the desire for connection . . . but [that] does not root these in identity or other group characteristics'. This is an important shift from seeing affects necessarily associated with particular groups, but enables us to mobilize via affective connection across differences.

Affective activism and associated concepts such as affect solidarity are helpful for thinking through the Paris march via a reparative framework. Firstly, the affective conditions of ambivalence or affective dissonance that emerge in response to the values promoted in debates over 'marriage' are not solely the property of lesbian and gays, they are accessible to all. For example, many feminists have stood against marriage because of its patriarchal history. Secondly, ambivalence can arise due to an analysis of the context in which debates about gay rights take place. If we reflect on the sheer numbers of people marching in Paris (possibly over 100,000) in comparison to the number that have signed up for civil partnerships in the UK over seven years (7,000), then something else is collectively at stake here other than lesbians and gays simply demanding the right to marry. The image holds certain clues as we see the French national motto 'Freedom, Equality, Fraternity' held high, along with a call for secularism. And this particular backdrop may explain why others, friends, allies and those generally motivated by a fight for key social values, will partake in broader based demands for social equality and justice beyond their own sexual identity. Yet, debates that expand to include issues of religion or nationalism also raise mixed emotions, and affective dissonances, for those on whose behalf the battles are being fought. Jasbir Puar (2007) eloquently describes this in her book *Terrorist Assemblages: Homonationalism in queer times* by considering how US imperialist practices are predicated on the basis of cultural and political distinctions evidenced by utilizing a gay and women's rights discourse to flaunt a liberal political agenda, while ignoring the massive gender, race and sexuality inequalities that remain at home. Thus, to be critically engaged with this process it is necessary for queer subjects to train their affective responses to seek out not only where we are co-opted for the purpose of neoliberalism, but also for the purpose of nationalism and racism – perhaps nowhere more so than in the old colonial capitals of Europe. At the same time, seeking out reparative readings of our affective responses can also draw us into unusual alliances that bring us together in a broader fight against social inequality with seemingly distinct identity collectives. To provide a final example, at one junction during the march we came alongside another protest that was being held back as we crossed over the bridge. This was a group comprising primarily men, many of North African descent. What are they marching for we asked? Migrant rights, the right to remain and to work in France. I could join them, my white, lesbian, Australian friend said. And yes potentially she could, as via different protests, different liberal reforms, out of place and without some of the many privileges that supported her in alternative contexts, it was the same rights that they were seeking – the right to live a life in France. We might also imagine that some of these men could have been marching in our parade, but single-issue politics erases our ability to articulate multiple oppressions and the mixedness of identities. Thus, in doing politics identities do matter to understand how groups of people come together into particular formations that express resistance to oppression, yet attending to affectivity and hybridity and to how our experiences might relate to those of others who also occupy the borders might open up new alliances to promote a broader challenge to oppressive practices and social inequalities.

> Doing politics refigures the perceptible, not so one can finally recognize one's proper place in the social order, but to make evident the incommensurability of worlds, the incommensurability of inegalitarian distribution of bodies with the principle of equality . . . rethinking collectivity allows us to reconsider those who are excluded, not as victims of exclusion, but as the invisible and imperceptible engine of socio-political transformation. (Stephenson and Papadopoulos, 2006, p. 138)

Affective activism, community and queer mental health

Despite the transformations in the social policy landscape achieved via identity politics and liberal reforms, a second key trope in contemporary debates about queer lives is a growing concern for elevated rates of mental health problems and suicidal distress (King et al., 2008). Drawing particularly on the UK context, it is clear that regardless of policy changes a legacy of marginalization and oppression lives on in many people's lives, experienced through psychological distress and social isolation (Johnson et al., 2007), exacerbated by poverty and poor housing (see Browne and Bakshi, 2013). Yet doing research on this topic is not straightforward if we are to resist reinstating pathologizing accounts of queer lives. Having 'come out' of the history of pathologization, the establishment and transformation of existing labels and categories remain a crucial point for the socio-political agenda of non-normative sexuality and gender identities and practices. Recent psychological research in the area of LGBT lives is often well-meaning in terms of trying to document trends in well-being and campaign for service provision but it does little to transform dominant forms of representation or the nexus of social relationships by which LGBT people become defined (e.g. suicidal risk). Community-based participatory research offers an alternative mode of engagement and it is an internationally recognized framework for developing culturally relevant research and addressing issues of marginalization, inequality and injustice. It operates within a Participatory Action Research (PAR) approach that aims to articulate knowledge production and transformative action and assumes there is an interdependence between action and knowledge (Lewin, 1946). This perspective also emphasizes the idea that the knowledge produced should be meaningful and relevant to the people involved in the research and the contexts in which it is being produced (Fals Borda, 2001; Montero, 2003). The participation of individuals or groups involved is a key principle aligned with the emancipation and empowerment goals of action research, whereby research is not for producing knowledge alone but for promoting research praxis that contributes to issues of social justice, as well as 'strengthening the capacity of the individual to play the role of actor in his or her own life' (Miller and Rose, 2008, p. 106). Within this framework projects aim to provide a 'methodological space' for working with groups and communities described as 'marginalized'

or 'oppressed' as a means to explore forms of recognition and representation while seeking to promote change in concrete and local
conditions. To explore these ideas further I present an analysis of
recent work on LGBT suicidal distress via a community-based
participatory project and argue that it offers an alternative form of
politics that works towards transformation via community, feelings
and experience.

Since 2005 I have been working in Brighton, UK with an
LGBT community mental health charity MindOut that delivers
advocacy and peer support to some of the most vulnerable LGBT
people in the local area. Despite being aware of the tensions in
doing research on mental health and suicide we have sought to
better understand the reasons why people feel suicidal and offer
opportunities to engage in transformative projects that enable participants to produce representations of their sexuality and mental
health and promote connections with the wider community.
Within the social sciences visual and aesthetic projects are increasingly acknowledged for their potential to engage participants and
offer transformative possibilities through the affective realm. For
example, aesthetic projects allow for connection through the act
of witnessing (Radley, 2009) via the increased capacity of images
to affect people, or participatory wit(h)nessing (Ettinger, 2006),
the passing on of 'events without witnesses' to those who were
not there. With this in mind, in the summer of 2008 we produced
a photographic exhibition that was displayed during the annual
Pride Festival for two weeks in the local art gallery, and again
during LGBT history month, 2011 (for further details about the
project see Johnson, 2011). The seven participants each displayed
three images they had taken with a short extract of text to contex-
tualize what they wished to convey to the audience. As a means
of creating a dialogue we had a sign requesting those who viewed
the exhibition to leave some feedback. In contrast to previous projects where participants had talked about their sexual and gender
identities, participants offered only incidental representations of
their 'gender' or 'sexual' identities within the images/texts picked
for display. Instead, the exhibition presented images/texts that
reflected emotions, disaffection with psychiatric practices such as

Bleak, Liz, 2008:

> It was a bit of a bleak day when I took this and that was sort of how I was feeling . . . I just wanted to be alone and not be bothered by anyone and not interact with anyone . . . I just wanted to sort of close down and shut everyone out. Because, when I get ill, and especially when I go into hospital . . . they expect you to talk about such personal things and you know, they get you to do it over and over again and to people you don't even know and they make judgements on everything you say and so that's why I like to go down to the sea and just pretend that I'm not with anyone and nobody can touch me and I'm all alone. I love that.

© Katherine Johnson and MindOut, Focusing the Mind, reproduced with permission.

medication, and strategies for coping via their relationships with animals, people and the natural environment.

The above photo and textual extract is one example from the exhibition. An image of a person on a deserted beach, contemplative, hood-up on a grey day might be construed in the context of 'representations of LGBT mental health' as sad, isolating, depressing. Yet something powerfully defiant is being constructed here in this self-portrait: anger at the intrusion of psychiatric services into the personal recesses of individual subjectivity and a refusal to participate in the map of social relations drawn up for the (queer) mental health service user. Here, in the use of image and text the participant manages to subvert the calcification of an existing identity representation 'LGBT mental health service user' by co-producing an occasion that 'escapes' medical construction and intrusions into experience. In the co-production of image and text, the participant reclaims ownership of her thoughts and feelings, however momentarily, in order to enjoy the experience of being alone. And, as Papadopoulos et al. argue, 'If experience is the ultimate target of the regime of life control, it is also the starting point for every politics of escape' (2008, p. 152). Thus, this new experience of 'momentary escape' offers the potential to transform experience.

The analysis of the feedback left by those who viewed the exhibition also suggests the project enabled an 'affective connection' between participants and viewers as they told stories of 'being moved' and 'touched' by the display. Again representations of gender and sexual identities were downplayed in favour of viewers' accounts of their own memories and narratives of psychological distress. Responses included the following examples:

> Wow. What an amazing moving exhibition. So personal and universal. Moved to tears . . . Uncomfortable viewing for some who want to pretend we are all ok. I love this – it's beautiful – thanks. Well done.

> I found the exhibition extremely moving and sad. R★★★'s photo of 'coping mechanisms' reminded me of my dad who died a year ago and who was an alcoholic. Even the medication is the same. I feel angry at how he was treated by the mental health services in Brighton. I think this project is invaluable in highlighting mental health problems and the effect they have on people. This project humanizes the issues of poor mental health. I think that those who took part are very brave and only wish that my dad had been able to have such support that the group offers.

I have argued that the exhibition offered a modest and contingent social intervention in the field of LGBT mental health and representations of identities via the affective realm, something that I have referred to as 'affective activism' (e.g. Johnson, 2011; Johnson and Martínez Guzmán, 2012). The concept *affective activism* is used to note a practice that offers the potential for surprising or hopeful connections across identity differences. It was introduced by Anne Allison (2009, p. 106) in a sociological paper on Japanese youth activism set against the precarious backdrop of the socio-economic conditions of flexibility and consumerism. Allison defines affective activism as 'a vitalist politics that creates forms of connection that literally, sustain people in their everyday lives'. This form of activism offers an alternative and more contingent one to that of identity politics that strives to achieve specific liberal reform. Instead, affective activism does not require us to give up on identities, but it opens us up to the possibility of finding new forms of relating across identity differences, while reimagining how we might be represented. One way of explaining this entails thinking about experience as a process, where there is no split between subject (the viewer) and object (exhibition), instead they meet in an 'actual occasion' (Whitehead, 1933). For Whitehead's account of the occasion, the 'subject has a "concern" for the object as a component in the experience of the subject with an affective tone drawn from this object and directed towards it' (Whitehead, 1933, p. 176, cited in Papadopoulos et al., 2008, p. 153). Thus transformation occurs through sensation rather than rationality, through a process of a becoming experience, or the withering of previous experience.

Thus, community-participatory approaches cannot be seen as rationalist projects that can be mobilized to enable the transformation from situation A to situation B. What these projects instead reveal is that we can be changed by our engagement, that connections do occur, but we cannot predict in what form this may take: there is always a 'risk' in the types of affective responses that may be experienced by both those participating in the project and the intended and unintended audience: we do not know exactly how, when or if we will be affected. When coupling this with the multi-modal form of representation available to visual methods the possibilities for interpretation, reading, affective responses and connectivity are amplified. In order to offer another

theoretical context for reflecting on the interconnections and link-
ages that might be happening in the affective space I turn to the
psychoanalyst and artist Bracha Ettinger's theory of the 'matrixial
borderspace'. Psychoanalysis is quite a departure for community-
based research, and process-orientated psychology, but for those
working in psychosocial and queer studies it offers another means
for rethinking the relationship between the psyche and the social
realm. Ettinger's work offers a rich theoretical engagement with
affect and art that is non-Oedipal in its consideration of sexuality
and thus non-pathologizing for queer subjectivity, and provides a
new conceptual framework that enables us to rethink relationality. By using the universalism of the intrauterine experience, and
the 'matrixial' as an alternative but parallel symbolic order to the
phallus, she argues we are always already in togetherness, always
already in relation to the Other. For her, we are born into trauma
and loss, a loss of connection to the (m)other and we are driven
towards linking with the Other. Her theory is a complex, dense,
looping development of Lacanian and Freudian psychoanalysis,
which does not seek to replace the notion of the phallic order,
rather indicate that there are alternative forms of connections
that we emerge from and desire. As Callum Neill (2008, p. 338)
describes, 'She furnishes us with an armoury of terminology that
itself forces a rethinking. . . . Matrix, matrixial, metramorphous,
copoesis, co-fading, cross-imprinting, com-passion, borderspace,
borderlinking, link-a, wit(h)nessing, relations-without-relating,
distance-in-proximity, trans-subjective unconscious web, severality.' This theory has potential for those interested in psychic life and
cultural transformation as well as for those interested in developing
a feminist ethics of care. Her theory is developed with particular
reference to visual culture as documented by Griselda Pollack and
her own artwork, specifically painting, is one way into the theory.
Within her account, there is little consideration of other forms of
artwork, and perhaps like others considering the relation between
psychology and art (e.g. Arnheim, 1986), she would be sceptical
of photography as an art form. That said, many of her observations
in relation to com-passion, wit(h)nessing and metramorphous via
Freud's account of the uncanny resonate with observations of the

processes at play in this visual participatory project: the process of feeling moved, transformed, by specific images that touch us in ways we may not have been prepared for.

In seeking to draw together epistemological and ontological engagements that enable a reconfiguration of representation as well as affective connection, Antar Martínez and I have sought to rethink participatory action research through a poststructuralist and affect theory informed lens (Johnson and Martínez Guzmán, 2012). We rework the concept participation as a process that entails co-producing artefacts (meaning and action) for the public domain that might also develop self-knowledge/consciousness raising. For us, 'artefact' suggests the combination or integration of art (creativity, invention, singularity) and fact (object, form, reality) and draws attention to the idea that action research and its achievements are 'artificially made', co-created in local contexts. In this example, image and text can be drawn together to move *and* restructure meaning, but the artefacts continue to mutate in affect–meaning–action as they are deployed in different spaces. Thus, what is produced in a community-participatory project is not *the* stories/representations of the participants, which pin them to particular identities, but rather an invitation to rethink representation and the opportunity to reconnect across identity differences, initiated by the process of feeling moved. Thus, community projects, particularly those that use the methods of visual arts, offer potential for alternative practices for transformative, via intersubjective, affective adventures in sociality and experience but, following Adrienne Rich (1986, p. 223), these movements for change 'live in feelings, actions and words'.

Transforming sexuality and the psychosocial subject

This chapter draws together theoretical and methodological resources to present a psychosocial approach that seeks to both understand and transform sexuality. It does this by weaving between binary oppositions introduced within the course of the book, including subjectivity/identity, regulation/resistance, paranoid/reparative, epistemology/ontology, and ultimately psychic/social. Drawing on the examples of gay marriage and mental health and concepts of reparative readings, hybridity and community it provides an analysis of 'feelings, actions and words' (Rich, 1986) in examples of political activism including a mass demonstration and a community visual arts projects. It is argued that both these examples help to illuminate the concept 'affective activism' which offers a vitalist politics that can sustain people through their everyday lives via new forms of relating across identity difference. Attending to the value of reparative encounters and experiences of being in and out of place opens up new modes for understanding privilege and difference across categorical differences including gender, sexuality, race and class, thus heralding new starting points for political action. As such, practices that hope for the transformation of sexuality (alongside other forms of social inequality within a global context of neoliberalism) require hybrid forms of politics that attend to the affective dynamics necessary for rethinking collectivity. This also requires acknowledging the ongoing place of identity as 'the formation and cultural representation of what gets marked out as "identity" is intrinsic to experiences of subjectivity' (Wetherell, 2012, p. 78).

7

A Psychosocial Manifesto for Queer Futures

A movement for change lives in feelings, actions and words.

Adrianne Rich, 1986, p. 223

In a manifesto the author is required to set out a prescriptive directive for the reader to follow or reject, or outline a set of intentions, policies or commitments to envision a new worldview, many of which might be wildly optimistic and utopian. In posing the title *Sexuality: A psychosocial manifesto*, this book does this only as far as outlining a set of practices for producing a psychosocial engagement with sexuality, rather than delivering a comprehensive psychosocial theory *of* sexuality. This final chapter summarizes the practices or modes of engagement that have been drawn on to constitute a psychosocial thesis by reimagining academic endeavours, transdisciplinarity, politics of marginalization and, ultimately, queer futures. While the application in this book has been to the field of sexuality it is hoped that in setting out some principles in this final reflection it will be of value to other fields of enquiry where there is the desire for transformation, and recognition that 'a movement for change lives in feelings, actions and words' (Rich, 1986, p. 223).

Transdisciplinarity: theory and methods

A psychosocial manifesto demands that we do not simply follow the disciplinary 'canon' – whether this is empirical psychology, sociology or queer studies. It requires us to engage with the margins, with the interstices, multiplicities, identifications and disidentifications that cross sexuality, gender, race and class lines. Thus, a psychosocial manifesto argues that we need not attempt to theorize queer subjectivity without recourse to psychology and psychoanalysis, rather we need to reimagine the psychological through theoretical enrichment with other disciplinary interpretation and critiques. Engaging with poststructuralism, phenomenology, psychoanalysis and affect theories that return us to object-relations or cognitivism and neuroscience is part of the disciplinarity criss-crossing that defines psychosocial studies. Queer perspectives share much with this process, introducing notions of *doing*, alongside concepts of 'hybridity' and/or 'mixedness' which can help rethink the relationship between categories of difference such as sexuality, gender, race and class and help hold multiple perspectives in tandem. These concepts can also be applied to theorize personal experiences of living in the borders, or to account for the theoretical stitching together of disciplinary polarizations between psychology and socio-historical accounts.

A psychosocial manifesto also demands engaging a range of methods for analysing experience. These include close textual reading, rich description, decoding of cultural representations, and empirical accounts that analyse language, images and feelings. In this book this has been demonstrated through weaving together analyses of comedy sketches with interview data and through reflections on participatory methods of engagement with political activism and community arts projects. Opening empirical methods up to more creative and artistic modes of engagement has the potential to shift the emphasis from language, knowledge and paranoid readings (epistemology) towards understandings of feelings, experience and community (ontology) that have been associated with the reparative turn. Yet, a psychosocial manifesto in maintaining its focus on stitching binaries together calls for attention to both – not a replacement of one with the other. As noted in chapter 4:

> hybridity forewarns us that we need to think more carefully about the ontology, politics and circumstances of subjectivity, it does so from a semantic field that is itself pluralised and wandering, with a to-ing and fro-ing between material and cultural definitions, and attempts to transport terms from one domain to the other (Yao, 2003). Discussions weave between the empirical, theoretical, technological and experiential and are spoken through the languages of the natural, social and human sciences, autobiography, fiction, literary criticism, art, activism and social policy. (Gunaratnam, 2014, p. 5)

In this book I have drawn on these ideas to develop a transdisciplinary psychosocial manifesto that shares many values with queer theoretical approaches. It has been acknowledged that those in psychosocial studies draw on queer theories, but here I would like to suggest that psychosocial studies *is* queer. It does this theoretically by emphasizing hybridity and mixedness, but it also demands engaging beyond cultural texts to explore lived experiences and everyday lives. What it also offers, with its criss-crossing of academic spheres, is the opportunity to document the way ideas, theories and methods translate. This enables us to say as much about disciplinarity as about the subject or topic we are studying.

Identity, subjectivity and the politics of marginalization

A limitation of a psychosocial manifesto might be that in attempting to stitch together categories that are often held in distinction such as psychic and social, identity and subjectivity, epistemology and ontology, it might appear as if other social categories of difference often associated with identities disappear. Some might suggest that an intersectional analysis is more primed to keep these distinctions alive. Having attempted to provide a psychosocial engagement with sexuality, I would agree that it is difficult to maintain sufficient analytic purchase across a proliferation of categorical distinctions and still say something meaningful about both the general and the particular (Wiegman, 2012). But, a psychosocial analysis aims to hold onto Sedgwick's axiom that people are different from one another, while acknowledging that categorical differences mark out different forms of marginalization that are not fixed to subjects, rather dependent on the location and context. In applying a psychosocial manifesto a focus on subjectivity need not mean giving up on identities. Rather it presupposes a requirement to attend to the way that multiplicity shapes our lives, and acknowledges that privilege and oppression while more attached to certain categories attach to subjects in more fluid ways. Attending to the fluidity of how we are positioned is central to accounts of hybridity and mixedness and offers a politics of hope through the potential for transformation.

Queer futures?

Queer theory has long drawn our attention to challenging normative ways of living and relating. In recent years more focus has been paid to affective and temporal engagements expressed through questions about futurity. Here, melancholic odes to feeling backwards (Love, 2007), or serious engagements with Freud's account of the death drive have been used to question future driven narratives of reproduction (Edelman, 2004) or progress towards the good life, with some seeking new future utopias or embracing 'slow death' in place of 'cruel optimism to find ways of flourishing in the historical present' (e.g. Berlant, 2011). Questions of queer temporality have been debated in relation to a so-called 'anti-social turn' (Halberstam, 2008) and as a battleground between the political potentiality of negative and positive affective engagements. Yet, what all of these approaches share is a frustration with the present day and questions of how to live better, how to connect better, how to eek out more optimistic lives than those currently offered during our contemporary neoliberal times. Some have asked whether we are after sex, and whether queer theory is now over, even passé (Halley and Parker, 2011), for others it is seeing a revival (e.g. Yekani et al., 2013), inspired by the addition of new queer icons such as Lauren Berlant, Sara Ahmed, José Esteban Muñoz, Judith Halberstam and Jasbir Puar, who are all grappling in various forms with questions that stretch queer from a primary focus on intimacy and erotic life to incorporate multiple forms of precarity that afflict experience in twenty-first-century lives. However, in the turn to affect, ontology and the body, to community, feelings and experience that have inspired these scholars it is important to acknowledge that others have been there before: that feminist theory, psychology and psychoanalysis have existing insights to help explore subjectivity, experience and political transformation; that marginal voices or those working at the margins of queer debates are as likely to fuel 'the invisible and imperceptible engine of socio-political transformation' (Stephenson and Papadopoulos, 2006, p. 138).

As we consider the potential of negative affects such as shame for social and political transformation we must hold on to the axiom that people are different and that some are more able to bear a conscious engagement with living in the historical present, with its cruel optimism, its fragility and disappointment. We must take seriously that hope, as has been argued by activists from Harvey Milk in the 1970s to the late, inspiring José Esteban Muñoz (2009), is central to the everyday survival of many – and that hopelessness is heavily implicated in explanations for suicide. We might also want to reflect on why international suicide rates are associated with the uptake of neoliberal economic policies and the dramatic cultural changes that ensue (Curtis and Curtis, 2012).

Following this, a psychosocial manifesto seeks to inspire strategies for political engagement and social transformation, with particular concern for the relationship between transformations for minority identity groups and broader challenges to the social and economic injustices of our times. There is an urgent requirement for hybrid forms of politics that, as Lisa Duggan (2003) notes, attend to both love and money. Certainly 'political commitments usually flow from [these] ties of identity and belonging that happen to lead some people into fighting for equality and justice, when puzzling over how to live' (Segal, 2008, p. 392), but identity politics alone will not achieve the necessary impacts that are required to reimagine the world we live in. Instead they are likely to win particular legislative reforms that regulate subjectivity, and rights that can be so easily taken away under new regimes. This is not to denigrate the way that liberal reforms have had an impact in countries like the UK, reshaping forms of intimacy and family dynamics, but these impact unevenly, always favouring the already more privileged. At the same time, many cultural anxieties about sexuality remain expressed through global media accounts of state intervention in Russia, in Australia and in India such that no 'right' to gay marriage, or to love a same-sex partner freely, can be taken for granted if the state decides to legislate to remove it. Similarly, a human rights discourse does not work as a transformative intervention to protect sexual minorities in countries that do not have strong forms of governance – here we need other modes of collective engagement to rethink relationality and our connection to others. Thus, participatory projects such as those that are used in community psychology offer another form of affective activism, particularly when delivered through visual and creative means, that permits subjects to challenge how they are represented, foster new affective bonds through processes such as participatory wit(h)nessing, and transform experience. Of course cultural projects such as these are not without their own risks as a political strategy, but they do allow another starting point. And, as we have seen throughout this book, a psychosocial manifesto asks us to rethink the impasse which requires finding another way to begin.

References

Abelson, R. P. (1981) Psychological status of the script concept. *American Psychologist*, 36(7): 715–49.

Ahmed, S. (2004) *The Cultural Politics of Emotion*. Edinburgh: Edinburgh University Press.

Ahmed, S. (2006) *Queer Phenomenology: Orientations, objects, others*. Durham, NC: Duke University Press.

Allison, A. (2009) The cool brand, affective activism and Japanese youth. *Theory, Culture and Society*, 26(2–3): 89–111.

Altman, D. (1971) *Homosexual: Oppression and liberation*. New York: Outerbridge and Dienstfrey.

Altman, D. (1999) From gay power to gay mardi gras. *The Harvard Gay and Lesbian Review*, 6(3): 27–9.

Altman, D. (2001) *Global Sex*. Chicago: University of Chicago Press.

Angelides, S. (2001) *A History of Bisexuality*. Chicago: University of Chicago Press.

Anzaldúa, G. (1987) *La Frontera/Borderlands: The new mestiza*. San Francisco: Aunt Lute Books.

APA (American Psychiatric Association) (1952) *Diagnostic and Statistical Manual of Mental Disorders*. Washington, DC: American Psychiatric Association.

Apperley, A. (1997) Foucault and the problem of Method. In M. Lloyd and A. Thacker (Eds.) *The Impact of Foucault on the Social Sciences and Humanities*. London: Palgrave Macmillan.

Arnheim, R. (1986) *New Essays on the Psychology of Art*. Berkeley: University of California Press.

Badgett, M. V. L. (2003) Employment and sexual orientation: disclosure and discrimination in the workplace. In L. Garnets and D. Kimmel (Eds.) *Psychological Perspectives on Lesbian, Gay and Bisexual Experience*. New York: Columbia University Press.

Bailey, J. M. (1995) Biological perspectives on sexual orientation. In A. R. D'Augelli and C. J. Patterson (Eds.) *Lesbian, Gay and Bisexual Identities over the Lifespan: Psychological perspectives*. Oxford: Oxford University Press.

Bailey, J. M. and Pillard, R. C. (1991) A genetic study of male sexual orientation. *Archives of General Psychiatry*, 48: 1089–96.

Bailey, J. M., Pillard, R. C., Neale, M. C. and Agyei, Y. (1993) Heritable factors influence sexual orientation in women. *Archives of General Psychiatry*, 50: 217–23.

Bailey, J. M., Dunne, M. P. and Martin, N. G. (2000) Genetic and environmental influences on sexual orientation and its correlates in an Australian twin sample: personal processes and individual differences. *Journal of Personality and Social Psychology*, 78(3): 524–36.

Barker, M. (2004) Including the B-word: reflections on the place of bisexuality within lesbian and gay activism and psychology. *Lesbian and Gay Psychology Review*, 5: 118–22.

Barker, M., Richard, C., Jones, R., Bowes-Catton, H. and Plowman, T. (2012) *The Bisexuality Report: Bisexual inclusion in LGBT equality and diversity*. Centre for Citizenship, Identities and Governance and Faculty of Health and Social Care, Open University. Available at http://www. open.ac.uk/ccig/files/ccig/The%20BisexualityReport%20Feb.2012. pdf [Accessed 18 July 2013]

Barnard, I. (1999) Queer race. *Social Semiotics*, 9(2): 199–212.

Bauman, Z. (2003) *Liquid Love*. Cambridge: Polity.

Beasley, C. (2005) *Gender and Sexuality: Critical theories, critical thinkers*. London: Sage.

Berger, P. L. and Luckmann, T. (1967/1991) *The Social Construction of*

Reality: A treatise in the sociology of knowledge (No. 10). Harmondsworth: Penguin.

Berlant, L. (2009) Neither monstrous nor pastoral, but scary and sweet: some thoughts on sex and emotional performance in *Intimacies* and *What Do Gay Men Want? Women and Performance: A Journal of Feminist Theory*, 19(2): 261–73.

Berlant, L. (2011) *Cruel Optimism*. Durham, NC: Duke University Press.

Berlant, L. and Warner, M. (1995) What does queer theory teach us about X? *pmla*, 110(3): 343–9.

Bersani, L. and Phillips, A. (2008) *Intimacies*. Chicago: Chicago University Press.

Bicknell, C. (2006) The sociological construction of gender and sexuality. *The Sociological Review*, 54(1): 87–113.

Bieschke, K. J. (2002) Charting the waters. *The Counseling Psychologist*, 30: 575–81.

Billig, M. (2005) *Laughter and Ridicule: Towards a social critique of humour*. London: Sage.

Blanchard, R. and Bogaert, A. F. (1996) Homosexuality in men and number of older brothers. *American Journal of Psychiatry*, 153(1): 27–31.

Blanchard, R., Cantor, J., Bogaert, A. F., Breedlove, S. M. and Ellis, L. (2006) Interaction of fraternal birth order and handedness in the development of male homosexuality. *Hormones and Behaviour*, 49: 405–14.

Blumenfeld, W. J. (Ed.) (1992) *Homophobia: How we all pay the price*. Boston: Beacon Press.

Bohan, J. S. (1996) *Psychology and Sexual Orientation: Coming to terms*. Oxford and New York: Psychology Press.

Bradford, M. (2004) The bisexual experience: living in a dichotomous culture. In R. C. Fox (Ed.) *Current Research on Bisexuality*. New York: Harrington Park Press/Haworth Press, Inc.

Brandzel, A. L. (2005) Queering citizenship? Same-sex marriage and the state. *GLQ: A Journal of Lesbian and Gay Studies*, 11(2): 171–204.

Brown, J. (2006) *A Psychosocial Exploration of Love and Intimacy*. London: Palgrave.

Brown, L. S. (1995) Lesbian identities: concepts and issues. In A. R. D'Augelli and C. J. Patterson (Eds.) *Lesbian, Gay, Bisexual Identities over the Lifespan: Psychological perspectives*. Oxford: Oxford University Press.

Brown, S. D. and Stenner, P. (2009) *Psychology without Foundations: History, philosophy and psychosocial theory*. London: Sage.

Brown, W. (2005) *Edgework: Critical essays on knowledge and politics*. Princeton, NJ: Princeton University Press.

Browne, K. and Bakshi, M. L. (2013) *Ordinary in Brighton? LGBT, activisms and the city*. Farnham: Ashgate.

Burkitt, I. (2008) Subjectivity, self and everyday life in contemporary capitalism. *Subjectivity*, 23(1): 236–45.

Burr, V. (2003) *Social Constructionism*. New York and London: Routledge.

Butler, J. (1990) *Gender Trouble and the Subversion of Identity*. New York and London: Routledge.

Butler, J. (1993) *Bodies that Matter*. New York and London: Routledge.

Butler, J. (2004) *Undoing Gender*. New York and London: Routledge.

Cantú, N. and Hurtado, A. (2012) Introduction. In G. Anzaldúa, (1987/2012) *La Frontera/Borderlands: The new mestiza* (4th ed.). San Francisco: Aunt Lute Books.

Cass, V. (1979) Homosexual identity formation: a theoretical model. *Journal of Homosexuality*, 4(3): 219–35.

Cass, V. (1984) Homosexual identity formation: testing a theoretical model. *Journal of Sex Research*, 20(2): 143–67.

Cass, V. (1990) The implications of homosexual identity formation for the Kinsey model and scale of preference. In D. McWhirter, S. Sanders and R. Reinisch (Eds.) *Homosexuality/Heterosexuality: Concepts of sexual orientation*. Oxford and New York: Oxford University Press.

Cass, V. (1996) Sexual orientation identity formation: a western phenomenon. In R. Cabaj and T. Stein (Eds.) *Textbook of Homosexuality and Mental Health*. Washington, DC: American Psychiatric Press.

Chandler, M. J., Lalonde, C., Sokol, B. and Hallett, D. (2003) Personal persistence, identity development, and suicide: a study of native and non-native North American adolescents. *Monographs of the Society for Research in Child Development*, Serial No. 273, 68(2). Malden, MA: Wiley-Blackwell.

Chesler, P. (1972) *Women and Madness*. Garden City, NY: Doubleday.

Clarke, V. and Peel, E. (2004) The social construction of lesbianism: a reappraisal. *Feminism and Psychology*, 14(4): 485–90.

Clarke, V. and Peel, E. (2007) From lesbian and gay psychology to LGBTQ psychologies: a journey into the unknown (or unknowable)?

In V. Clarke and E. Peel (Eds.) *Out in Psychology: Lesbian, gay, bisexual, trans and queer perspectives.* Chichester: John Wiley and Sons.

Clough, P. T. (2007) Introduction. In P. T. Clough and J. Halley (Eds.) *The Affective Turn: Theorizing the social.* Durham, NC: Duke University Press.

Cochran, S. and Mays, V. (2006) Estimating prevalence of mental and substance-using disorders among lesbians and gay men from existing national health data. In A. Omoto and H. Kurtzman (Eds.) *Sexual Orientation and Mental Health.* Washington, DC: American Psychological Association.

Cohen, J. (2005) *How to Read Freud.* London: Granta.

Cooley, C. H. (1902/2001) Looking-glass self. In J. O'Brien (Ed.) *The Production of Reality: Essays and reading on social interaction.* London: Sage.

Cover, R. (2012) *Queer Youth Suicide Culture and Identity: Unliveable lives?* Farnham: Ashgate.

Cowan, K. and Valentine, G. (2006) *Tuned Out: The BBC's portrayal of lesbian and gay people.* London: Stonewall.

Coyle, A. (1992) My own special creation? The construction of gay identity. In G. M. Breakwell (Ed.) *Social Psychology of Identity and the Self Concept.* London: Academic Press.

Coyle, A. (2004) Subverting psychology and prioritizing politics: reflections on the social construction of lesbianism from an irritated youth. *Feminism and Psychology*, 14(4): 507–10.

Crenshaw, K. (1989) Demarginalizing the intersection of race and sex: a Black feminist critique of antidiscrimination doctrine, feminist theory and antiracist politics. *University of Chicago Legal Forum*, 140: 139–67.

Crenshaw, K. (1991) Mapping the margins: intersectionality, identity politics, and violence against Women of Colour. In M. Shanley and V. Narayan (Eds.) *Restructuring Feminist Political Theory: Feminist perspectives.* Cambridge: Polity.

Curtis, C. and Curtis, B. (2012) The operation of a suicidal cohort and its socio-economic origins. In C. Walker, K. Johnson and L. Cunningham (Eds.) *Community Psychology and the Socio-economics of Mental Distress: International perspectives.* London: Palgrave Macmillan.

Cvetkovich, A. (2012) *Depression: A public feeling.* Durham, NC: Duke University Press.

Dank, B. M. (1971) Coming out in the gay world. *Psychiatry*, 34(2): 180–97.

D'Augelli, A. and Grossman, A. H. (2001) Disclosure of sexual orientation, victimisation, and mental health among lesbian, gay, and bisexual youths. *Suicide and Life Threatening Behaviour*, 31: 250–64.

D'Augelli, A. R. and Patterson, C. J. (Eds.) (2001) *Lesbian, Gay and Bisexual Identities among Youth: Psychological perspectives*. New York: Oxford University Press.

Dean, T. (2000) *Beyond Sexuality*. Chicago: University of Chicago Press.

Dean, T. and Lane, C. (Eds.) (2001) *Homosexuality and Psychoanalysis*. Chicago: University of Chicago Press.

Deleuze, G. and Guattari, F. (1972/1983) *Anti-Oedipus: Capitalism and schizophrenia*. Minneapolis: University of Minnesota Press.

Diamond, L. M. (1998) Development of sexual orientation among adolescent and young adult women. *Developmental Psychology*, 34(5): 1085–95.

Diamond, L. M. (2003a) Was it a phase? Young women's relinquishment of lesbian/bisexual identities over a 5 year period. *Journal of Personality and Social Psychology*, 84(2): 352–64.

Diamond, L. (2003b) New paradigms for research on heterosexual and sexual-minority development. *Journal of Clinical Child and Adolescent Psychology*, 32(4): 490–8.

Diamond, L. M. (2005) A new view of lesbian subtypes: stable versus fluid identity trajectories over an 8 year period. *Psychology of Women Quarterly*, 29(2): 119–28.

Diamond, L. M. (2008) Female bisexuality from adolescence to adulthood: results from a 10 year longitudinal study. *Developmental Psychology*, 44(1): 5–14.

Dickson, N., Paul, C. and Herbison, P. (2003) Same-sex attraction in a birth cohort: prevalence and persistence in early adulthood. *Social Science and Medicine*, 56(8): 1607–15.

Dörner, G., Schenk, B., Schmiedel, B. and Ahrens, L. (1983) Stressful events in prenatal life of bi- and homosexual men. *Experimental and Clinical Endocrinology*, 81(1): 83–7.

Downing, L. and Gillett, R. (2011) Viewing critical psychology through the lens of queer. *Psychology and Sexuality*, 2(1): 4–15.

Draganski, B., Gaser, C., Kempermann, G., Kuhn, H. G., Büchel, C. B.

and Ma, A. (2006) Temporal and spatial dynamics of brain structure changes during extensive learning. *The Journal of Neuroscience*, 26(23): 6314–17.

Drescher, J. (1996) Psychoanalytic subjectivity and male homosexuality. In R. P. Cabaj and T. S. Stein (Eds.) *Textbook of Homosexuality and Mental Health*. Washington, DC and London: American Psychiatric Press.

Drummond, K. D., Bradley, S. J., Peterson-Badali, M. and Zucker, K. J. (2008) A follow-up study of girls with gender identity disorder. *Developmental Psychology*, 44(1): 34–45.

Duggan, L. (2003) *The Twilight of Equality: Neoliberalism, cultural politics and the attack on democracy*. Boston: Beacon Press.

Dworkin, S. L. and O'Sullivan, L. F. (2005) Actual versus desired initiation patterns: tapping disjunctures within and departures from tradition male sexual scripts. *Journal of Sex Research*, 42(2): 150–8.

Dworkin, S. L., Beckford, S. T. and Ehrhardt, A. A. (2007) Sexual scripts of women: a longitudinal analysis of participants in a gender-specific HIV/STD prevention intervention. *Archives of Sexual Behavior*, 36(2): 269–79.

Edelman, L. (2004) *No Future: Queer theory and the death drive*. Durham, NC: Duke University Press.

Edwards, D. (1997) *Discourse and Cognition*. London: Sage.

Edwards, J. (2008) *Eve Kosofsky Sedgwick*. London: Routledge.

Eliason, M. J. (1995) Accounts of sexual identity formation in heterosexual students. *Sex Roles*, 32(11/12): 821–34.

Ellis, H. and Symonds, J. A. (1897/1936) Sexual inversion. In H. Ellis (Ed.) *Studies in the Psychology of Sex*, vol. II, part 2. New York: Random House.

Ellis, L., Ames, M. A., Peckham, W. and Burke, D. (1988) Sexual orientation of human offspring may be altered by severe maternal stress during pregnancy. *Journal of Sex Research*, 25(1): 152–7.

English, J. F. (1994) *Comic Transactions: Literature, humor and the politics of community in twentieth-century Britain*. Ithaca, NY: Cornell University Press.

Epstein, S. (1994/2002) A queer encounter: sociology and the study of sexuality. In C. Williams and A. Stein (Eds.) *Sexuality and Gender*. Oxford: Blackwell Publishers.

Erhardt, A. and Money, J. (1967) Progestin-induced hermaphroditism: a study of 10 girls. *Journal of Sex Research*, 3(1): 83–100.

Eribon, D. (2004) *Insult and the Making of the Gay Self*. Durham, NC: Duke University Press.

Erikson, E. (1959) *Identity and the Life Cycle*. New York: International Universities Press.

Ettinger, B. (2006) *The Matrixial Borderspace*. Theory Out of Bounds, vol. 28. Minneapolis: University of Minnesota Press

Evans, D. T. (1993) *Sexual Citizenship: The material construction of sexualities*. London: Routledge.

Fairclough, N. (1992) Discourse and text: linguistic and intertextual analysis within discourse analysis. *Discourse and Society*, 3(2): 193–217.

Fals Borda, O. (2001) Participatory (action) research in social theory: origins and challenges. In P. Reason and H. Bradbury (Eds.) *Handbook of Action Research*. London: Sage.

Fassinger, R. E. and Miller, B. A. (1997) Validation of an inclusive model of sexual minority identity formation on a sample of gay men. *Journal of Homosexuality*, 32(2): 53–78.

Fausto-Sterling, A. (2000) *Sexing the Body: Gender politics and the construction of sexuality*. New York: Basic Books.

Flowers, P. and Buston, K. (2001) 'I was terrified of being different': exploring gay men's accounts of growing-up in a heterosexist society. *Journal of Adolescence*, 24(1): 51–65.

Foucault, M. (1967) *Madness and Civilization: A history of insanity in the Age of Reason*. London: Tavistock Press.

Foucault, M. (1969) *The Archaeology of Knowledge*. London: Tavistock Press.

Foucault, M. (1979/1990) *The History of Sexuality, Volume 1: An introduction*. Harmondsworth: Penguin Books.

Foucault, M. (1984) What is enlightenment? In P. Rabinow (Ed.) *The Foucault Reader*. New York: Pantheon Books.

Foucault, M. (1988) Truth, power, self: an interview with Michel Foucault. In L. Martin, H. Gutman and P. Hutton (Eds.) *Technologies of the Self*. Amherst: The University of Massachusetts Press.

Fox, D. R. and Prillentensky, I. (Eds.) (1997) *Critical Psychology: An introduction*. London: Sage.

Fox, R. C. (1996) Bisexuality in perspective: a review of theory and research. In B. A. Firestein (Ed.) *Bisexuality: The psychology and politics of an invisible minority*. Thousand Oaks, CA: Sage.

Fox, R. C. (Ed.) (2004) *Current Research on Bisexuality*. New York: Harrington Park Press.

Freeman, E. (2010) *Time Binds: Queer temporalities, queer histories*. Durham, NC: Duke University Press.

Freud, S. (1905/1991) Three essays on the theory of sexuality. In A. Richards (Ed.) *The Penguin Freud Library, vol. 7 On Sexuality: Three essays on the theory of sexuality and other works*. London: Penguin.

Freud, S. (1920/2001) Beyond the pleasure principle. In J. Strachey (Trans.) *The Standard Edition of the Complete Psychological Works of Sigmund Freud*, vol. XVIII (1920–1922). London: Vintage.

Freud, S. (1925/1991) Some psychical consequences of the anatomical distinction between the sexes. In A. Richards (Ed.) *The Penguin Freud Library, vol. 7 On Sexuality: Three essays on the theory of sexuality and other works*. London: Penguin.

Frith, H. and Kitzinger, C. (2001) Reformulating sexual script theory: developing a discursive psychology of sexual negotiation. *Theory and Psychology*, 11(2): 209–32.

Frosh, S. (2010a) *Psychoanalysis Outside the Clinic: Interventions in psychosocial studies*. London: Palgrave.

Frosh, S. (2010b) Psychosocial textuality: religious identities and textual constructions. *Subjectivity*, 3(4): 426–41.

Frosh, S. (2012) *For and Against Psychoanalysis*. London: Routledge.

Frosh, S. and Baraitser, L. (2008) Psychoanalysis and psychosocial studies. *Psychoanalysis, Culture and Society*, 13(4): 346–65.

Gagnon, J. H. (1977) *Human Sexualities*. Glenview, IL: Scott, Foresman.

Gagnon, J. H. (1990) The explicit and implicit use of the scripting perspective in sex research. *Annual Review of Sex Research*, 1: 44–56.

Gagnon, J. H. and Simon, W. (1968) Social meaning of prison homosexuality. *Federal Probation*, 32(1): 23–9.

Gagnon, J. H. and Simon, W. (1973) *Sexual Conduct: The social sources of human sexuality*. London: Hutchinson and Co.

Garnets, L. and Kimmel, D. (Eds.) (2003) *Psychological Perspectives on Lesbian, Gay and Bisexual Experience*. New York: Columbia University Press.

Gergen, K. J. (1973) Social psychology as history. *Journal of Personality and Social Psychology*, 26(2): 309–20.

Gergen, K. J. (2009) *An Invitation to Social Construction* (2nd ed.). London: Sage.

Giddens, A. (1991) *Modernity and Self-identity: Self and identity in the late modern age*. Cambridge: Polity.

Giddens, A. (1992) *The Transformation of Intimacy: Sexuality, love and eroticism in modern societies*. Cambridge: Polity.

Giffney, N. (2009) Introduction: the 'q' word. In N. Giffney and M. O'Rourke (Eds.) *The Ashgate Research Companion to Queer Theory*. Farnham: Ashgate.

Giffney, N. and O'Rourke, M. (2007) The 'E(ve)' in the(e)ories: dream-reading Sedgwick in retrospective time. *The Irish Feminist Review*, 3: 6–21.

Gillies, V., Harden, A., Johnson, K., Reavey, P., Strange, V. and Willig, C. (2004) Women's collective constructions of embodied practices through memory work: an exploration of memories of sweating and pain. *British Journal of Social Psychology*, 43(1): 99–112.

Gillies, V., Harden, A., Johnson, K., Reavey, P., Strange, V. and Willig, C. (2005) Painting pictures of embodied experience: the use of nonverbal data production for the study of embodiment. *Qualitative Research in Psychology*, 2(3): 199–212.

Goffman, E. (1961) *Asylums: Essays on the social situation of mental patients and other inmates*. New York: Anchor Books.

Gonsiorek, J. C. (1995) Gay male identities: concepts and issues. In A. R. D'Augelli and C. J. Patterson (Eds.) *Lesbian, Gay, and Bisexual Identities over the Lifespan: Psychological perspectives*. New York: Oxford University Press.

Gonsiorek J. C. and Rudolph, J. R. (1991) Homosexual identity: coming out and other developmental events. In J. C. Gonsiorek and J. D. Weinrich (Eds.) *Homosexuality: Research implications for public policy*. Thousand Oaks, CA: Sage.

Goodwin, J., Jasper, J. M. and Polletta, F. (Eds.) (2001) *Passionate Politics: Emotions and social movements*. Chicago: Chicago University Press.

Gould, D. (2001) Rock the boat, don't rock the boat, baby: ambivalence and the emergence of militant AIDS activism. In J. Goodwin, J. M.

Jasper and F. Polletta (Eds.) *Passionate Politics: Emotions and social movements*. Chicago: University of Chicago Press.

Greco, M. and Stenner, P. (Eds.) (2008) *Emotions: A social science reader*. London: Routledge.

Green, R. (1979) Biological influences on sexual identity. In H. A. Katchadourian (Ed.) *Human Sexuality: A comparative and developmental perspective*. London: University of California Press.

Grosz, E. (1995) *Space, Time and Perversion*. London and New York: Routledge.

Gunaratnam, Y. (2014) Rethinking hybridity, interrogating mixedness. *Subjectivity*, 7: 1–17.

Halberstam, J. (2008) The anti-social turn in queer studies. *Graduate Journal of Social Science*, 5(2): 140–56.

Hall, D. E. and Jagose, A. (2013) Introduction. In D. Hall and A. Jagose (Eds.) *The Routledge Queer Studies Reader*. New York: Routledge.

Hall, J. A. Y. and Kimura, D. (1994) Dermatoglyphic assymmetry and sexual orientation in men. *Behavioural Neuroscience*, 108: 1203–6.

Halley, J. and Parker, A. (Eds.) (2011) *After Sex? On writing since queer theory*. Durham, NC: Duke University Press.

Halperin, D. M. (1990) *One Hundred Years of Homosexuality and Other Essays on Greek Love*. New York and London: Routledge.

Halperin, D. M. (1993) Is there a history of sexuality? In H. Abelove, M. A. Barale and D. M. Halperin (Eds.) *The Lesbian and Gay Studies Reader*. London: Routledge.

Halperin, D. M. (1995) *Saint Foucault: Towards a gay hagiography*. Oxford: Oxford University Press.

Halperin, D. M. (2004) *How to Do the History of Homosexuality*. Chicago and London: Chicago University Press.

Halperin, D. M. (2007) *What Do Gay Men Want? An essay on sex, risk, and subjectivity*. Ann Arbor: University of Michigan Press.

Halperin, D. M. and Traub, V. (Eds.) (2009) *Gay Shame*. London and Chicago: University of Chicago Press.

Hamer, D. and Copeland, P. (1994) *The Science of Desire: The search for the gay gene and the biology of behaviour*. New York: Simon and Schuster.

Hamer, D., Hu, S., Magnuson, V., Hu, N. and Pattatucci, A. M. L. (1993) A linkage between DNA markers on the X chromosome and male sexual orientation. *Science*, 261: 321–7.

Hanna, P. (2013) Reconceptualizing subjectivity in critical social psychology: turning to Foucault. *Theory and Psychology*, 23(5): 657–74.

Harding, C. (2001) *Sexuality: Psychoanalytic perspectives*. Hove: Brunner-Routledge.

Harper, G. W. and Schneider, M. (2003) Oppression and discrimination among lesbian, gay, bisexual, and transgendered people and communities: a challenge for community psychology. *American Journal of Community Psychology*, 31(3/4): 243–52.

Hegarty, P. (2004) Getting past divide and conquer: a statement from the new Chair of the Section. *Lesbian and Gay Psychology Review*, 5(1): 4–5.

Hegarty, P. (2007) What comes after discourse analysis for LGBTQ psychology? In E. A. Peel and V. C. Clarke (Eds.) *Out in Psychology: LGBTQ perspectives*. Chichester: John Wiley and Sons.

Hegarty, P. (2009) Toward an LGBT-affirmative informed paradigm for children who break gender norms: a comment on Drummond et al. (2008) and Rieger et al. (2008). *Developmental Psychology*, 45(4): 895–900.

Hegarty, P. (2011) Sexuality, normality, intelligence: what is queer theory up against? *Psychology and Sexuality*, 2(1): 45–57.

Hemmings, C. (2005) Invoking affect: cultural theory and the ontological turn. *Cultural Studies*, 19(5): 548–67.

Hemmings, C. (2012) Affective solidarity: feminist reflexivity and political transformation. *Feminist Theory*, 13(2): 147–61.

Henriques, J., Hollway, W., Urwin, C., Venn, C. and Walkerdine V. (Eds.) (1984/1998) *Changing the Subject: Psychology, social regulation and subjectivity*. London and New York: Methuen.

Herek, G. (2003) Psychology of sexual prejudice. In L. Garnets and D. Kimmel (Eds.) *Psychological Perspectives on Lesbian, Gay and Bisexual Experience*. New York: Columbia University Press.

Heyes, C. J. (2007) *Self-transformations: Foucault, ethics, and normalized bodies*. New York: Oxford University Press.

Hillier, L. and Harrison, L. (2004) Homophobia and the production of shame: young people discovering the fault lines in discourse about same sex attraction. *Culture, Health and Sexuality*, 6(1): 79–94.

Hocquenghem, G. (1978/1993) *Homosexual Desire*. Durham, NC and London: Duke University Press.

Hoffman, R. M. (2004) Conceptualizing heterosexual identity development: issues and challenges. *Journal of Counseling and Development*, 82(3): 375–80.

Hoggett, P. (2008) What's in a hyphen? Reconstructing psychosocial studies. *Psychoanalysis, Culture and Society*, 13(4): 379–84.

Hollway, W. (1989) *Subjectivity and Method in Psychology: Gender, meaning and science*. London: Sage.

Hollway, W. (2006) Paradox in the pursuit of a critical theorization of the development of self in family relationships. *Theory and Psychology*, 16(4): 465–82.

Hollway, W. (2008) Doing intellectual disagreement differently. *Psychoanalysis, Culture and Society*, 13(4): 385–96.

Hu, S., Pattatucci, A. M. L., Patterson, C., Lin, L., Faulkner, D., Cherny, S. S., Kruglyak, L. and Hamer, D. H. (1995) Linkage between sexual orientation and chromosomal Xq28 in males but not in females. *Nature Genetics*, 11(3): 248–56.

Hubbard, R. and Wald, E. (1993) *Exploding the Gene Myth*. Boston: Beacon.

Huffer, L. (2010) *Mad for Foucault: Rethinking the foundations of queer theory*. New York: Columbia University Press.

Hyde, J. S. (Ed.) (2005) *Biological Substrates of Human Sexuality*. Washington, DC: American Psychological Association.

Icard, L. D. (1986) Black gay men and conflicting social identities: sexual orientation versus racial identity. *Journal of Social Work and Human Sexuality*, 4(1–2): 83–93.

Irving, J. M. (2009) Shame comes out of the closet. *Sexuality Research and Social Policy: Journal of NSRC*, 6(1): 70–9.

Israel, G. E. and Tarver, D. E. (1997) *Transgender Care: Recommended guidelines, practical information and personal accounts*. Philadelphia: Temple University Press.

Jackson, S. and Scott, S. (2010) Rehabilitating interactionism for a feminist sociology of sexuality. *Sociology*, 44(5): 811–26.

Jeffreys, S. (2003) *Unpacking Queer Politics: A lesbian feminist perspective*. Cambridge: Polity.

Johns, D. J. and Probst, T. M. (2004) Sexual minority identity formation in an adult population. *Journal of Homosexuality*, 47(2): 81–126.

Johnson, K. (2007) Changing sex, changing self theorizing transitions in embodied subjectivity. *Men and Masculinities*, 10(1): 54–70.

Johnson, K. (2011) Visualising mental health with an LGBT community group. In P. Reavey (Ed.) *Visual Methods in Psychology: Using and interpreting images in qualitative research*. London: Routledge.

Johnson, K. and Martínez Guzmán, A. (2012) Rethinking concepts in Participatory Action-Research and their potential for social transformation: post-structuralist informed methodological reflections from LGBT and Trans-Collective projects. *Journal of Applied Social and Community Psychology*. DOI: 10.1002/casp.2134.

Johnson, K., Faulkner, P., Jones, H. and Welsh, E. (2007) *Understanding Suicidal Distress and Promoting Survival in the LGBT Communities*. Brighton: Brighton and Sussex Community Knowledge Exchange Project.

Johnson, P. E. (2001/2013) 'Quare' studies, or '(Almost) everything I learnt about queer studies I learnt from my grandmother'. In D. E. Hall and A. Jagose (Eds.) *The Routledge Queer Studies Reader*. New York: Routledge.

King, M., McKeown, E., Warner, J., Ramsay, A., Johnson, K., Cort, C., Wright, L., Blizard, R. and Davidson, O. (2003) Mental health and quality of life of gay men and lesbians in England and Wales: controlled, cross-sectional study. *British Journal of Psychiatry*, 183: 552–8.

King, M., Semlyen, J., Tai, S. S., Killaspy, H., Osborn, D., Popelyuk, D. and Nazareth, I. (2008) A systematic review of mental disorder, suicide, and deliberate self harm in lesbian, gay and bisexual people. *BMC Psychiatry*, 8: 70. Available at http://www.biomedcentral.com/1471-244X/8/70 [Accessed 28 July 2009]

Kinsey, A. C., Pomeroy, W. B. and Martin, C. E. (1948) *Sexual Behaviour in the Human Male*. Philadelphia: W. B. Saunders Company.

Kinsey, A. C., Pomeroy, W. B., Martin, C. E. and Gebhard, P. H. (1953) *Sexual Behaviour in the Human Female*. Philadelphia: W. B. Saunders Company.

Kitzinger, C. (1987) *The Social Construction of Lesbianism*. London: Sage.

Klein, F. (1993) *The Bisexual Option: A concept of one hundred percent intimacy* (2nd ed.). New York: Harrington Park Press.

Klein, F., Sepekoff, B. and Wolf, T. J. (1985) Sexual orientation: a multivariable dynamic process. *Journal of Homosexuality*, 11(1–2): 35–49.

Knizek, B. L. and Hjelmeland, H. (2007) A theoretical model for interpreting suicidal behaviour as communication. *Theory and Psychology*, 17(5): 697–720.

Kristeva, J. (1980) *Desire in Language: A semiotic approach to literature and art*. New York: Columbia University Press.

Laumann, E. O. and Gagnon, J. H. (1995) A sociological perspective on sexual action. In R. G. Parker and J. H. Gagnon (Eds.) *Conceiving Sexuality: Approaches to sex research in a postmodern world*. New York: Routledge.

Lee, I.-C. and Crawford, M. (2007) Lesbians and bisexual women in the eyes of scientific psychology. *Feminism and Psychology*, 17(1): 109–27.

Lester, D. (1997) The role of shame in suicide. *Suicide and Life-Threatening Behavior*, 27(4): 352–61.

Le Vay, S. (1991) A difference in hypothalamic structure between hetero-sexual and homosexual men. *Science*, 253: 1034–7.

Le Vay, S. (1993) *The Sexual Brain*. Cambridge, MA: MIT Press.

Levine, H. (1997) A further exploration of the lesbian identity development process and its measurement. *Journal of Homosexuality*, 34(2): 67–78.

Levine, H. and Evans, N. J. (1991) The development of gay, lesbian and bisexual identities. In N. J. Evans and V. A. Walls (Eds.) *Beyond Tolerance: Gays, lesbians and bisexuals on campus*. Alexandria, VA: American College Personnel Association.

Lewin, K. (1946) Action-research and minority problems. *Journal of Social Issues*, 2(4): 34–46.

Leys, R. (2011) The turn to affect: a critique. *Critical Inquiry*, 37(3): 434–72.

Local Government Act (1988). London: HMSO. Available at http://www.legislation.gov.uk/ukpga/1988/9/pdfs/ukpga_19880009_en. pdf [Accessed May 2014]

Lorde, A. (1984) *Sister Outsider: Essays and speeches*. New York: The Crossing Press.

Love, H. (2007) *Feeling Backward: Loss and the politics of queer history*. Cambridge, MA: Harvard University Press.

Lynd, H. M. (1958) *On Shame and the Search for Identity*. London: Routledge and Kegan Paul.

Macey, D. (1993) *The Lives of Michel Foucault*. London: Hutchinson.

MacKinnon, C. A. (1992) Does sexuality have a history? In D. C. Stanton (Ed.) *Discourses of Sexuality: From Aristotle to AIDS*. Ann Arbor: University of Michigan Press.

Marcuse, H. (1955) *Eros and Civilization*. Boston: Beacon Press.

Marcuse, H. (1969) *An Essay on Liberation*. Boston: Beacon Press.

Markus, H. and Zajonc, R. P. (1985) The cognitive perspective in social psychology. In G. Lindzey and A. Aronson (Eds.) *Handbook of Social Psychology*. New York: Harper and Row.

Massumi, B. (2002) *Parables for the Virtual: Movement, affect, sensation*. Durham, NC: Duke University Press.

McCall, L. (2005) The complexity of intersectionality. *Signs*, 30(3): 1771–800.

McCarn, S. R. and Fassinger, R. E. (1996) Revisioning sexual minority identity formation: a new model of lesbian identity and its implications for counseling and research. *Counseling Psychologist*, 24(3): 508–34.

McConaghy, N. (1999) Unresolved issues in scientific sexology. *Archives of Sexual Behavior*, 28(4): 285–318.

McDermott, E., Roen, K. and Scourfield, J. (2008) Avoiding shame: young LGBT people, homophobia and self-destructive behaviours. *Culture, Health and Sexuality: An International Journal of Research, Intervention and Care*, 10(8): 815–29.

McIntosh, M. (1968/1981) The homosexual role. In K. Plummer (Ed.) *The Making of the Modern Homosexual*. London: Hutchinson.

McNay, L. (1994) *Foucault: A critical introduction*. Cambridge: Polity.

Mead, G. H. (1934/1967) *Mind, Self, and Society*. Chicago: University of Chicago Press.

Medhurst, A. (2007) *A National Joke: Popular comedy and English cultural identity*. Oxford: Routledge.

Medical News Today (2011) Homo or hetero? The neurobiological dimension of sexual orientation. Available at http://www.medicalnewstoday.com/releases/226963.php [Accessed 20 July 2013]

Merrell Lynd, H. (1958) *On Shame and the Search for Identity*. Oxford: Routledge.

Meyer, I. H. (2003) Prejudice, social stress, and mental health in lesbian, gay, and bisexual populations: conceptual issues and research evidence. *Psychological Bulletin*, 129(5): 674–97.

Meyer-Bahlburg, H. F. L. (1995) The role of prenatal estrogens in sexual orientation. In L. Ellis and L. Ebertz (Eds.) *Sexual Orientation: Toward biological understanding*. Westport, CT and London: Praeger.

Miller, P. and Rose, N. (2008) *Governing the Present*. Cambridge: Polity.

Minton, H. L. (1997) Queer theory: historical roots and implications for psychology. *Theory and Psychology*, 7(3): 337–53.

Money, J. (1988) *Gay, Straight and In-between*. Oxford: Oxford University Press.

Money, J. and Erhardt, A. (1972) *Man and Woman, Boy and Girl*. Baltimore: Johns Hopkins University Press.

Monro, S. (2010) Sexuality, space and intersectionality: the case of lesbian, gay and bisexual equalities initiatives in UK local government. *Sociology*, 44(5): 996–1009.

Montero, M. (2003) *Teoría y práctica de la psicología comunitaria: la tensión entre comunidad y sociedad*. Barcelona: Paidós.

Moore, P. (2004) *Beyond Shame: Reclaiming the abandoned history of radical gay sexuality*. Boston: Beacon Press.

Muñoz, J. E. (1999) *Disidentifications: Queers of color and the performance of politics*. Minneapolis and London: University of Minnesota Press.

Muñoz, J. E. (2006) Feeling brown, feeling down: Latina affect, the performativity of race, and the depressive position. *Signs*, 31(3): 675–88.

Munt, S. (1992) Sex and sexuality. In A. Millwood Hargrave (Ed.) *Broadcasting Standards Council Annual Review*. London: John Libbey and Company.

Munt, S. (2008) *Queer Attachments: The cultural politics of shame*. Aldershot: Ashgate.

Murphy, T. F. (1997) *Gay Science: The ethics of sexual orientation research*. New York: Columbia University Press.

Mustanski, B. S., DuPree, M. G., Nievergelt, C. M., Bocklandt, S., Schork, N. J. and Hamer, D. (2005) A genome wide scan of male sexual orientation. *Human Genetics*, 116(4): 272–8.

Nash, J. C. (2008) Rethinking intersectionality. *Feminist Review*, 89: 1–15.

Neill, C. (2008) Severality: beyond the compression of the cogito. *Subjectivity*, 24(1): 325–39.

Nelkin, D. and Lindee, S. M. (1995) *The DNA Mystique: The gene as a cultural icon*. New York: W. H. Freeman.

Nightingale, D. J. and Cromby, J. (1999) *Social Constructionist Psychology: A critical analysis of theory and practice*. Maidenhead: Open University Press.

ONS (2012) *Civil Partnerships in the UK*. London: ONS. Available at

http://www.ons.gov.uk/ons/rel/vsob2/civil-partnership-statistics--un
ited-kingdom/2012/stb-civil-partnerships-2012.html#tab-Key-find
ings [Accessed 18 December 2013]

O'Rourke, M. (2011) The afterlives of queer theory. *Continent*, 1(2):
102–16.

Osborne, P. and Segal, L. (1993) Gender as performance: an interview
with Judith Butler. *Radical Philosophy*, 67: 32–9.

Papadopoulos, D., Stephenson, N. and Tsianos, V. (2008) *Escape Routes:
Control and subversion in the 21st century*. London: Pluto Press.

Parker, I. (1989) *The Crisis in Modern Social Psychology, and How to End it*.
London and New York: Routledge.

Parker, I., Georgaca, E., Harper, D., McLaughlin, T. and Stowell Smith,
M. (1995) *Deconstructing Psychopathology*. London: Sage.

Patterson, C. J. (2008) Sexual orientation across the life span: introduction to the special section. *Developmental Psychology*, 44(1): 1–4.

Pease, A. and Pease, B. (1998) *Why Men Don't Listen and Women Can't
Read Maps: How we're different and what to do about it*. Mona Vale, NSW:
Pease Training International.

Phelan, S. (1990) Foucault and feminism. *American Journal of Political
Science*, 34(2): 421–40.

Plummer, K. (1975) *Sexual Stigma: An interactionist's account*. London:
Routledge.

Plummer, K. (1981) *The Making of the Modern Homosexual*. London:
Hutchinson.

Plummer, K. (1982) Symbolic interactionism and sexual conduct: an
emergent perspective. In M. Brake (Ed.) *Human Sexual Relations:
Towards a redefinition of sexual politics*. New York: Pantheon.

Plummer, K. (1995) *Telling Sexual Stories*. London: Routledge.

Plummer, K. (1996/2003) Intimate citizenship and the culture of sexual
story telling. In J. Weeks, J. Holland and M. Waites (Eds.) *Sexualities
and Society*. Cambridge: Polity.

Potter, J. and Wetherell, M. (1987) *Discourse and Social Psychology: Beyond
attitudes and behaviour*. London: Sage.

Probyn, E. (2005) *Blush: Faces of shame*. London: Minneapolis
Press.

Prosser, J. (1998) *Second Skins: The body narratives of transsexuality*. New
York: Columbia University Press.

Puar, J. (2007) *Terrorist Assemblages: Homonationalism in queer times.* Durham, NC: Duke University Press.

Radley, A. (2009) *Works of Illness: Narrative, picturing and the social response to serious disease.* InkerMen Press.

Reiger, G. Linsenmeier, J. A. W., Gygax, L. and Bailey, J. M. (2008) Sexual orientation and childhood gender nonconformity: evidence from home videos. *Developmental Psychology*, 44(1): 46–58.

Rice, G., Anderson, C., Risch, N. and Ebers, G. (1999) Male homosexuality: absence of linkage to microsatellite markers at Xq28. *Science*, 284: 665–7.

Rich, A. (1986) Notes towards a politics of location. *Blood, Bread, and Poetry: Selected prose, 1979–1985.* New York: Norton.

Richardson, D. (1996) Heterosexuality and social theory. In D. Richardson (Ed.) *Theorising Heterosexuality.* Buckingham: Open University Press.

Riggs, D. W. (2006) *Priscilla, (White) Queen of the Desert: Queer rights/race privilege.* New York: Peter Lang.

Riggs, D. W. and Walker, G. A. (Eds.) (2004) *Out in the Antipodes: Australian and New Zealand perspectives on gay and lesbian issues in psychology.* Perth: Brightfire Press.

Rivers, I. (1998) Lesbian, gay and bisexual development: theory, research and social issues. *Journal of Community and Applied Social Psychology*, 7(5): 329–43.

Roen, K., Scourfield, J. and McDermott, E. (2008) Making sense of suicide: a discourse analysis of young people's talk about suicidal subjecthood. *Social Science and Medicine*, 67(12): 2089–97.

Rosario, V. A. (1997) *Science and Homosexualities.* London: Routledge.

Rosario, V. A. (2002) Science and sexual identity: an essay review. *Journal of the History of Medicine and Allied Sciences*, 57(1): 79–85.

Rose, N. (1998) Governing risky individuals: the role of psychiatry in new regimes of control. *Psychiatry, Psychology and Law*, 3(2): 17–96.

Rose, N. and Miller, P. (2008) *Governing the Present.* Cambridge: Polity.

Roseneil, S. (2002) The heterosexual/homosexual binary: past, present and future. In D. Richardson and S. Steidman (Eds.) *Handbook of Lesbian and Gay Studies.* London: Sage.

Rubin, G. (1984) Thinking sex: notes for a radical theory of the politics of sexuality. In C. Vance (Ed.) *Pleasure and Danger: Exploring female sexuality.* Boston: Routledge.

Rubin, G. and Butler, J. (1994) Sexual traffic. *Differences*, 6(2–3): 62–99.

Russell, G. M. and Gergen, K. J. (2004) The social construction of lesbianism: resistance and reconstruction. *Feminism and Psychology*, 14(4): 507–10.

Rust, P. (1993) Coming out in the age of social constructionism: sexual identity formation among lesbians and bisexual women. *Gender and Society*, 7(1): 50–77.

Rust, P. C. (2000). Bisexuality: a contemporary paradox for women. *Journal of Social Issues*, 56(2), Special Issue: Women's sexualities: New perspectives on sexual orientation and gender: 205–21.

Rutherford, J. (2007) *After Identity*. London: Laurence and Wishart.

Savic, I. and Lindström, P. (2008) PET and MRI show differences in cerebral asymmetry and functional connectivity between homo- and heterosexual subjects. *Proceedings of the National Academy of Sciences of United States*. Available at http://www.ncbi.nlm.nih.gov/pmc/articles/PMC2453705/ [Accessed 18 June 2014]

Savin-Williams, R. C. (2001) A critique of research on sexual-minority youths. *Journal of Adolescence*, 24(1): 5–13.

Savin-Williams, R. C. and Diamond, L. M. (2000) Sexual identity trajectories among sexual-minority youths: gender comparisons. *Archives of Sexual Behaviour*, 29(6): 607–27.

Schank, R. C. and Abelson, R. P. (1977) *Scripts, Plans, Goals, and Understanding*. Hillside, NJ: Lawrence Erlbaum.

Schneider, B. (2008) Arguments, citations, traces: Rich and Foucault and the problem of heterosexuality. *Sexualities*, 11(1–2): 86–93.

Schneidman, E. (1993) *Suicide as Psychache: A clinical approach to self-destructive behavior*. New York: Jason Aronson.

Schulman, S. (2009) *Ties that Bind: Familial homophobia and its consequences*. New York: The New Press.

Seal, D. W. and Ehrhardt, A. A. (2003) Masculinity and urban men: perceived scripts for courtship, romantic, and sexual interactions with women. *Culture, Health, and Sexuality*, 5(4): 295–319.

Sears, J. T. (1989) The impact of gender and race on growing up lesbian and gay in the South. *National Women's Studies Association Journal*, 1(3): 422–57.

Sedgwick, E. K. (1985) *Between Men: English literature and male homosocial desire*. New York: Columbia University Press.

Sedgwick, E. K. (1990) *Epistemology of the Closet*. Oakland: University of California Press.

Sedgwick, E. K. (1991) How to bring your kids up gay: the war on effeminate boys. *Social Text*, 29: 18–27.

Sedgwick, E. K. (1993) *Tendencies*. Durham, NC and London: Duke University Press.

Sedgwick, E. K. (2003) *Touching Feeling: Affect, pedagogy, performativity*. Durham, NC and London: Duke University Press.

Sedgwick, E. K. (2007) Melanie Klein and the difference affect makes. *South Atlantic Quarterly*, 106(3): 625–42.

Sedgwick, E. K. (2008) *Epistemology of the Closet* (2nd ed.). Oakland: University of California Press.

Sedgwick, E. K. and Frank, A. (Eds.) (1995) *Shame and its Sisters: A Silvan Tomkins reader*. Durham, NC and London: Duke University Press.

Segal, L. (1994) *Straight Sex: Rethinking the politics of pleasure*. London: Virago Press.

Segal, L. (1999) *Why Feminism? Gender, psychology, politics*. New York: Columbia University Press.

Segal, L. (2008) After Judith Butler: identities, who needs them? *Subjectivity*, 25: 381–94.

Seidman, S. (2003) *The Social Construction of Sexuality*. New York: Norton.

Simon, W. and Gagnon, J. H. (1967) Homosexuality: the formulation of a sociological perspective. *Journal of Health and Social Behavior*, 8(3): 177–85.

Simon, W. and Gagnon, J. H. (1984) Sexual scripts. *Society*, 22(1): 53–60.

Simon, W. and Gagnon, J. H. (1987) A sexual script approach. In J. H. Geer and W. T. O'Donohue (Eds.) *Theories of Human Sexuality*. New York: Plenum.

Simpson, M. (Ed.) (1996) *Anti-gay*. New York: Freedom Editions.

Socarides, C. (1968) *The Overt Homosexual*. New York: Grune and Stratton.

Socarides, C. (1995) *Homosexuality: A freedom too far*. Phoenix, AZ: Adam Margrave Books.

Stein, A. (2006) *Shameless: Sexual dissidence in American culture*. New York: New York University Press.

Stein, E. (Ed.) (1990) *Forms of Desire: Sexual orientation and the social constructionist controversy*. New York: Garland.

Stenner, P. (2004) Is autopoietic systems theory alexithymic? Luhmann and the socio-psychology of emotions. *Soziale Systeme*, 10(1): 159–85.

Stenner, P. (2007) The adventure of psychosocial studies: revisioning the space between the psychic and the social. Inaugural lecture (18 May 2007). Available at http://www.brighton.ac.uk/sass/contact/staffpro files/stenner/inaugural_lecture.pdf [Accessed 28 January 2009]

Stenner, P. and Moreno, E. (2013) Liminality and affectivity: the case of deceased organ donation. *Subjectivity*, 6(3): 229–53.

Stephenson, N. and Papadopoulos, D. (2006) *Analysing Everyday Experience: Social research and political change*. Basingstoke: Palgrave Macmillan.

Stockton, K. B. (2006) *Beautiful Bottom, Beautiful Shame: Where black meets queer*. London: Duke University Press.

Sullivan, N. (2003) *A Critical Introduction to Queer Theory*. New York: New York University Press.

Swaab, D. (2005) The role of hypothalamus and endocrine system in sexuality. In J. S. Hyde (Ed.) *Biological Substrates of Human Sexuality*. Washington, DC: American Psychological Association.

Szasz, T. S. (1960) *The Myth of Mental Illness*. New York: Harper Perennial.

Taylor, G. (2002) Psychopathology and the social and historical construction of gay male identities. In A. Coyle and C. Kitzinger (Eds.) *Lesbian and Gay Psychology: New perspectives*. Oxford: Blackwell.

Taylor, Y., Casey, S. and Hines, S. (Eds.) (2010) *Theorizing Intersectionality and Sexuality*. Basingstoke: Palgrave Macmillan.

Terry, J. (1999) *An American Obsession: Science, medicine and homosexuality in modern society*. Chicago: University of Chicago Press.

Troiden, R. R. (1979) Becoming homosexual: a model of gay identity acquisition. *Psychiatry*, 42(4): 362–73.

Ussher, J. M. (1989) *The Psychology of the Female Body*. New York: Routledge.

Ussher, J. M. (2009) Heterocentric practices in health research and health care: implications for mental health and subjectivity of LGBTQ individuals. *Feminism and Psychology*, 19(4): 561–7.

Ussher, J. M. (2010) Are we medicalizing women's misery? A critical review of women's higher rates of reported depression. *Feminism and Psychology*, 20(1): 9–35.

Venn, C. (2006) *The Postcolonial Challenge: Towards alternative worlds.* London: Sage.

Venn, C. and Terranova, T. (Eds.) (2009) Special Issue on Michel Foucault. *Theory, Culture and Society*, 26(6): 1–272.

Vitellone, N. (2011) What do gay men want? An essay on sex, risk and subjectivity, by David M. Halperin. *Psychology and Sexuality*, 2(1): 102–3.

Von Krafft-Ebing, R. (1886) *Psychopathia sexualis: eine klinisch-forensische Studie.* Stuttgart: Enke.

Walkerdine, V. and Jimenez, L. (2012) *Gender, Work and Community after De-industrialisation: A psychosocial approach to affect.* London: Palgrave Macmillan.

Warner, M. (Ed.) (1993) *Fear of a Queer Planet: Queer politics and social theory.* Minneapolis and London: University of Minnesota Press.

Warner, J., McKeown, E., Griffin, M., Johnson, K., Ramsay, A., Cort, C. and King, M. (2004) Rates and predictors of mental illness in gay men, lesbians and bisexual men and women: results from a survey based in England and Wales. *British Journal of Psychiatry*, 185: 479–85.

Weeks, J. (1977) *Coming Out: Homosexual politics in Britain from the nineteenth century to the present.* London: Quartet Books.

Weeks, J. (1978) *Preface to the 1978 Edition of G. Hocquenghem, Homosexual Desire.* Durham, NC and London: Duke University Press.

Weeks, J. (1985) *Sexuality and its Discontents: Meanings, myths and modern sexualities.* London: Routledge.

Weeks, J. (1989) *Sex, Politics and Society: The regulation of sexuality since 1800* (2nd ed.). London: Longman.

Weeks, J. (1995) *Invented Moralities: Sexual values in an age of uncertainty.* Cambridge: Polity.

Weeks, J. (1998) The homosexual role after 30 years: an appreciation of the work of Mary McIntosh. *Sexualities*, 1(2): 131–52.

Weeks, J. (2000) *Making Sexual History.* Cambridge: Polity.

Weeks, J. (2007) *The World We Have Won: The remaking of erotic and intimate life.* London: Taylor and Francis.

Weinberg, M. S., Williams, C. J. and Pryor, D. W. (1994) *Dual Attraction: Understanding bisexuality.* New York: Oxford University Press.

Weinrich, J. D. and Klein, F. (2003) Bi-gay, bi-straight, and bi-bi: three bisexual subgroups identified using cluster analysis of the Klein Sexual Orientation Grid. *Journal of Bisexuality*, 2(4): 109–39.

Wetherell, M. (2008) Subjectivity or psycho-discursive practices? Investigating complex intersectional identities. *Subjectivity*, 22(1): 73–81.

Wetherell, M. (2012) *Affect and Emotion: A new social science understanding*. London: Sage.

Whittier, D. K. and Simon, W. (2001) Intrapsychic sexual scripting. *Sexualities*, 4(2): 139–65.

Wiegman, R. (2012) *Object Lessons*. Durham, NC: Duke University Press.

Wiegman, R. (2014) The times we're in: queer feminist criticism and the reparative 'turn'. *Feminist Theory*, 15(1): 4–25.

Worthington, R. L. and Mohr, J. J. (2002) Theorizing heterosexual identity development. *The Counseling Psychologist*, 30: 491–5.

Worthington, R. L., Savoy, H., Dillon, F. R. and Vernaglia, E. R. (2002) Heterosexual identity development: a multidimensional model of individual and group identity. *Counseling Psychologist*, 30(4): 496–531.

Worthington, R. L., Navarro, R. L., Savoy, H. B. and Hampton, D. (2008) Development, reliability, and validity of the Measure of Sexual Identity Exploration and Commitment (MoSIEC). *Developmental Psychology*, 44(1): 22–33.

Yekani, E. H., Kilian, E. and Michaelis, B. (Eds.) (2013) *Queer Futures: Reconsidering ethics, activism, and the political*. Farnham: Ashgate.

Zhou, J. N., Hofman, M. A., Gooren, L. J. G. and Swaab, D. F. (1995) A sex difference in the human brain and its relation to transsexuality. *Nature*, 378: 68–70.

Zucker, K. and Bradley, S. (1995) *Gender Identity Disorder and Psychosexual Problems in Children and Adolescents*. New York: Guilford Press.

Zucker, K. J., Drummond, K. D., Bradley, S. J. and Peterson-Badali, M. (2009) Troubled meditations on psychosexual differentiation: reply to Hegarty (2009). *Developmental Psychology*, 45(4): 904–8.

Index